CONTROL FREAKS WRIT LARGE
Modern Political literature

Patrick Morgan

Connor Court Publishing

Published in 2022 by Connor Court Publishing Pty Ltd

Copyright © Patrick Morgan

All rights reserved. No part of this book may be reproduced or transmitted in any form or by any means, electronic or mechanical, including photo copying, recording or by any information storage and retrieval system, without prior permission in writing from the publisher.

Connor Court Publishing Pty Ltd
PO Box 7257
Redland Bay QLD 4165
sales@connorcourt.com
www.connorcourt.com

Printed in Australia

ISBN: 9781922815132

Front cover painting: Vasily Perov, Public domain, via Wikimedia Commons

Front cover design: Maria Giordano

Printed in Australia.

First, how foolish and dangerous it is, in thinking out the nature of the Soviet system, to minimize the difference between our experience and theirs, our opportunities and theirs, our ways and theirs, of managing the relations between the state and the citizen. Secondly: how foolish it would be to imagine that the desires and fears which help to sustain their system, in all its reaches, are not perfectly recognizable everywhere about us and within us.

Dan Jacobsen *The London Review of Books*

CONTENTS

Preface   7

Introduction   11

1   The Underground Man Emerges   23
2   Portents of Trouble   39
3   Takeover Tactics   59
4   Total Domination   83
5   Endless Domination   107
6   Coming Out Abruptly   129
7   Inside The Leviathan   151
8   The Adversary Culture   169
9   Coming Out Gradually   191
10 The American Pushback   213
11 The Afterlife of Literature   237

Bibliography   249

Acknowledgements   254

Index   256

PREFACE

At university in the 1960s two events particularly affected many of us, the tragic death of Albert Camus, the hero of the existentialists, and the publication of *One Day In The Life of Ivan Denisovich* (1963) by Alexander Solzhenitsyn, soon to become leader of the dissident movement in the Soviet Union. Patrick White's novel *Riders in the Chariot* (1961) included a character who had survived the Holocaust. At the same time I caught up with George Orwell's *Nineteen Eighty-Four* (1949) and Hannah Arendt's *The Origins of Totalitarianism* (1951), two seminal works of the previous decade which set me on a course of reading political literature as a preferred interest. The structural strengths and weaknesses of *Nineteen Eighty-Four* particularly intrigued me. The literature then emerging from the Soviet Union and Eastern Europe I found more enthralling than that of the West. In 1967 I published an article 'Three Dissident Movements in the Soviet Union' in *Quadrant*, a magazine from the Congress For Cultural Freedom stable, and in 1969 an article on Ukrainian dissidents in *The Bulletin*, and I continued to publish on political literature thereafter.

A gulf gradually emerged in these years between two common views. On one side were those who in opposing the Vietnam War played down the deformities of Communism, and who as a result admired the protest movement and the counter culture, and in doing so drew attention to major fault lines, as they saw them, in Western societies. On the other side were those who saw the Soviet invasion of Czechoslovakia in 1968 as pivotal, confirming Orwell's and Arendt's analyses. To see Western protest movements as similar to those in the East we thought misleading. We continued to use Arendt's concept of 'totalitarianism' as a useful interpretative tool, to be modified as events developed, whereas in the United States university analysts quickly consigned it to the dustbin of history. In these circles the views I developed became minority ones, though still mainstream in Western societies generally. A strong attraction to political activity often exists among other strains in the modern make-up; under pressure it can evolve into a troubling will to power. Much political literature reveals individuals swept up by larger ideological worldviews, sometimes against their will. It is the drastic change from a normal to an abnormal situation, and then back again, which marks many forms of political literature. Much of it can be justly called anti-political or counter-political literature.

My wife Ann studied Russian literature for a year in 1967-8 at Leningrad University. During a sabbatical year in 1980-1 we both attended a seminar course, organized by Professor Leonard Shapiro and Peter Reddaway at the London School of Economics on contemporary Russian and East European politics. At the same time I attended a course on George Orwell at Birkbeck College by his biographer, Professor Bernard Crick. It was a tense year. At Soviet instigation the Polish Communist government was planning to clamp down on the Solidarity movement, with the Polish General Jaruzelski declaring martial law. The legitimacy of Communism was soon to be in tatters, so its former sympathizers in the West relinquished it, and instead devoted their energies to finding fault at home. I had a six month appointment teaching at Charles University in Prague in 1994 which helped further my knowledge of Eastern Europe. We visited Poland, Lithuania and Ukraine immediately before the Maidan uprising in Kyiv, which deposed the pro-Russian Ukrainian government in 2014.

By this time the dominance of literary theory had replaced many previous ways of assessing literature. Conundrums abounded. The new theorists argued that Dickens and Conrad were unconsciously supporting the industrialization and colonialism they thought they were opposing. But they kept away from the East, as it would have been hard to argue that Solzhenitsyn was an unwitting supporter of Communism. The recent aggressive behaviour of ISIS, and of Putin's

Russia and Xi's China, can be fitted into a modified totalitarian paradigm. In the West political correctness has developed as a new form of thought control whereby words like 'diversity' and 'inclusiveness' are strewn around, in a double-think kind of way, to achieve ends which are monochrome and exclusive.

My main interest is in political literature. But I found over the long haul that to appreciate these works it was necessary to understand their political and historical contexts, especially with East European and Russian literature. So my project gradually became of necessity not just lit. crit., but a two track one, with the literature and its political settings informing each other.

INTRODUCTION

Civil society has a number of interconnected layers: the public realm, intermediate layers consisting of society's many diverse organizations (educational, business, communal, and so), and the private realm of the family and individuals. We focus on our own lives, and on the public realm which since the 20th century has attracted enormous attention. However in a properly functioning civil society it is the middle realm, not the political one, which is the lynch pin and should be the focus. One role of governing organs is to allow the middle realms to flourish, and to protect them from intrusion. In modern times the state has often reversed these priorities, either by a revolutionary dissolving of long ingrained structures, or less dramatically by suborning the middle realms of society as a new means of maintaining control. Players in the middle and private realms can be drawn, often to their detriment, into the political sphere.

The 18th century political thinker Edmund Burke understood that civil societies grew up as a process of long natural organic growth. Regimes aiming at dominance had to sunder these deep rooted links in the process of imposing themselves. The leaders of newly formed institutions did not represent the interests of their constituents to a wider audience, as with past rulers; instead they attacked their own citizens, trying to convert them to the new paradigm. Edmund Burke understood the mentality of the new takeover merchants when he wrote of them in his *Reflections on the Revolution in France*:

> The temporary possessors and life-renters, unmindful of what they have received from their ancestors, or of what is due to their posterity, should act as if they were the entire masters; that they should not think it amongst their rights to commit waste on the

inheritance, by destroying at their pleasure the whole original fabric of their society; hazarding to leave to those who come after them, a ruin instead of an habitation. By this unprincipled facility of changing the state as often, and as much, and in as many ways as there are floating fancies or fashions, the whole chain and continuity of the commonwealth would be broken.[1]

This type of behaviour is the subject matter of much political literature. Burke reveals fanatics were wreaking societal havoc a century before Dostoievsky depicted them in *The Devils*. Burke distinguished between two types of organizations: organic ones which rise naturally in civil society over time, in contrast to artificial, instant, top-down structures, like the misnamed Committee for Public Safety during the French Revolution, conjured into existence out of nowhere. In the aftermath of the English Revolution of the 1640s, the poet Andrew Marvell described a society-wide meltdown and reformation, similar to that described by Burke, in the activities of Cromwell who

> Could by industrious valor climbe
>
> To ruin the great work of time
>
> And cast the kingdome old
>
> Into another mold.
>
> Though justice against fate complain,
>
> And plead the antient rights in vain:
>
> But those do hold or break
>
> As men are strong or weak.

What was new in totalitarianism? In the past, as long as citizens kept their heads down and didn't actively revolt, they could survive, as authoritarian regimes left them more or less alone. The romantic rebel and the outsider became stock heroes in modern literature. This was appropriate for depicting reactions to traditional types of rule, where instruments of oppression were brought out on particular occasions to coerce known opponents. Rulers were separated from their subjects,

---

1   Edmund Burke *Reflections on the Revolution in France*, 1790, Yale University Press, New Haven & London, 2003, p. 81.

who were seen at worst as potential enemies. But this template created difficulties in describing a totalitarian regime, where citizens are not remote from the means of control, but have to undergo rituals of complicity in the regime's actions on a frequent basis.

As the US political scientist Robert Nisbet pointed out, one way of defining totalitarianism is as an invasion by the state of its own civic culture. It is a form of internal imperialism by which the dominant political organs freeze autonomous social activity.[2] Such regimes try to cannibalize their own societies, breaking down its sinews. The German dramatist Bertolt Brecht joked that the East German Communist government should dismiss the people and elect another, but in a way that's what was routinely happening. Totalitarian regimes exist not just to govern a nation but to change it, to rearrange its constituents so that the building blocks of society take on radically new shapes. Existing groups are as a result diminished in influence and replaced by new ones formed in the regime's image. Through this process the political realm forms an alliance with supportive groups against the citizenry and civil society as a whole.

Many works of political literature are based on the understanding that Nazi and Communism were similar. Hence use of allegories – plague (Camus), rhinoceros (Ionesco), gangsters (Brecht) – which fit either case. Literature reveals that ideological distinctions between left and right were not crucial, but ideological drive was. But in some academic circles and among the progressive left the concept of totalitarianism has never been accepted as a useful explanatory tool, because its severe condemnation of Communism did not sit well with those who retained various degrees of attachment to Communism or the Soviet Union, or at least gave them the benefit of the doubt. And the left, for whom Nazism was the great beast, had to reject a family connection between Communism and Nazism, which use of the concept of totalitarianism leads to. But they still vilified Nazi Germany in terms very similar to those used in totalitarian analysis, while rarely using the word. Some of the US left were however happy to employ

---

2   Robert Nisbet, 'The Artist as Prophet', *National Interest*, Spring, 1992.

the notion of totalitarianism to describe their own country, since that was the prime target of their animus. The progressive US academic Abbott Gleeson's book *Totalitarianism* is a typical ridiculing of the concept, which he believes was illegitimately highjacked by Western Cold Warriors for internal political ends. Some US revisionist historians used the idea of 'totalitarianism from below' to justify Stalin's excesses on the ground that he was merely following the urgings of his people. Daniel Goldhagen's book *Hitler's Willing Executioners* revealed an analogous situation in Nazi Germany.

The term 'totalitarian' first arose in connection with Mussolini's Fascist regime, and gained wider currency when the more thoroughgoing regimes of Hitler and Stalin came to power from the late 1920s onwards. Totalitarianism was first identified in its apocalyptic form, regimes which tried to control all aspects of public and private life, including the minds of citizens. The notion came naturally into vogue to explain the dictatorships, concentration camps, extreme violence, and the resulting unprecedented dislocations which arose when these regimes destroyed civil society. Soviet and Nazi deformations were collectively stamped on the public mind as quintessential signs of a new phenomenon, different in kind from previous authoritarian regimes. People naturally thought this was totalitarianism's defining form. But totalitarianism was unusual in that its extreme form appeared first. It was seen as abnormal from the start, and was thought to be imposed from above as a political force. But did it always have to be total, as its label suggested; was this its essential form? Was it a purely political phenomenon, and did it arise exclusively from above?

Totalitarian behaviour did not arise out of the blue, as it appeared to when, in response to new horrors, the concept arose as a useful analytic tool. A similar but more circumscribed impulse to dominate had an earlier genesis in the later 19th century below the level of political visibility. Just as people were trying to cope with the difficult challenges of modernity, a new strategy combining thinking and action arose. It went largely unrecognized as a new form of human behaviour, though it is now sometimes retrospectively attributed to a proto-totalitarian personality. Ordinary people had been accustomed to think, in the standard way, that categories like subjective and objective were opposites. Radical activists began to subvert such neat divisions, and to employ more complex behaviours, such as aggressive defence, which confused people who thought in standard binary categories. This became a control device, an early form of the behaviour Orwell was many decades later to describe as 'double-think'. It employed thought categories in a 'creative' way to determine behaviour. Gifted authors were preternaturally sensitive to these new mind games.

Dostoievsky's *Notes From Underground* (1864), we now see in retrospect, revealed the existence of such a complex will to dominate in personal relations. Nietzsche tried in a discursive manner to describe this phenomenon. Perpetrators of this new kind of behaviour are today familiarly known as 'control freaks'. Totalitarianism acted like a virus in its incubation phase, being invisible, infectious and malign, but below the level of public visibility. This takeover behaviour, the basis of a new personality type, may be its normal form, and the Hitler-Stalin type an epiphenomenon, in which this new mode of behaviour expanded its reach into the public realm and, using new technologies available in the 20th century, took the will to power to its logical conclusion, where it became a grave danger to whole realms. The totalitarian personality can exist on the level of ordinary human interactions. JLTalmon, Hannah Arendt, Albert Camus, George Mosse and others have retrospectively traced its origins, but few were sensitive enough to recognize it as it developed, as Dostoievsky did. In its pre-political farm, totalitarian behaviour appeared before Mussolini, Lenin, Hitler and Stalin. Their radical behaviour was so unprecedented it disguised its true origins. Totalitarianism did have a pre-history, an incubation phase, which being subliminal and non-political, assumed a less than total, and a less than visible, form. It arose at the same time as modernity, roughly 1870 to 1920, which caused great confusion. Unused to coping with the mixed messages sent out by totalitarian personalities and regimes, the public mind found it difficult to understand the connections between modernity and totalitarianism, and the differences between them. Some embraced totalitarianism by mistakenly thinking it was just a more intense form of modernity.

After this preparatory, pre-political phase, came the takeover or installation phase, when a new power group escalated its control mechanisms to dominate a whole society, moving it from a normal to an abnormal situation. The outcome of such a successful revolution was a coercive, highly politicised society. The meltdown of social structures near the end of the first world war prepared the ground for takeovers by Mussolini and Lenin. A similar disintegration after the Great Depression ushered in Hitler's regime and Mao's in the chaos after the second world war. Would-be totalitarian tyrants needed both to take over a country, and then to keep the masses they ruled under permanent thrall. Lenin and Mussolini came to power after *coup d'etat* style revolutions, with the ground not prepared, so the societal revolution had to take place subsequently. Hitler was preparing the ground by winning over the populace before coming to power in 1933, but he also needed to obtain the permanent allegiance of citizens thereafter. The next stage was a society under a permanent condition of heightened terror, the period of concentration camps, purges and mass terror, where domination was more or less complete, and the chances of avoiding it negligible. The heightened phase in both Germany and Russia came in the early 1930s to middle 1940s. But whereas the German regime was terminated quickly in 1945 by external military intervention, the Soviet regime continued in its apocalyptic form until Stalin's death in 1953. The two cases thereafter had quite different trajectories. A further phase came after a regime was confident it has consolidated its grip on power, as in Russia and East Europe in the decades after Stalin's death. The imposed domination diminished to an intermediate stage, where overt terror and fear were lessened, and where resistance was at least possible, if still unlikely to succeed. Finally there was a stage when (either abruptly or gradually) repression was overcome. All these stages are exhaustively covered in political literature. As well as political dominance, literature also reveals various modes of surviving, resisting and overcoming these intrusions, as totalitarian regimes, despite their name, were of greatly varying intensity.

INTRODUCTION

The post-war situation in East Europe and the Soviet Union raised new problems, as domination reduced its intensity, as we see in *Nineteen Eighty-Four*. The new situation revealed both public and private forms of subservience. The regimes retained the essential characteristics described in the classic accounts of totalitarianism, but the methods of coercion were more indirect and less visible – some *modus vivendi* between citizen and state had been tentatively arrived at. The traditional separation of regime and society was now more blurred, and complicit attitudes had just as important a role to play as structural domination. It became a species of massive endemic collusion as much as a naked tyrannical display, as many individuals participated in spreading the contagion. In the Soviet Russia, where it had existed for seven decades by the 1980s, the totalitarian mentality was more thoroughly internalized than it had been in Nazi Germany, where it had only little over a decade to flourish, or in the east European Communist satellites where it had existed for just over four decades.

The concept of totalitarianism had therefore to be modified to encompass the post-Stalin Communist regimes of the Soviet Union and East Europe. A more normalized form of control was present, somewhat akin on a personal level to Dostoievsky's Underground Man, but more virulent from having learnt from the past. The Russian novelist Zinoviev believed the new *modus vivendi* so reached was the next form of bureaucratic organization in modern societies. To cope with this new situation (victors and victims sharing roles, complicity from below, and so on), new definitions have been advanced to suggest a continuity between the all stages (pre, extreme and later), which allowed for a spectrum linking totalitarianism and normality. The Hungarian writer Miklos Haraszti distinguished between 'hard' and 'soft' totalitarianism, John Westling between its *grand mal* form and the *petit mal* form noticeable in the West, and the Russian Natalia Lubomirova between its vertical and horizontal ('silent, daily, non-active') forms. This was also known as 'totalitarianism from below'. These were attempts to see the totalitarian malady not as an epiphenomenon, something wildly different from all other forms of behaviour, but as having connections with more routine events, while still acknowledging that the regimes of Lenin, Hitler, Stalin. Mao and Pol Pot were unique. This provided a continuity, connecting it with the other periods, and with the more disturbed situation in the West from the 1960s onwards.

The new totalitarians had themselves in their early careers been radical dissidents and revolutionaries, experts in civil destruction. This was their formative experience, which never left them; even in power they never relinquished this deep adversary stance, never fully admitting to authority, always continuing to play the radical outsider, though they wielded centralized power ruthlessly. They were always claiming they were victims of the current situation, never content with the status quo, never admitting they were the new establishment, always calling for an ongoing revolution, a permanent stirring of the porridge, with the result that a skeletal form of an opposition was less likely to arise. This helped keep themselves in control. This contrary position – power and dissidence combined in the supreme leader – necessitated a double-think mentality to encompass it. Double think, a notion first described by George Orwell, is the ability to keep contrary notions in one's head at the same time, and to be able to switch seamlessly between them, as a control mechanism over others, and a rationalization mechanism for oneself.

The revolutionary changes sought and brought about by Fascist and Communist regimes didn't automatically come into being after the first imposition of power. As physical revolution and violence lost their efficacy over time, various forms of complicity-inducing indoctrination became a principal tool of change. Trotsky's notion of permanent revolution, whereby skeletal social structures had to be continually broken down through new ideological impositions, was a natural response to this situation. Radical dissatisfaction with current reality became, paradoxically, the permanent stance of rulers. The new strategy was for those in control to cozen up to the populace, to make people identify with the new mentality, as though both had similar objectives. In the place of straight forward arguments those in power situations insinuated their unlikely paradoxical, contradictory notions into the populace at large. Regimes inveigled their citizenry into a form of self-generating complicity, converting them from functioning subjects into compromised objects. Instead of frontal attack, as in the past, they disarmed their targets and co-opted them – each individual participated at the same time in the roles of both oppressor and victim familiar to the dictator, and so passed on the domination virus, as well as being subject to it. We have in us drives to domination, submission and resistance in various measures. These are not impulses external to us, not entirely imposed from above, nor existing only in the political realm. The new political apparatchiks were unique in inducing their subjects to become accomplices in generating the domination virus themselves. They mobilized for political ends new psychological insights into techniques of domination and complicity, such as the return of the repressed and the carrot and the stick, which had been developing to cope with modern life.

Of course with totalitarian rulers the threat of the periodic use of force was always present, and often employed, but a battery of other, more subtle, means of coercion was utilized as well. Both coercion and complicity, a double-think combination, were necessary tools of control in totalitarian societies. In the early stages, as illustrated in Dostoievsky's works, complicity was at the forefront and physical coercion was minimal. In its heightened stage, as in the Hitler and Stalin regimes, coercion was pre-eminent. But as regimes 'normalized' themselves complicity, which had never disappeared, again became the favoured control mechanism. The aim of totalitarian regimes has always been to have their populations in spiritual thrall to them; they want their citizenry to have internalized the regimes' Big Brother mentality, preferably voluntarily.

Many political science theories of totalitarianism emphasized structural domination from above, and separation of the ruling powers from ordinary society. Control was seen to be imposed by dictators and their henchmen on passive and unwilling populations, the suffering victims. In other words, it was seen as essentially a political phenomenon. But modes of domination can arise not only nor primarily from above, but from other structures in society, and in the hearts and minds of ordinary people. The political science approach to the problem is instructive and necessary, but incomplete. Take physical violence as an example, which is rightly emphasized in the classic accounts. It seemed a defining feature, yet in post-war East European Communist societies, it was not as pervasive or central as previously. In the past police torture, visits at 4 am, camps, and long prison sentences were the norm; now control was maintained without these being at the forefront. Political science typologies could explain only some parts of the new mentality, the overt part.

Political literature, which covers all these developments, is especially important in describing societies in their middle level or pre-political phase, and in revealing the first tremors of absorption into the political realm. Political literature also reveals the processes by which social structures can be totally replaced by new regimes. Conversely it can show how societies are able to de-escalate from a dangerous over-preoccupation with overtly political matters. Middle level organizations can, and should, combine with the private realm to ward off too great intrusion from the state, which is not meant to be paramount, as Burke understood. In contrast political literature enables us to get a more complete inner understanding of regimes which play control games. The double-think arguments loved by power seeking ideologues are scarcely amenable to straight forward, rational analysis. Only through a novel like Koestler's *Darkness at Noon* can we fully come to understand the tortuous logic by which a show trial victim like Rubachev becomes complicit in his own elimination. Literature can operate on many layers at the same time, conveying different effects. This takes it beyond monochrome linear prose analysis. Literature can thus simultaneously mimic, and re-enact, competing layers of political activity. By operating on more than one level at the same time, it is suited to recreating the complex nature of double-think mind games, and in doing so revealing them. For this reason we can first discern in political literature the pre-political phase of totalitarian activity. Poets may or may not be the unrecognised legislators of the world, but authors often act as canaries in the mine, sensitive enough to pick up at an early stage underground seismic shifts in behaviour patterns. Some authors became ideological barrackers of tyrants, but the majority in their literary works recreated, and abhorred, the new moves in society in a more revealing way than the standard analyses of political commentary.

A form of intimate human manoeuvring exists even in apocalyptic situations, though in this case the personal side is often hidden from view by the immensity of the imposed domination. Literature reveals that personal complicity exists in all stages, even in extreme circumstances, as in Solzhenitsyn's *One Day in the Life of Ivan Denisovich*. Characters in literature engage in opposing roles, such as domination and resistance, simultaneously. Literature reveals that the will to power, the urge to dominate, is potentially in all of us. In this way processes of intimidation can come to have a momentum of their own. Authors revealed how domination first appeared in personal form, and how potentially all people can carry the virus, and some are able to develop, and some to halt, it. Literature also reveals non-visible levels of domination, which were evident in post-war East Europe, and in the politically correct realms of Western society. A tolerance trick is played by the politically correct: tolerance is granted to those who hold acceptable views, but not to those who don't. This is having it both ways, an example of double-think, holding opposite views in mind at the same time. As a result normal argument can itself become the problem, not the solution.

Today we are left with the post-totalitarian societies of East Europe on the one hand, and the West on the other. The rise of Islamist terrorism and the increasingly repressive regimes in China and Russia are reviving the questions first raised in confronting totalitarian regimes. Are there any similarities or connections between them? Some critiques of the West describe it as unfree, a place where the establishment maintains control by Big Brother propaganda techniques. Social analysts like Adorno and Marcuse, members of the Frankfurt School which set up the notion of the authoritarian personality, believed the West's rulers controlled society subliminally by dulling revolutionary aspiration through media and consumer saturation. From an opposite perspective others believed that the clampdown on tolerance and free expression, now known as 'political correctness', itself has a soft totalitarian underlay. The rise in today's society of control freaks who strive to manipulate everything around them for their own benefit suggests that a word like 'totalist' is best used to describe this drive, rather than the word 'totalitarian', which is too strong for our condition in the West. But evidence exists of features of totalitarianism in its *petit mal* form into our society, just as the East Europeans are coming out of it.

1

THE UNDERGROUND MAN EMERGES

Julian Assange is by no means a unique phenomenon. To understand him we have to go back to the later nineteenth century, where a new personality type, intent on domination in the personal and social spheres, arose. It achieved this by becoming adept at psychological understanding of his own and others' motivations, and by developing an ability – subtle, persuasive and insinuating – to manipulate his milieu for his own ends. In Russia this new type was known as the 'superfluous man'. He was usually a male thinker lacking a useful profession, disenchanted with society and living outside it, at least in his mind. The great literary expression of the type is the 'hero' of Dostoievsky's early novella *Notes From Underground* (1864). The title refers to one who lives beneath the level of the floorboards in a small basement (today he might inhabit an embassy nook). Symbolically the title means one who has haughtily withdrawn from mainstream society, because in his own mind he clearly sees its defects. His aim is to justify himself, which he does to his own satisfaction by revealing society's stupidities, like the anti-heroes of many modern novels such as Camus' *The Outsider*, Donleavy's *The Ginger Man* and Boll's *The Clown*. He is an intelligent, isolated male, in whom all experience is refracted through the prism of his critical consciousness, the jumbled thoughts coursing uncontrollably through his brain.

Dostoievsky's Underground Man is self-obsessed, subject to frequent mood-swings and suffers from a too fervid imagination. In the first half of the novella he engages in an argument with himself, but it is also a dialogue with an imagined interlocutor. He is an adept thinker who can handle complex ideas; he anticipates any objection to his flow of thought and readily counters it. He enjoys this argumentative mode, as he is seeking to persuade his interlocutor (and the reader) of the justice of his arguments. His existence consists of a long, remorseful reverie in which past embarrassments and future Walter Mitty-like escapades of imagined incidents roll through his mind as though on film. He is seeking to persuade the interlocutor of the sense of his arguments, but also to exert some control over him. He exults in startling paradoxes, at stages saying: 'too great a lucidity is a disease' (p. 93) and also 'consciousness is man's greatest plague' (p. 118).[3] He is deadly serious, yet playing with us all.

All possible contingencies, and every possible (and self-serving) reply to them, are thought up by him, but the self-referring dialogue (half confession, half accusation) has little necessary relation to reality. It is dictated primarily by his personal urges, and is imposed upon reality. He puts himself through the wringer, playing out the roles of both tormentor and victim in the dramas being acted out in his own mind. By undergoing all emotional states, and by living dangerously, he understands them when they occur in others and can therefore exploit their weaknesses. It is a dress rehearsal for future encounters, both personal and political. His consciousness, which alternates between spasms of passion and boredom, gratifies him, as he finds the contemplation of his own tortuously brilliant 'logic' the greatest satisfaction of all.

He sets it down because it relieves him to do so. He is doing it primarily for himself. He is not so much self-questioning as self-torturing: 'We can at least lacerate ourselves from time to time, which does liven us up a bit.' (p. 118). He is a 'lover of paradoxes' (p. 203) who has discovered the more he is made abject, the more he

---

3   All page references are to editions listed in the bibliography.

can take advantage of a situation and become dominant (in the past such a person would have felt incapacitated by his depression and slunk away). He gets a sadistic thrill by putting others and especially himself through the ropes: 'I derived pleasure precisely from the blinding realisation of my degradation' (p. 94). These are strange contradictions. (The underground man's moodswings may reflect Dostoievsky's memory of his earlier gambling compulsion, which involved swings between fantasy, hope and deep self-loathing.)

Of one character we are told 'he becomes passionate as he expostulates upon human interests...Then, exactly fifteen minutes later, without any apparent external cause...he pirouettes and starts saying exactly the opposite of what he was saying before.' (pp. 106-7).[4] The narrator is himself prey to these quick changes of mood; one minute he is dominant, the next submissive, he is happy, then sad, confident then depressed, meek then aggressive, powerless then powerful, and so on:

> It is noteworthy that I usually thought of "the sublime and the beautiful" during my dissipation, often just when I hit the rock-bottom of abjection. These thoughts...seemed to spice it up by contrast and, like a good sauce, helped bring out the taste. This sauce, concocted of contradictions and suffering, contained painful self-analysis, and the resulting agonies and torments added piquancy and even meaning to my dissipation. (pp. 136-7)

He enjoys this mental gymnastics in which each polarity stimulates its opposite. Characters like the narrator are an apparently mercurial mass of contradictions, but they use these sudden switches of moods to destabilize others while remaining in control of the situation themselves: 'I kept shifting from one extreme to the other for no apparent reason: one day I'd despise them, the next I'd feel they were my betters.' (p. 125) This rapid, seemingly irrational shifting between contradictory roles reveals a character adept at an early private form

---

4   Regime propaganda in *Nineteen Eighty-Four* similarly alternates at the flick of a switch from reviling Eastasia to reviling Eurasia; the Underground Man's combining the roles of bully and victim was replicated on a larger canvas in later political literature.

of double-think. Strange magnetic attractions of opposites occur; the Underground Man doesn't like his servant Apollon, but depends on him. Who is running the show in this relationship? Role reversals abound. Self-hatred leads to bullying of others, despising oneself leads to feeling superior to one's companions. About the prostitute Lisa the Underground Man realizes: 'the more repulsive she finds me, the better I'll like it', a familiar masochistic form of enjoyment (p. 163). Power games towards a classmate are evident: 'I was already a tyrant at heart and wanted to be the absolute ruler of his mind...It was as though I'd only wanted his total friendship just for the sake of winning it and making him submit to me.' (p. 147)

The Underground Man develops a mode of ideological thinking which is very difficult to defeat on its own terms, since it can always produce arguments to justify itself, the more daring and breathtaking the better. These arguments have no stable, objective 'content'. In his mind he has, like Mr Kurtz in *The Heart of Darkness*, 'lost all restraint'. It's a very daring and dangerous game he's playing at, but in the end, with all his attempts to ensnare others, it's only himself he is bogging down. His realization that vengeance 'will hurt itself a hundred times more than it will hurt the one against whom its revenge is directed' (p. 97) is one of the lessons the hero learns in his attempt to pay back his school friends. With those he knows he plays a taunting game. His aim is to achieve psychological mastery of any situation by a complicated game of self-abasement. He wishes to torture others by humiliating himself – 'humiliation is purification' (p. 202). His basic method is to establish at the outset his victim status – apparently inferior, vulnerable and powerless – to disarm people with this 'admission' and to then use this as a cover for a takeover operation. He understands emotions like shame, guilt, humiliation, and embarrassment, since he undergoes them himself, and uses them to get power over others. These are destructive strategies. We know them today as text book examples of control mechanisms, deployed personally in the nineteenth century, and later politically in the twentieth.

In the first half of the novella the hero reveals his devious character. The second half displays him as a control freak in action in a series of revealing incidents: his school friends' party, his visit to the prostitute Lisa, his relations with his servant Apollon, and a return visit from Liza, all structured so they psychologically play off against each other. The underground man carries out his initial foray at a party of his old schoolfellows, into whose company he insinuates himself. On the previous evening he has disoriented his former colleagues by his self-invited presence. Naturally tolerant and polite, their inability to exclude him at the start incapacitates them later from taking action against him. At the party next evening he dominates the scene for his own ends, imposing his own agenda on it, in the process destroying it, even though he is an outsider to the company. He turns the event into a power struggle between himself and a past acquaintance, Zverkov, and as a result ruins the evening as a festive occasion: 'It was still within my power to start trouble'. (p. 130) He contrives to make himself, not the guest-of-honour, Zverkov, the centre of attention. He uses controlled moodswings to destabilize his fellow guests. He insults Zverkov and then profusely apologizes, the carrot-and-stick method of breaking human resilience, familiar from later brainwashing episodes. He implicates others in this charade so they in turn play out the roles of both aggressor and victim he assigns to them. Since he understands the 'contemptible stratagems' of his opponents and of himself, he acts with great daring or chutzpah, as when he asks to borrow money from a colleague, Simonov, at the end of the party in order to show he has broken him. His school friends have no ability to mount effective resistance to him. All this is not done purely by previous design; as the event unfolds he feels driven by his self-destructive bent to improvise more devilish designs. He despises ordinary bourgeois people like his former school friends; they are people who in his mind aren't daring, who don't have his heightened consciousness. He is intent on destroying what Edmund Burke called the 'small platoons', the essential building blocks of any society.

During an episode later that evening with the prostitute Liza he plays a similar taunting game. Finding himself bored and in a nasty mood, with 'vicious zest' (p. 167) he gets a sadistic thrill by detailing her grim future of decline rather than marriage, thereby destroying her romantic illusions about love. He dissolves her stable sense of herself by the stratagem of suddenly alternating his mood between sentimentality and brutal frankness, thus achieving control over her, his basic aim. Telling her the potential truth of her situation does not help her, on the contrary. He destroys her with this revelation, and thus enjoys humiliating her. He claims to be removing her from one form of slavery (prostitution) but is indoctrinating her into another form, being in thrall to him who is only toying with her. She sees him as a saviour figure, whereas he is in it for manipulative than rather sexual pleasure. Enjoying her humiliation, he disarms her with his frankness: 'Although I may defile and degrade myself, I'm still no one's slave'. (p. 169) She is now his psychological slave. Though in hock to a madam ('you've sold your soul to the devil') she is now just as much in debt to him psychologically. He passes on to Liza his own role-reversal virus: 'I've been made a doormat, so I wanted to show my power and wipe my feet on someone else' (p. 195) Arbitrarily and swiftly switching sides between subjection and dominance becomes a control device which is hard to counter.

'You're just like a book' (p. 174) Liza remarks, and he later adds, in another reference to literature: 'What I was really after at that moment were power and a role to play.' (p. 196). He is playing with her as though she is a character in a romantic novel, whereas she is deadly serious and taken in by him: 'my cynicism had crushed her.' (p. 195). Dostoievsky is drawing attention here to a perverse similarity between literature and the personal domination of another – in both the ability to imagine oneself in others' shoes is paramount. This is a sadistic destruction of a vulnerable helpless being for his own ends. The Underground Man enjoys driving her to despair, at the same time partly hating himself for doing it. This is a classic early case of gradual personal brainwashing – domination by cozening up and getting her confidence, grooming her so she is now in his grip. But he is also deceiving, and brainwashing, himself.

In the next incident these roles are neatly reversed: his servant

Apollon becomes the initiating force, and deals out a similar kind of humiliation to the Underground Man as he has to his school comrades and to Liza, the same contradictions, roles reversal and switching. The narrator first tries a detached Napoleonic demeanour towards Apollon, but this does not work, and he soon becomes the victim of his servant's superior stratagems. Apollon puts on an air of being haughty, distant, calmly in control, and won't give an inch. The two have psychologically swapped their formal roles of master and servant. The Underground Man becomes angry with him, calls him a 'vicious bully', and tries to punish him by withholding his wages. Apollo was the Greek god of calm rationality in contrast to the Dionysian extremes of the Underground Man, who juggles excess and control: 'I instinctively want to live, to exercise all the aspects of life in me and not only reason.' (p. 112). Apollon successfully plays the controller role, previously so familiar to the Underground Man, who can't break his servant's will. Apollon is overbearing, supercilious and sarcastic like his master. Apollon despises him, just as the Underground Man despises his old school friends and Liza. The domination/humiliation virus is beginning to up set up a chain reaction in society.

In modernist literature the liberated hero feels he lives under no thrall, countenances no taboos, and acknowledges no domain outside his own resources. Arrogant, paranoid, perverse, sadistic and self-pitying, he egoistically expands his own personality to fill the void. This leads to narcissism and the wish for power for its own sake. The Underground Man is an early example of the adversary thinker – he wishes to destroy whatever is a going concern. His is potentially a takeover operation, but in this particular case Dostoievsky's hero wants only to temporarily control others, but not to permanently hog-tie them. He is only playing with personal power and discloses no larger design for a better world. He understands the subtle mechanisms of a new form of domination, just as Solzhenitsyn later imagined, in his *Lenin in Zurich*, the feverish, manipulative mind of Lenin as a deracinated radical thinker before he came to power. The Underground Man is a proto-totalitarian personality.

In this early novella Dostoievsky explored mechanisms of personal domination. But the novella is not just about personal psychopathology. Dostoievsky tentatively developed in it an argument about the way a whole society organises itself; he was interested here in the wider connections between civilisation and tyranny. Dostoievsky rejected the commonly held view that 'man mellows under the influence of civilization and becomes less bloodthirsty and less prone to war.' (p. 107) Instead his narrator points out a strange anomaly: 'Have you noticed, for instance, that the most refined, bloodthirsty tyrants, compared to whom the Atillas and Stenka Razins are mere choirboys, are often exquisitely civilised?' (p. 108) Refinement and brutality hold hands: this anticipates later behaviour by Nazis and Communists, such as concentration camp supervisors who enjoyed classical music in the evening after a hard day's 'work'. High civilization is paradoxically linked with tyranny; boredom will lead to torture being welcomed. Dostoievsky also explored and deplored a possible future society being organised on scientific, planned, utopian lines. His images for this were the immense Crystal Palace (built in London in 1851) and the ant-hill. He saw danger in utopian schemes, in 'all the classifications and tables drawn up by humanitarians for the happiness of mankind'. (p. 107)

Dostoievsky later expanded these early insights in one of his major novels, *The Devils*, where the same drives to domination are deployed but on a wider social canvas. In its society-wide manifestation the engorging hubris of the Underground Man leads to megalomaniac state power, which appropriates to itself all rights, meanings and controls. The combination of a destructive, anti-establishment personality with the ability to gain political control later led to totalitarian rule, which Dostoievsky was one of the first to foresee. Dostoievsky understood that utopian schemes for the betterment of mankind did not allow for the nasty, dark side of human nature which the Underground Man himself displays.

Nietzsche developed a strong fellowship feeling with Dostoievsky, admiring his writings. Their great works came out at the same time, the decades of the 1870s and the 1880s. Preternaturally sensitive to the embryonic currents of modernism, they took up similar themes but in different forms: Nietzsche explored these new ideas in discursive philosophic commentary, not in imaginative fiction as Dostoievsky did. We notice the personality of the Underground Man displays many of the characteristics Nietzsche was to delineate, but not necessarily endorse. Like the Underground Man, Nietzsche advanced radical, shocking views. In the writings of both we notice an oscillation between an Apollonian outlook (harmonious, balanced) and a Dionysian (frenzied, bohemian) one. Nietzsche set up this polarity as the basis of his first work *The Birth of Tragedy*, which appeared in 1872, eight years after Dostoievsky's *Notes From Underground*, so it is possible Nietzsche was influenced by it. Nietzsche believed the two qualities, Dionysian and Apollonian, in combination were needed to produce a true tragic hero, who had great insights aspiring to the condition of art. We sense that in later life the Underground Man will become an unbalanced character, in whom the Dionysian strain may become ascendant.

Nietzsche's announcement of the death of God situated an individual, like the Underground Man, in a challenging realm where he had to overthrow accepted verities and moralities, and yet forge a new path so as not succumb to the temptation of nihilism, which the collapse of religious belief invited. Christianity was rejected by Nietzsche as a slave mentality, the province of the week who wallow in the crippling emotion of pity. In its place individuals had to move beyond conventional mentality based on good and evil, and have the confidence to be masters of their destiny rather than be slaves to it. They had to develop from their own resources the will to power, to lift themselves by personal striving to become masterful *ubermenschen*, courageously inhabiting a lonely landscape of the mind, a form of creativity akin to art, the highest expression of the Dionysian spirit.

This congruence between some of Nietzsche's and Dostoievsky's insights in *Notes From Underground* should not surprise us (though Dostoievsky remained a Christian), as both were ahead of the pack in discerning the first underground tremors of larger disruptions which lay ahead. This does not mean that Nietzsche was a pathfinder for Fascist or other totalitarian projects, since we cannot assume when Nietzsche describes some new condition that he is automatically supporting it, nor does he set out any political agenda. But his views did have consequences, which, rightly or wrongly, were developed by his followers in subsequent decades.

Dostoievsky expanded his psychological insights into personal domination in *Notes From Underground* to a wider canvas, potentially the whole of society, in *The Devils* (first published in magazine form in 1871-2), itself an early premonition of events in Russia. The aspiring revolutionaries, led by the young squires, Peter Verkhovensky and Nicholas Stavrogin, deliberately sow despair, confusion and fear among ordinary people as they try to hollow out the weak structures of the Tsarist regime, as a preliminary to destroying the 'small platoons' of its society. They are able to operate effectively because, as Dostoievsky understood, Russian society has lost belief in itself. The mood of the upper classes was frivolous and loose, silly behavior was abroad, people were bored, the foundations of a hierarchically structured order, necessary as a social cement, were crumbling 'as though they had become uprooted or as though the floor had suddenly given way under their feet.' (p. 332). The out-of-touch provincial gentry, whose children in reaction have become revolutionaries, is tellingly satirized. And rudderless liberals like the novelist Karamazinov (based on Turgenev), who embraced modernity and liberalism in a desperate bid to get on with the new wave, display how enlightened they believe they are. They mistakenly assume the revolutionaries are on the same wave-length as themselves, whereas the revolutionaries want to shut down liberties for everyone.

The revolutionaries incite their small band of followers by artificially creating an atmosphere of expectation and heightened tension. They cast a spell over their disciples, like Kurtz in *Heart of Darkness* and the devils of the Gospel story who infect the Gardarene swine with their demented behavior. (pp. 647-8). (An alternative translation of the novel's title is *The Possessed*.) The plot is loosely based on the activities of the Nechayev circle, extreme nihilist terrorists who killed one of their circle as a blood bond to implicate the rest. The Russian revolutionary tradition fused Marxist anti-bourgeois class theory, the revolutionary activism of Nechayev and his like, and the Dionysian frenzy anatomized by Nietzsche, a combination which produced the Russian meltdown that Dostoievsky sensed.

Members of the new generation, epitomized by the youthful Verkovensly and Stavrogin, exhibit in a more developed form and on a wider canvas the proto-totalitarian personality exhibited by the Underground Man. Stavrogin presents himself as utterly calm, detached, confident and in control: 'It seemed as though nothing could embarrass him…His articulation was amazingly clear; his words fell from his lips like large smooth grains, always carefully chosen, and always at your service'. This duplicitous style, this dissembling reminiscent of the Underground Man, makes him hard to handle: 'At first you could not help liking it [his verbal facility], but later on you hated… this string of every-ready words'. (p. 188). The would-be revolutionaries first move is to use words and arguments as weapons, they employ plausible but faulty logic, a series of arguments which sound impressive at first blush, but which are internally contradictory and which in the cold light of day lack commonsense. One of the group, Kirilov, believes (like Ibsen's Hedda Gabler) that suicide is liberating: 'Everyone who desires supreme freedom must dare to kill himself… He who dares to kill himself is a god'. Such beguiling paradoxes and language games in fact contradict reality – death in this context is not freedom but escapism, a death wish – and confuse one's followers. It follows that atheism and nihilism are necessary preconditions for revolutionary commitment, which by a perverse reasoning follows logically: 'So now every one can make it so there shall be no God and there shall be nothing.' (p. 126). To which Shatov, who dissents from these views, later replies: 'The first sign of the decay of nations is when they begin to have common gods' (p. 257). The death of God spawns a multiplicity of new ones, as Chesterton later understood.

In the novel ideas which present themselves as noble turn out to have malign underpinnings. Shatov rightly accuses the rebels, who have gone beyond right and wrong, of blurring the distinction between a brutish and an heroic act. He understands why the impressive Stavrogin marries a crippled woman: 'Just because the infamy and absurdity of such a marriage reached the pitch of genius...You got married because of your passion for cruelty...It was a case of morbid hysteria. The challenge to common sense was too tempting to be resisted!' (pp. 260-1) Stavrogin uses his wife for his own thrill-seeking ends, just as the Underground Man uses Liza. Shatov, in many respects a spokesman for the author's views, understands the revolutionaries' high minded but contradictory ideals:

> It's all because of their servile thoughts. There's also hatred there. They would be the first to be unhappy if Russia was suddenly to be reorganized even according to their own ideas...They would have no one to hate then; no one to despise; no one to laugh at. It's just an everlasting animal hatred of Russia which has corroded their organism. (pp. 146-7)

Shatov's warning is: Don't give credence to their arguments, but note their underlying motivations, which are exactly opposite. They are part of what we today call the adversary culture, those who despise their own country while claiming to be its cheerleaders and saviours.

Much later in the action, Dostoievsky provides his own riposte to the notion that this 'supreme freedom' is liberating. Shigalyov, a chastened rebel, recalls the perverse path his thinking took: 'My conclusion is in direct contradiction to the original idea with which I start. Starting from unlimited freedom, I arrived at unlimited despotism'. (p. 404). 'Unlimited despotism' is on the same level as Kurtz's terrible cry near the end of *Heart of Darkness*: 'Exterminate all the brutes'. The revolutionary's claimed desire for freedom leads to murder, a glaring anomaly. From this follows their idea of a lowest common denominator society, where equality is produced by reducing all ranks, including the aristocracy, to the level of slavery. Verkhovensky attests: 'Slaves must be equal: without despotism there has never been any freedom or equality'. (p. 418) It is a peculiar form of equality: 'Every member of the society spies on the other, and he is obliged to inform against them', a prophetic insight of Russia under Stalin. The revolutionary 'rejects morality as such and is in favour of the latest principle of general destruction for the sake of the ultimate good. He already demands more than a hundred million heads for the establishment of common sense in Europe'. (p. 106). This strange self-defeating logic – evil is needed to do good, coercion produces freedom – unsurprisingly leads to mass killings, a premonition of the regimes of Lenin, Stalin, Hitler, Mao and Pol Pot.

Dostoievsky was also prescient in anticipating the method – crushing civil society by giving power to the soviets – by which the Bolsheviks were able to take over Russia half a century after he was writing:

> A picture of Russia covered with an endless network of small groups. Each of these active groups…aims by systematic propaganda to expose the local authorities and to undermine their prestige, to throw the village population into confusion, to promote cynicism and public scandals, utter disbelief in everything under the sun…to throw the country at a given moment, if necessary, into a mood of despair. (p. 544)

Then 'when society – sick, depressed, cynical, and godless… had been brought to the point of collapse, they would suddenly seize power, raising the banner of revolt.' (p. 662) Their real aim was to tear everything down, not to revivify society: 'We shall proclaim destruction – why? why? – well, because the idea is so fascinating!... an upheaval will start. There is going to be such a to-do as the world has never seen. Russia will become shrouded in a fog, the earth will weep for its old gods'. (p. 422) This is the paradoxical notion, really a contradiction, that wholesale destruction will lead to a new, better, type of society. The revolutionaries and their followers are depicted in religious terms, like the swine in the Biblical story, possessed by devil spirits beyond their control. (p. 647) Dostoevsky shared the Slavophile belief that only deep Orthodox Christian beliefs could save his country: 'An atheist at once ceases to be a Russian.' 'Do you know who are now the only 'god-bearing' people on earth, destined to regenerate and save the world?...It is the spirit of life, as the Scripture says, 'rivers of living water', the running dry of which is threatened in Revelation'. (pp. 255-6) Later Bulgakov similarly invoked, in his novel *The Master and Margarita*, the presence of devils to depict the Bolsheviks.

Dostoievsky's devils have many of the 'soft totalitarian' characteristics of modern adversary culture: aggressive defense, destabilizing society, intellectual language games, hating one's own, escalating one's demands, pseudo tolerance, power seeking above all, and so on. Their idea that suicide is liberating is a typical false paradox by which one can prove (by contorted logic) anything one desires. But some components of a society-wide takeover are missing at this early stage in *The Devils*: the rebels are not yet in charge of society, and don't have the means to carry out their program. Except for the murder of Shatov, it all remains in the provinces and as a notion in their heads. But the spark (*iskra*) is there.

With his British Isles upbringing Edmund Burke understood the need for societies to build up over time a network of strong civic institutions, and how they could be radically corroded by extremist eruptions. In *The Devils* Dostoievsky demonstrated how, as also in the French case, a fading ruling aristocracy which still held power could suffocate the natural functions of civil society, and so open the way for revolutionaries to shatter its moribund structure.[5] The failure of aristocratic regimes to modernize created opportunities for tyrannies to arise in France in 1789 and in Russia in 1917. The further demoralization of the old ruling classes after the deluge incapacitated them from taking effective action against their new overlords. These intrusions were made easier by widespread social breakdown, typically in times of war and depression, as happened with the rise of the dictators between the world wars. For the *grand mal* form of totalitarianism, the

---

5   In Donald Smith's *Former People: The Last Days of the Russian Aristocracy*, Pan Books London, 2013, the Russian ruling class is shown as incapable of facing the Bolshevik threat.

first world war was an obvious candidate as enabler. The war led to loss of stability, the collapse of patriotism and other strong belief systems, which in turn produced disillusionment and cynicism. The war atomized Russian society, leading to Lenin's *coup d'etat*, but with the ground not fully prepared. Mussolini's takeover was part coup, part popular agitation in the chaotic post-war situation. The Weimar period and the Great Depression fatally weakened Germany. Hitler's coming to power was part parliamentary election, part popular extra-parliamentary support. Mao rose to power after the Chinese society was destroyed by civil strife in the 1930s followed by the second world war.[6]

---

6   Likewise ISIS, a terrorist group with a totalitarian ideology, took control for a time in parts of Iraq and Syria in the vacuum caused by civil strife in those countries.

2

PORTENTS OF TROUBLE

Believing himself to be an advanced thinker, the Underground Man exclaims contemptuously of Liza: 'That's only to be expected of these stupid, pure-hearted romantics! Ah, damn them, these filthy, stupid, rotten, sentimental souls.' (p. 185) The Underground Man here reveals himself changing from a romantic to a more advanced attitude. The half century from 1870 to 1920 was a disturbed, transitional period, as Matthew Arnold understood: 'We stand between two worlds, one dead/ The other powerless to be born'. What shape would new alignments take? In this period literature exemplified a new approach known as modernism, while at the same time giving hints of more daring strategies to come. Modernity looked to the future not the past, rejecting previous belief systems such as religions as superstitions which enslaved men's minds. Former ages had been held together by widely shared social mores. Without these sustaining systems, people felt lost and despairing, unable to orient themselves and find purpose. The former consolations of life – family, occupation, identification with one's locality or country – no longer sufficed. For the first time people felt they were living in a period where no system of values which gave meaning to life was generally accepted. The world now presented itself as bleaker, hard edged, and without resonances or coherence, which required a more detached perspective. Modernism was therefore secular in relation to ideologies which attempted to explain everything.

In reacting against the self-indulgent passions associated with romanticism, modernism revived the Enlightenment values of pluralism and tolerance. No particular set of values attached to modernism, but value-free attitudes were possible part replacements. All views were now provisional – you were on your own, with doubt a permanent condition. In this directionless universe consciousness took on a kaleidoscopic, nightmarish quality, as individual perception varied according to mood and situation. The personality became more fluid and malleable at will. A general sense of the separation of the individual from the life around him, which came to be known as alienation, arose. Public breakdown and personal disintegration reinforced each other – one's ego fractured like society itself. These developments, which implied a break with the past, created a new elite, which designated itself an *avant garde*, separate from ordinary society and superior to it. A new type of society was coming into being, whose self-appointed task was to puncture accepted certainties, but at this non-political stage modernists thinkers were not aiming to take it over.

But some still wanted coherence, if not certainty. As a result worldviews which attempted to connect the disparate components of life together were a feature of this unsettled period, as they provided an antidote to incoherence. Major thinkers of the time – Freud, Darwin, Marx, Nietzsche, Sir James Frazer and others – developed wide ranging, 'big picture' ways of thinking which displaced the old verities. Marx rejected the bourgeois order and laid plans for its coming overthrow. A belief in inevitably evolving progress, called Social Darwinism, arose. Nietzsche upturned Christian morality by moving beyond conventional good and evil and extolling a new *ubermensch*. In investigating former rituals and taboos, Frazer and Freud resurrected old deities: Frazer unearthed a cyclical death cult as the basis of many European cultures, and Freud discovered an unconscious side of human behaviour. These thinkers, though regarded as innovative, were aware of darker regressive currents lurking beneath the surface. Civilization itself was revealed as a thin veneer which could easily be stripped away. This penchant for worldviews combining progressive and regressive elements had a slow burning, solvent effect on society, loosening its bonds and making dramatic changes possible.

The modernist personality, with no fixed beliefs, found it hard to maintain a steady state position. Very quickly, almost as soon as modernism itself came into existence, more radical activists went beyond it. The rampant, free floating ego now constituted the self's indispensable moral compass. A radical outsider could now launch attacks on a society viewed as tone deaf to higher aspirations, rather than on defenseless targets, like the individual victims of the Underground Man's wiles. Like the Underground Man the new breed explored more daring modes of personal interaction, including new psychological strategies which could eventually be deployed in the public realm. Now that all bets were off, there arose a late Romantic drive for risk taking, a yearning for possible self-destruction, to see how deep into the mire one could go in order to jettison the carapace of one's old self. The beguiling paradox, perhaps a contradiction, was that willed self-destruction might produce a new creativity, just as the revolutionary sweeping away of the old order might produce a new, more fulfilling, type of society. Such redemptive, transgressive moves went beyond modernism. Radical personalities admired the Nietzschean superman, who had passed beyond the standard stages of human development – ordinary rules did not apply to him. Megalomania on a public as well as personal level was in evidence. The American critic Lionel Trilling saw this type as the forerunner of today's 'adversary culture'

In the decades before and after 1900 a number of novels introduced these new forms of behavior which contained a hint of things to come. One was Herman Melville's *Billy Budd, Sailor: An Inside Narrative*, written in 1889-1891, but published in various versions only from 1924 onwards after Melville's death. The late publication of the novel, delayed until after the first world war, assisted its acceptance as a masterpiece in the new disturbed Weimar climate. The story takes place against the background of the French Revolution, described as counter-productive since it had an outcome opposite to that intended: 'the Revolution itself became the wrongdoer, one more oppressive than the kings'. (p. 7) The Bill of Rights and the conflicting interpretations of Thomas Paine and Edmund Burke on the French Revolution, mentioned in the novella, are in the air. (p. 13) The revolutionary spirit of the age sparks a Great Mutiny by British naval seamen, with another unexpected outcome: the mutiny leaders are hung, but their protests eventually spark reform. In disagreeing with the revolutionaries Captain Vere, Master of the Billy Budd's ship *Indomitable*, does not rely on defending past privileges: 'While other members of that aristocracy to which by birth he belonged were incensed at the innovators mainly because their theories were inimical to the privileged classes, not alone Captain Vere disinterestedly opposed them because they seemed to him incapable of embodiment in lasting institutions, but at war with the peace of the world and the true welfare of mankind'. (p. 26) With his understanding that the incendiaries' ideas are 'incapable of embodiment in lasting institutions' Captain Vere is here advancing arguments along Burkean lines. He is opposed to both influential groups, being neither a class conscious conservative nor a destructive radical, a position later taken by standout authors like Orwell and Camus.

The novella is the story of a leading seaman Billy Budd, an innocent, well-meaning and generous personality. Described as 'The Handsome Sailor' Budd is attractive but an unsophisticated spawn of nature, a relic of a more romantic age. He is not equipped for the subtle tactical manoeuvring on board ship, a cauldron more complex than his previous milieu: 'To one essentially such a novice in the complexities of factitious life', Billy Budd finds difficult 'the abrupt transition from his former and simpler sphere to the ampler and more knowing world of a great warship' (p. 15), a particular instance of a transition from an individual to an organizational role, and from romantic to modern mores. The decent Billy Budd is out of his depth in the intricate moves on deck. He initially impresses his superiors with his free spiritedness and natural superiority: 'with little or no sharpness of faculty or any trace of the wisdom of the serpent, nor yet quite a dove, he possessed that kind and degree of intelligence going along with the unconventional rectitude of a sound human creature.' (p. 16) His weakness, apart from guilelessness, is an easily provoked impulsiveness. The-master-at-arms on board ship, the man whose duty it is to keep order on the lower decks, is Claggart, who is envious of Billy Budd's easy-going nature and winning ways. The two are contrasted, with Billy outgunned: 'The sailor [Budd] is frankness, the landsman [Claggart] is finesse. Life is not a game with the sailor, demanding the long head; no intricate game of chess where few moves are made in straightforwardness, and ends are attained by indirection; an oblique, tedious, barren game hardly worth that poor candle burnt out in playing it'. (p. 47) Billy Budd is admirable, but as an innocent abroad, likely to be outmanoeuvred.

The functioning civil society which shapes the life of the crew on board the warship could be disrupted by a possible mutiny, which Captain Vere fears. A cloud of suspicion hovers over the crew because of the recent Great Mutiny at Spithead on the Nore, which increases paranoia and strange conduct on the *Indomitable*. The two protagonists are again contrasted: 'The will to it [satire] and the sinister dexterity were alike wanting [in Billy Budd]. To deal in double meanings and insinuations of any sort was quite foreign to his nature.' (p. 14) Claggart however is an expert in the subtle politics of shipboard life. It is an uneven battle between two personalities, the inside narrative of the novella's title. Billy Budd's mind is an open book, but Claggart's is deceptive, and does not disclose its full hand.

Here is a complex, modern case where devious moves and motives are deployed. It is Billy's good looks and openness which both attract and annoy Claggart. Envy and antipathy co-exist in Cloggart's mind, a double-think love-hate oscillation, not simple hatred: 'as if Claggart could even have loved Billy but for fate and ban'. (p. 48) The two share a strange, mirror-image bond, at once alike and opposite (as with the Underground Man and Apollon, with the two main characters in Conrad's novella *The Secret Sharer,* and with the Pontius Pilate and Yeshua in Bulgakov's novel *The Master and Margarita*). Claggart is suspicious like a detective or secret policeman, ferreting out discord in his supervising role whether it exists or not. He is, confusingly, pleasant to Budd because he's down on him which disarms Budd. Dislike is paradoxically called forth by his harmlessness: 'For what can more partake of the mysterious than an antipathy spontaneous and profound, such as is evoked in certain exceptional mortals by the mere aspect of some other mortal, however harmless he may be, if not called forth by this very harmlessness itself?' (p. 35) Similarly the harmlessness of the prostitute Liza stirs up in the protagonist in *Notes From Underground* not pity, as we would normally expect, but a chance for her humiliation. Between Claggart and Budd a 'deadly space' opens up because of Claggart's dark designs. Claggart, with 'the wisdom of the serpent', disguises the malignity of his aims under a 'cool judgement'. The victim, Billy Budd, finds the combination of affection and disdain (the carrot and the stick) harder to handle than if each were administered separately.

Shipboard harmony is disrupted by a supposed conspiracy, dreamt up by the disturbed mind of Claggart, who reports to the captain his suspicions of an alleged mutiny led by Budd, all based on vague circumstantial inferences without reliable evidence. An investigation ensues, with the informer Claggart also the prosecutor, a conflict of roles. The victim, Billy Budd, is found guilty: his guileless exterior must, to suspicious minds, be a mask for inner guilty intent. It is paradoxically Billy Budd's good qualities of innocence, personal nobility, and straightforwardness which bring him down. Claggart projects his own duplicitous designs on to Billy. The investigation amounts to a show trial, as the 'evidence' brought forward is a mixture of rumour and supposition, and as such irrefutable. Budd is condemned by these factors before the inquiry's actual decision. When the guilty verdict is put to Billy Budd, he, outraged and lost for words, impulsively fells and kills Claggart with one blow, for which he is eventually executed. Superior human virtue has been brought low by lesser men who out of envy ('silent reproach') destroy the well-functioning civil society on board ship. Complex modern power games of attraction and repulsion, mirror-imaging each other, are at play here.

Personal power, the ability to manipulate other human beings towards one's agendas, is also an important motif in the Norwegian playwright Henrik Ibsen's *Hedda Gabler*. The play was written at the same time as *Billy Budd*, and first staged in 1891. Hedda, the bored wife of a journeyman scholar, Jörgen Tesman, and Brack, a judge, are both arch manipulators. A third figure, Lövberg, an errant genius who is working on a scholarly masterpiece, is an academic rival of Hedda's husband Tesman. Tesman and Lövberg exhibit contrasting Apollonian and Dionysian poles of behaviour. Characters in the play who are not devious but more open and given to affection and co-operation, like Lövberg and Thea Elvsted, Tesman's assistant, lose out, like Billy Budd, to those for whom rivalry and control are pre-eminent. Hedda exclaims 'I want for once in my life, to have power over a human being's fate', an aim Claggart achieves. (p. 324). Later Hedda confides to Brack: 'I'm heartily thankful you have no hold or power over me'. (p. 338) Brack, the most subtle manipulator, uses sexual blackmail as a form of control over Hedda until she realizes: 'So I am now in your power'. These are forms of the Nietzschean master-slave symbiosis.

Hedda exists in only two extreme states, boredom and exhilaration, which are strangely connected. She encourages personal rivalries to inject dramatic conflict into life, which is to manage things the wrong way round. A great liberating breakout which defies the conventions, like some inspirational deed, is necessary to make life meaningful to her (it's the same for political revolutionaries). The more bored one is, the more extreme the breakout needed. With each extreme reinforcing the other, the moodswings become more violent. (We notice a similar pattern in some of Sylvia Plath's poems, and in Robert Lowell's line: 'Each drug that numbs alerts another nerve to pain'.) In this regard Hedda resembles the Underground Man – both are manipulative, both induce pseudo-crises, and both create personal sadistic tyranny as a relief from the mundane. Exhilaration itself has to be artificially induced.

In the Romantic era love and death went hand in hand, as in *Wuthering Heights*, and in the *liebestod* of Wagner's *Tristan and Isolde*. This fatal combination was superseded in the modern age by the connection between power and death. The manuscript of Lövberg's masterpiece has been found by Tesman. Hedda encourages Lövberg to commit suicide and then burns his manuscript, a joint work of Lövberg and his friend Thea Elvsted. (The burning of a manuscript was also a key factor in Bulgakov's life and in his novel *The Master and Margarita*, a similar linking of literature and life). Striving for artistic success becomes the highest goal in life, an ecstatic state beyond religious morals. The destruction of a work of art is paralleled with the destruction of Lövberg. Hedda eventually calls Brack's bluff by committing suicide herself, because she wants to be free, not a slave to anyone. Her phrase 'boring myself to death' becomes literally true. In her swings between boredom and breakout, between highs and lows, she ultimately seeks in her suicide a combination of both: death (nothingness) amalgamates itself with boredom (nothingness) to become the final and irreversible breakout, the ultimate high. Hedda admires actions which are aesthetically pleasing; by this inverse morality suicide becomes for her the highest moral act, and the highest form of art. In these beliefs she resembles Kirilov's stance in Dostoievsky's *The Devils*. Hedda is a Nietzschean in her vacillating master-slave relationship with Brack, and in her belief that aesthetic strivings transcend conventional notions of good and evil. Modern characters become adept at these complex mind games. Strange, contradictory swings between opposites became a feature of modern life and literature, but may also be pre-totalitarian, as they contain the seeds of wider manipulations.

Joseph Conrad did not like to be referred to as merely a spinner of nautical tales, believing, correctly, he was displaying the way human nature conducted itself in our times. He was writing in the period when the outlines of the modernist personality and its likely successors were taking shape. In his novella *The Secret Sharer* (1910) a ship's mate, having accidentally killed a crew member on another vessel, has escaped to the narrator's ship to avoid the gallows, a story so close to *Billy Budd* (which had not been published at this time) that it presents itself as an alternative ending to the Melville story. The two main characters in *The Secret Sharer*, the captain and the stowaway, are each alike and not alike, bonded magnetically together by a common but unknowable fate. In the story the two characters reverse their roles, with the stowaway (like the servant Apollon) determining the moves and the captain, who now feels himself a stranger on his own ship, in thrall to the stowaway's needs. The captain behaves well by taking a good share of guilt on himself and thus helping the man to swim to freedom and avoid execution.

A magnetic connection between two opposite characters is a common but not accidental feature of twentieth century literature, and especially of political literature – think of O'Brien and Winston in *Nineteen Eighty-Four*. Individuals became skilled at subtly manoeuvring in daily situations, usually for their own benefit, in a society where there were now no guidelines. Modern rulers understood, by inspecting their own drives, the motivation of their opponents, and were able to project this understanding on to them in order to draw them to their own mode of thinking. In this way they could both understand and defeat them. Opponents were seen as potential recruits as much as enemies, secret sharers in their own designs. The expected gap between victor and victim closed. The Underground Man, Claggart and Brack share these traits. The modern pre-totalitarian mind therefore had some strange analogies to the literary one, as both utilized their own internal imaginations to exploit the world.

Joseph Conrad's *Heart of Darkness* (1902), based on Belgian misrule of its colony in the Congo, is a more political tale of an egomaniac drive for total power which destroys the structures of the target society. An internal colonialism cannibalizes, almost literally, the colony's structures. Kurtz makes himself a god-like Deity, a Big Brother, whose followers adore him, showing signs of absolute subjection. (p. 94-5). His rampant all-devouring ego expands to fill the space left by the society he is destroying, an unstoppable drive for total power which brings in its train total ruin. The Russian manager in the colony is a fellow-travelling disciple of Kurtz. He can't break the mystical spell Kurtz casts on him, exhibiting a mixture of fear, admiration and envy towards him. He defends Kurtz, even though he senses Kurtz's weaknesses. He remembers a Kurtz conversation, with its 'big picture' notions and enormous ambitions; Kurtz's magnificent but meaningless eloquence transfigures the Russian, even though he can't remember its content. (Hitler's listeners had the same reaction to his speeches.) The skulls as trophies reveal that 'Mr Kurtz lacked restraint in the gratification of his various lusts, that there was something wanting in him'. The whisper he heard within himself 'had proved irresistibly fascinating. It echoed loudly within him because he was hollow at the core'. (p. 97)

Like *The Devils,* this novel contains on a restricted canvas a premonition of annihilations to come. The potential horror of twentieth century political life is not yet present in all its intensity and overreach. Kurtz lacks the technological means to take over a society. He proceeds partly by primitive brainwashing methods, aligning himself with the locals' atavistic cult beliefs. To succeed he also needs to exert coercion: his cry 'exterminate all the brutes' is a genocidal regression to an irrational primitive barbarism like the Nazis' *Gotterdammerung*; Lenin similarly called for extermination soon after he obtained power. Kurtz is a man who, like modern megalomaniac tyrants, considers himself a universal genius but has gone over the edge of extremity, turning on his own subjects. An antidote to this madness is introduced at the beginning of the novel by the Belgian doctor's advice: 'Du calme' (keep calm). (p. 38) The counter-strategy to figures like Kurtz is the steadiness and sense of perspective of Conrad's narrator (and of Conrad himself), which inoculate citizens from being carried away by wild current fanaticisms.

Conrad's later novel *The Secret Agent* (1907) does not describe a full takeover of society, as in *Heart of Darkness*. Both Conrad's *The Secret Agent* and Dostoievsky's *The Devils* deal with terrorists in the Russian revolutionary tradition, and both are loosely based on actual events, but in *The Secret Agent* the revolutionaries are a banal lot, dropouts never wanting to work. They are 'superfluous men' but without the Underground Man's focus. Their crazy utopian fantasies of regeneration coming out of destruction, their need for a great breakout like Hedda's, mask from themselves their own inner dissatisfaction with their present existence. They don't have the upper class élan of the conspirators in *The Devils*, being domestic, small minded and pathetic. As in *The Devils* fashionable emancipated high society, exemplified in this case by the Lady Patroness, embraces the revolutionary cause in the mistaken belief the terrorists are just liberals like themselves, but of a more daring and advanced kind. The Lady Patroness is described as a bleeding-heart fellow traveller: 'She was not an exploiting capitalist herself, she was, as it were, above the play of economic conditions. And she had a great capacity for pity for the more obvious forms of human miseries, precisely because she was such a complete stranger to them that she had to translate her conception into terms of mental suffering before she could grasp the notion of their cruelty'. (p. 122) The upper classes believe the terrorist Michaelis is, like themselves, a 'humanitarian sentimentalist'. (p. 123) Liberal modernity and revolutionary destruction were appearing in the same era, with many people unable at this early stage to distinguish between them.

Conrad understood the psychology of the potential revolutionary, men who, living on the fringes of society (like Conrad's own father), get their energy out of imagining a larger ideological vision which is in fact unrealistic. As Conrad explained: 'History is made by men, but they do not make it in their heads…No one can tell what form the social organization may take in the future. Then why indulge in prophetic phantasies? At best they can only interpret the mind of the prophet, and can have no objective value'. (p. 73) One terrorist is characterized as 'an insolent and venomous evoker of sinister impulses which lurk in the blind envy and exasperated vanity of ignorance…in all the hopeful and noble illusions of righteous anger, pity and revolt' (p. 78) In addition 'there are natures too, to whose sense of justice the price exacted looms up monstrously enormous, odious, oppressive… intolerable'. (p. 82) Unlike the grounded Conrad, his secret agents are common-garden unrealistic fanatics, dupes of a radical outbreak which yearns for destruction to compensate for personal failure.

Conrad's father was a Polish nationalist active against Russia in the uprising of 1863, an event which affected him greatly. Conrad admired his father's yearning for a freer state in Poland, but also acknowledged, as we notice in *The Secret Agent*, the futility of pursuing utopian drives and adversary beliefs which lead to the unreality of revolutionary politics. His father's actions, which led to exile in Russia, wrecked the family's life, with the young Conrad leaving Poland for good as a result. This ambiguous stance towards revolution forms a background angle to the novel. Conrad's father's futile actions and his mother's tragedy may be reflected in Conrad's sympathy for the failed secret agent Verloc and his wife, and his own perhaps in the destruction of the innocent young Stevie.

The German Nobel Prize winning novelist Herman Hesse published *Steppenwolf* in 1927. The novel combines dark subterranean Wagnerian romanticism with Nietzschean elements. *Steppenwolf* was written during the Weimar years, a period when longing for fatal love or bourgeois respectability no longer sufficed. The untamed Dionysian side of the personality comes to the fore. The Steppenwolf, Henry Heller (a name with echoes of Hermann Hesse himself), has a fluid personality: 'Man is not by any means a fixed and enduring form... He is much more an experiment and a transition.' (p. 74) His being has no predetermined unity, no grounding, but is split by modern traumas into many contending shards: 'His life oscillates not merely between two poles, such as body and spirit, the saint and the sinner, but between thousands, between innumerable poles'. (p. 70). His personality is malleable. alternating between higher and animal forms, between the civilized and the wild. His personality has a 'thin veneer of the human' (p. 51), a nod to Freud's' idea that civilization rests on a thin crust of rationality which is easily breached.

The novel illustrates Lionel Trilling's idea that the contemporary seeker finds himself by deliberately going down into the depths of his being, to personal degradation, as a necessary preliminary to self-understanding and redemption: 'my downfall...sees the ruins of being as fragments of the divine'. (p. 166) The hero 'stood with the slightest foothold on the peak of a crag' (p. 59) courting danger, the *vita periculoso* of Nietzsche and Mussolini. A conflict raised by the Underground Man re-emerges in the novel: 'self-hate is really the same thing as sheer egoism'. (p. 16) The hero's 'sickness of the soul...is not the eccentricity of a single individual, but the sickness of the times themselves, the neurosis of that generation to which Heller belongs'. It is a sickness of 'those who are strongest in spirit and richest in gifts'. (p. 27) The Steppenwolf, a textbook Nietzschean figure who goes well beyond the adversary culture, strives mightily, unaided, through a superhuman effort of the will to overcome all the daunting hurdles in his path: 'A journey through hell, a sometime fearful, sometimes courageous, journey through the chaos of the world...to give battle to chaos, and to bear the evil to the full'. (pp. 27-8) 'Only the strongest of them force their way through the atmosphere of the Bourgeois-Earth and reach the cosmic'. (p. 66) The Wagnerian end of the road is a triumph: "The laughter of the immortals...was a laughter without an object. It was simply light and lucidity. It was that which is left over when a true man has...got through to eternity and the world of space.' (p. 181). The Steppenwolf has been through the wringer and come out the other end. The immortals are the true creative artists and thinkers, brave, lonely pioneers of the spirit, whose liberating drives are considered, like Hedda Gabler's, the high point of art and morality.

The masked ball at the end of *Steppenwolf* prefigures that in Bulgakov's *The Master and Margarita*. Here it is a triumph of the new dispensation, where all rules are broken, and everything flows into everything else, as in magic realism. But in the late 1920s a fearful premonition of coming barbarism hangs over all, blighting the frivolity: 'the next war is being pushed on us with enthusiasm by thousands upon thousands day by day...Of course there will be another war. One doesn't need to read the papers to know that'. (pp. 138-9) The future portends not a revolutionary utopia but a cataclysm. *Steppenwolf* had a second life as a cult novel of the counter-culture of the 1960s, when such ideas were revived.

During the meltdown of the first wold war whole societies suffered from massive breakdown, which intensified previous fragmentation. The resulting power vacuum produced a mixture of anarchy and naked bids for power. The war's utter meaninglessness and the scale of its destruction numbed people, making previously admired virtues like loyalty and patriotism hard to justify, and giving rise to public feelings of amorality. The *avant garde* in general, and Lenin in particular, welcomed this change as a beneficial clearing away of the old, decayed parts of society, giving the new order a chance to thrive. A direct changeover from romanticism to revolution, with the modernist stage elided, is clearly illustrated in Lenin's reflections recorded by Maxim Gorky in his *V.I. Lenin* (1924):

> I know of nothing better than the Appassionata and could listen to it every day. What astonishing, superhuman music! It always makes me proud, perhaps with a childish naiveté, to think that people can work such miracles!...But I can't listen to music very often, it affects my nerves. I want to say sweet, silly things, and pat the little heads of people who, living in a filthy hell, can create such beauty. These days, one can't pat anyone on the head nowadays, they might bite your hand off. Hence, you have to beat people's little heads, beat mercilessly, although ideally we are against doing any violence to people. Hm – what a devilishly difficult job!

Like the Underground Man, Lenin is here caught in the process of extirpating the sentimental instincts and personal indulgences which accompany romanticism, but going further, inducing in himself a sharp, willed break, and forming a hardened personality, which subjugates everything, including others and his own former self, to this new goal.

From the late 1930s Solzhenitsyn had been asking himself what had brought about the tragedy of his own country's adoption of Communism. During his post-concentration camp literary career he compiled at intervals materials on the rise of Lenin in order to fill a crucial gap in understanding. He envisaged a novel cycle which would retrospectively imagine how a prolonged national tragedy, initiated by the Russian revolution of 1917, had come about in his own country. The first volume of the *Red Wheel* cycle, *August 1914*, appeared in 1971. A group of chapters extracted from it, entitled *Lenin in Zurich*, was published in 1975. This short work is an imaginative re-construction of events, based on available historical material, but infused with the drive of Lenin's personality. Solzhenitsyn had already penned a devastating imaginative portrait of Stalin from the inside in *The First*

Circle. He now attempted to similarly take down Lenin in literature, by entering into the deepest recesses of his personality in *Lenin in Zurich*. Half a century after the Russian Revolution, he now had a mind to dethrone its only true begetter. By stating in *The First Circle* that 'having a great writer is like having an alternative government', Solzhenitsyn was covertly announcing his long-term aim of creating an alternative in his own country, which came to pass, as Solzhenitsyn became the individual most responsible for dethroning Communism itself. Solzhenitsyn partly understands Lenin through an imaginative mirror-imaging of his own activities. Lenin brought down Tsarism, just as he aimed to bring down Communism. Both were workaholics with indomitable wills, exiled in Zurich, non-compromisers, leaders on a long term mission, and utilizing at times the 'silence, exile and cunning' which James Joyce recommended. All this is not to say that Solzhenitsyn and Lenin were au *fond* alike. Lenin advocated mass suppression, whereas Solzhenitsyn was a victim and opponent of such activity.[7]

Lenin's entourage was very different from the would-be revolutionaries of *The Secret Agent*, whom Lenin would have despised as bourgeois romantics. In *Lenin in Zurich* Lenin emerges as an unstoppable force, a totally devoted and ruthless workaholic, who puts political goals before human needs: 'there can be no such relationship between human beings as simple friendship transcending political, class and material ties.' (p. 20). Many of his comrades, not just his opponents, are sacrificed for his conspiratorial designs: 'The first rule is not to trust your ally.' (p. 129). He is himself a victim of this strategy, as he feels the strain of it on body and mind. Lenin tries to split most organizations he is involved with to increase his own power: 'he had cast off all allies, fragmented all his forces.' (p. 133) He sees great advantage in destruction – the worse the better. He is always manipulating and changing tactics, moving left in his ideological purity to a more extreme minority position, but triumphing by having the stamina, unlike others, to stick it out to the bitter end without deviating

---

7   Joyce lived in Zurich at the same time as Lenin; Tom Stoppard's play *Travesties* (1974) imagines them together in Zurich.

from his ultimate gaol. Lenin has 'the savage, intolerant narrowness of the born schismatic.' (p.116)

Most European socialists opposed the first world war and favoured peace, but Lenin with foresight supported it as an engine of destruction of existing social arrangements, a necessary prelude to his takeover plans. Lenin sensed the first tremors of great seismic shifts, with structures fracturing underneath. He believed 'it was in the power of a tiny group of extremely resolute men to stop this iron hurricane (and change its direction).' (p. 153) In his reconstruction Solzhenitsyn focusses on certain crucial events centering around Parvus (real name Alexander Helphand) a wealthy businessman-cum-revolutionary. Parvus acted as a go-between, persuading the German army chiefs to send Lenin and his entourage on a sealed train to Russia to cause further disintegration, just as revolution broke out in Russia in 1917. A stalemate in the war had already brought Russia to its knees. A personal dynamic of opposites is portrayed in *Lenin in Zurich* between Parvus, a wealthy, sybaritic businessman with a short-term strategy, and the adamantine Lenin, who wins the battle of wills and is able to use Parvus because Lenin denies himself all diversions from his gaol of Russia's ruin: *'the destruction of Russia now held the key to the future history of the world!'* (p. 115) Solzhenitsyn homes in on this episode which was crucial in bringing Communist rule to his own country, Russia, for seven decades.

Dostoievsky and Conrad had both personally experienced the downside of Tsarist autocracy. Early on they understood that some late nineteenth century rebels had, in confronting contemporary dilemmas, taken a different path from liberal reformers. Liberal society mistakenly believed it was supporting new modernist attitudes, whereas in some cases it was giving comfort to intolerant proto-totalitarian fanatics. Modernism was already considered insufficiently committed by these new thinkers and activists. The new boys on the block, like Lenin and Mussolini and their followers, rejected tolerance, which they considered a sign of weakness, as they committed themselves to takeover tactics. For the Fascists Mussolini adopted the slogan *vita periculosa* (live dangerously), a notion claiming a Nietzschean origin. For the Bolsheviks Parvus and Trotsky developed the analogous notion of permanent revolution: never rest, keep stirring the societal porridge. These were ways of grasping and keeping power by constantly destabilizing one's opponents (and supporters). The focus shifted beyond modernism, from the personal to the political, from the all-encompassing ego to an all-encompassing drive to control society.

Large ideological constructs which seemed to make everything coherent were in the air again. Spengler and Toynbee added theirs in the early twentieth century. As four European empires (Russian, Austrian, German and Ottoman) collapsed as a result of the first world war, they wrote 'big picture' history of civilizations falling and new ones rising, a perspective encompassing vast eons of time, like the conspiratorial circle of thinkers in *The Devils*. Lessons from the whole sweep of history were now shoehorned into internally coherent ideologies, and were taken up by ambitious power-seeking autodidacts like Lenin, Mussolini, Hitler and Stalin. The new ruthless activists were not really modernists: they had coherent (if distorted) ideological worldviews, and could not allow doubt, nor comprehend the complexities of life over the long haul, as the modernists did. Daunted by the bleak prospects of the contemporary condition, and finding it hard to live with uncertainty and without meaning, these extremists took a short cut, embracing a new kind of certainty, which by replicating the thought structures of religious belief, salvaged their deepest hopes. They aimed to destroy and rebuild society at the same time, and to keep doing both.

One element literary works by Dostoievsky, Melville, Ibsen, Conrad and Solzhenitsyn have in common is that the transgressive figures (the Underground Man, Claggart, Brack and Hedda, Kurtz and Lenin) seek revenge out of all proportion to the weaker, more vulnerable souls on whom they prey. It is as though they have a pre-determined, inbuilt will to power as their basic personality structure. They act aggressively because of what they *are*, not just because circumstances or ideology tempt them to it. The usual cause and response process is not in evidence. These destroyers do not merely react to perceived threats – they initiate and then escalate their actions. No matter what way they are treated they are basically unsatisfiable.

Totalitarianism wasn't just a political program, nor just a worked out ideology. It was *au fond* based on a distinctive and original personality type intent on messing with people's consciousness, which came to the fore in modern times. Its prime movers – Lenin, Mussolini, Hitler, Stalin, Mao and Pol Pot – were not (with the possible exception of Lenin) great political theorists. What set them apart was their strange, distorted and extreme personalities, by turns driven, vindictive, megalomaniac, cruel, paranoid and manipulative. They employed their own deep understanding of these new behaviours, which they divined in themselves, in their utter strivings for power, domination and control. They possessed an unholy grab-bag of thought disorders with which they played mind games with themselves and others. Their great 'achievement' was to impose the distorted state of their own consciousness on to the public realm, forcing it to behave in a way which reflected their own inner turmoil. They strived to change reality so that it lived up to their desired image of it. This, rather than any fixed preconceived program of political action, was the key. Ideologies of various sorts, often based on race or class, which they deployed, were ultimately veneers designed to convince others, to be abandoned or changed at will. Mussolini and Hitler moved from being socialists to being fascists while hardly missing a beat. Their permanent focus was on power, a boot stamping on a human face forever, as Orwell put it, more than on ideas. As it was basically a *forma mentis*, a unique way of engaging with the world more than a discrete political program, this behavior was first clearly disclosed to the world in certain 19th century works of political literature. Similarly modern totalitarian dictators had far reaching schemes; they worked out in their minds an all-encompassing 'big picture' worldview which provided a *post hoc facto* rationalization of what they were going to do anyway. They prided themselves on being, like artists, creative intellectuals in the Nietzschean mould. The central characters in many modern novels follow the Underground Man in constantly unfurling in their imaginations a narrative which rationalizes their present situation.

As a reaction to the uncertainty inherent in modernism, and because of fear of freedom, insistent drives for coherence, assurance and belief returned. People couldn't bear to live without strong ideas. Some more radical thinkers, the aspiring totalitarians like Lenin, wished to restore a new religioid 'morality' imposed from on high. They restored certainty, they were guru leaders, with followers and fellow travelers who accepted the new revelation; they had cults, rituals, purging of heretics, a closed world intolerant of those without the 'truth'. The wheel had turned full circle. It was not just *politique d'abord* (politics above all else). Control, uniformity and power triumphed over applied skepticism. Liberal modernity and its nemesis, revolutionary break-out imposing a new order, confusingly arose together at the same time.

Though the apostles of the new order had a self-image of themselves as advanced thinkers, leading mankind forward on a new adventure, there existed many throwbacks to the past in their strategies. Their search for certainty and orthodoxy replicated in a new form the religious beliefs they had been so anxious to expunge. The new secular ideologies were regressive in other ways, imitating the thought structure of tribal societies and of discredited earlier ideologies. Orwell commended Zamyatin for his 'intuitive grasp of the irrational side of totalitarianism: human sacrifice, cruelty as an end in itself, the worship of a Leader who is credited with divine attributes'.[8] *Heart of Darkness, The Tin Drum* and *Lord of the Flies* likewise illustrate the dark, regressive underside of such regimes. This is the attraction of brute power, a sadistic connection between rulers and ruled, as the character O'Brien reveals. Zygmunt Bauman pointed out that totalitarian regimes employed a strange mixture of advanced technological means and regressive, atavistic yearnings. The Underground Man, Kurtz and the Devils are hardly avatars of the progressive mind: 'After us the savage gods.'

---

8   George Orwell *The Collected Essays*, Vol. IV, p. 75.

3

TAKEOVER TACTICS

Political literature focuses on the way a new insurgency undermines the morale of a citizenry before coming to power. This was often achieved by slow, imperceptible changes, called 'salami tactics', so that at each stage the victim group accepted a piecemeal lessening of agency without realizing it was on a slippery slope it couldn't get off. The visible top-down coups of dictators are well known, but what was happening beneath the surface beforehand was less clear. As a result political literature often covers the murky pre- and post-history of takeovers more than the coups themselves, which are amenable to structural political analysis. It focuses on techniques of subtle coercion more than outright force, as it investigates the motivations of the actors at ground level.

The revolutionary changes sought about by Fascist and Communist regimes didn't automatically come into being after the first imposition of power. It was not, as in the past, just a one-off operation. Once a regime gained political power, it still had to ensure a country kept relinquishing its old ways and moved towards radically new forms. Radical dissatisfaction with current reality became, paradoxically, the permanent stance of rulers – they had to continually renew the brew. As Marvell understood of Cromwell's regime: 'The same arts that did gain/a power must it maintain'. As we have seen, in the early 1920s both Mussolini, with his idea of the *vita periculosa*, and Trotsky, with his notion of permanent revolution, devised schemes of continual disruption. Skeletal social structures had to keep being broken down and regenerated through ideological impositions. These were ways of grasping and keeping power by constantly destabilizing one's opponents (and supporters).

This similarity between permanent revolution and *vita periculosa* tactics was more fundamental than the notional left-right differences between contending alignments. Authors generally believe revolutionary changes damage the polity and lead to tragedy, and warn us not to let it happen again. 'The plague has not yet ended' Camus tells us. This is literature itself acting as a countervailing force to abnormal political intrusion. The leaders of the newly forming institutions did not represent the interests of their constituents, as past rulers usually did. Instead they attacked their own comrades as much as their formal opponents. As Marvell understood, the revolutionary actor Cromwell

> Did thorough his own side
>   His fiery way divide.
> For 'tis alone to courage high
>   The emulous or enemy,
> And with such to inclose
>   Is more than to oppose.

The Underground Man disrupts his own school friends, Hedda Gabler attacks herself by suiciding, in *Catch-22* the pilots are endangered by the idiocy of their commanders more than by the enemy, in *Lenin in Zurich* many of his comrades, not just his opponents, are sacrificed for his conspiratorial designs: 'The first rule is not to trust your ally.' (p. 129). Stalin had his former comrade in arms Trotsky murdered; in the 1930s perhaps the most dangerous occupation in the Soviet Union was to be a member of its Central Committee. Mao directed his Cultural Revolution against China's Central Committee. Zhi recently purged top party operatives in China.

Frisch in *The Fire Raisers*, Camus in *The Plague,* Grass in *The Tin Drum* and Pinter in *The Caretaker* feature both oppressors and victims. But some works concentrate on one group only. Brecht's *Arturo Ui* play and Plath's poem 'Mushrooms' are written from the point of view of the takeover merchants, though they do not sympathize with them; both depict mechanisms of personal domination leading to an ultimate changeover of power. On the other hand Camus *The Plague* and Ionesco's *Rhinoceros* focus on how victims succumb to takeover pressures. They don't investigate in any detail the internal working of tyranny and imposed terror; they let the appearance of a plague or rhinoceroses stand for diverse takeover attempts. Camus' *The Plague* and Grass' *The Tin Drum* cover all three phases of control (takeover, extreme period and denouement), and the changes between them.

Some works of political literature have a close relation to actual events, others work more remotely by employing analogies. Novels like Solzhenitsyn's *August 1914* on the Bolshevik takeover in Russia have a close relation to actual events, whereas Silone's *Fontemara* on the Fascist takeover in Italy is less direct. Brecht's *The Resistible Rise of Arturo Ui* and Grass's *The Tin Drum* point by analogy to the Nazi regime; Brecht's play replicates the progress of events in Germany in the 1930s, but situates them in a Chicago gangster milieu. Frisch's play *The Fire Raisers* works in a similar way. Golding's *Lord of the Flies* operates on a realistic level. Though it dissects hunger for power and social breakdown in a youthful group, we recognize it is as a parable with wider political implications. These works cover a spectrum from normal to totalitarian behaviour, and probe the connections between them.

The Russian author Mikhail Bulgakov's ground-breaking novel, *The Master and Margarita* (finished in 1940 and published in book form only in 1967), was written during the worst times in the Soviet Union. It reveals how power was gained during the early Leninist takeover phase, and how it became all-encompassing in the 1930s Stalinist terror phase. Unlike many authors Bulgakov was in the middle of the maelstrom, and was also writing at the time these events were taking place, not retrospectively digesting them. In addition as an admirer of Dostoievsky Bulgakov had preternatural insights into how Russia was becoming the first nation to install a totalitarian regime. He had to devise new techniques, including magic/metaphysical realism, to comprehend (and oppose) the unprecedented events he was experiencing as citizen, dramatist, novelist and victim. Bulgakov moved to the centre of the storm, Moscow, in 1921 and wrote plays, short fiction, journalism and satire. He had to deal personally at a number of stages with Stalin, who liked his popular play *The Days of the Turbins*, and protected him for a period, but his other plays were banned in the late 1920s; he was a victim of the carrot and stick technique. In 1929 he wrote to Stalin, asking to leave Russia. Stalin personally phoned him, suggesting that he wouldn't thrive outside his own country. Bulgakov had no choice but to defer to Stalin's opaque threat, so he remained to work at home in the theatre.

The basic story of *The Master and Margarita* is of a mysterious, terrifying magician, Woland, who we come to realize is a devil-like figure. Woland arrives in Russia from Germany with a creepy, demonic entourage. This scenario seems based on Lenin (Woland) and the Bolsheviks (the troupe) importing a foreign ideology, German-based Marxist Communism, into Russia, as later depicted in Solzhenitsyn's *Lenin in Zurich*. The troupe proceed to disrupt important institutions in Moscow, including literary and union groups. Fashionable Moscow 'society' and its social climbers (like similar groups in *The Devils* and *The Secret Agent*) humiliatingly defer to these upstarts, and are satirized for their blind instant conformity to the new mode. A poet named Bezdomny ('homeless') tries to warn people about this new intrusion, but is confined to an asylum, where he meets a disillusioned author, the Master, who resembles Bulgakov.

A subplot, interpolated into the novel's dominant narrative, retells the story of Pontius Pilate (a tyrant who resembles Stalin) and his trial in Jerusalem of Yeshua (Jesus). The Master is writing a novel on this theme, an early draft of which is burned in despair by the author, who then scorns his lover, Margarita, and society. This has parallels with actual events in Bulgakov's life: an early draft of his great novel was burnt, and had to be reconstituted by his later partner. (Already complex parallels between literature and life are becoming evident). The show trial of Yeshua reveals a strange affinity (secret sharers) between the two protagonists, Pilate and Yeshua, rather than the old fashioned separation characteristic of authoritarian regimes. Pilate identifies in some strange way with the defendant, even though he ultimately condemns him. The testy symbiotic conversations between Pilate and Christ in part recapitulate Bulgakov's dealings with Stalin. Submerged religious imagery was common at this time: Akhmatova wrote in a poem 'Judas and the Word/Are stalking each other.' Bulgakov was a real life sacrificial victim of Stalin (as Jesus was of Pilate), who was playing with him like a giant spider, inveigling him into his web. The Jerusalem subplot gradually eddies out so that it is integrated into the main lines of the novel.

Psychological takeover techniques are the subject of Chapter Nine in the novel, 'Koroviev's Tricks', where ordinary people are softened up for a change. A self-satisfied tenant's association bureaucrat, Bosoi, holds all the cards at the start when he comes across a stranger in his flat, whom he is naturally determined to eject (later on this is also the plot of Pinter's play *The Caretaker*) But the stranger, Woland's assistant, Koroviev, adroitly avoids answering questions directly, throwing the burden of disclosure back on to Bosoi. The intruder's diversionary chutzpah tactics give him the upper hand and quickly destroy the self-confidence of the flat manager, putting him on the defensive. The bureaucrat reacts to outlandish events by saying 'it must all be put down on paper', as though bureaucratic norms will control further unrealities. A role reversal has occurred, with the intruder in psychological control. As Koroviev accurately says: 'Who is official and who is unofficial these days? It all depends on your point of view. It's all so vague and changeable. Today I'm unofficial, tomorrow, hey presto! I'm official.' (p. 105), reflecting the tactical changeability of revolutionary designs.

In this strange absurd world reality itself is malleable, and can be distorted, destroyed and replaced. The stranger now initiates a series of daring moves which take the befuddled manager's breath away, so that something unimaginable in normal times happens: the manager meekly agrees to the intruder becoming a tenant. After Bosoi insists things 'must be done properly', the stranger, understanding Bosoi's Achilles heel is greed, bribes him with wads of money, then reports him to the authorities. This is one way people were suborned and outed in denunciations and show trials in the 1930s. As he is led away to be tried, the defeated chairman plays his last card by exclaiming: 'the forces of evil are in this house', the only true thing he has said, but too late, as who would believe such a metaphysical explanation, which couldn't be put down on paper.

There exists a realm beyond the patently obvious which many find it hard to define, or imagine. Latin American writers who wanted to acknowledge an extra dimension to life developed a literary form known as magic realism. An early exponent of a similar device, before the Latin American novelists, was Bulgakov, who believed in the existence of evil, and made it a central component of his writing, both to reveal its essentially malign nature, and also to reject it. Bulgakov's use of magic/metaphysical realist devices (his father was a professor of theology) to encompass the disconcerting role of takeover strategies has pioneering features – he took this device to a new level. The totalitarian mind (unlike the modern mind) is innately aware of the existence of evil, and of how to manipulate it to achieve dominance. Bulgakov made this insight a central component of his writing in order to reveal its essentially destructive nature. This more comprehensive approach of Bugakov can be designated as metaphysical realism, of which magic realism is a component, but not the totality. Bulgakov's techniques prefigure Frisch, Ionesco, Pinter and the theatre of the absurd.

In the second part of the novel evil is more overt and widespread. People are mysteriously disappearing from their flats as though vaporized (as happened during the great Stalinist terror of the 1930s). Fear is everywhere, normality is deformed and out of sorts, expected roles are inverted. No natural explanation suffices; a deeply unnatural atmosphere is evident. This new dimension of radical evil becomes overt in the set-piece ball scene at midnight on Walpurgis Night (the witches' Sabbath) on Good Friday. An underground realm opens up to reveal the dead emerging from their resting places, with devils cavorting with witches and the revellers, when the 'spirit of evil and the lord of the shadows' is abroad (p. 378). The Margarita figure becomes the hostess with Woland at the great ball. Bulgakov believed the Soviet system was metaphysically evil, with the regime having made a Faustian bargain with the Devil, as predicted in Dostoievsky's *The Devils*. Lenin's and Stalin's henchmen, represented by Woland and his troupe, are fanatics, possessed like the Gadarene swine, taking the Russian people with them in their headlong rush over the cliff to perdition.

Radical evil is scary – ordinary linear argument can't convey its reach. New literary devices beyond those available to Dostoievsky were called for. Bulgakov employs a complex mixture of techniques, operating on many levels, to convey this eerie and disconcerting atmosphere: time switches, allegories, dark comedy in various gruesome guises, magic and fantastical events, bizarre disjunctions of elements, with the banal and the demonic morphing into each other, and distorted time and place sequences. Magic realism, breaking down constraints of time and place, is invoked: levitation, flying magicians, sleight of hand, and preternatural insights into the future. Internal exile forced Bulgakov into becoming a novelist, but he was initially a playwright. His novel is a theatrical experience, with play acting and references to the world of the theatre common. His characters take on the unreality of actors. All is staged, unnatural, carried out with a sense of exaggerated but creepy playfulness. Cowardice and courage, guilt and innocence, freedom and entrapment, and humour and dread, are all presented as part of a grotesque tragi-comedy.

Margarita implores the Devil to free the Master so she can live in poverty with him (reflecting Bulgakov's *modus vivendi* with Stalin). His wife keeps him going but can't avert his fate. Love does not triumph over politics. In his struggle to survive, the Master realizes sex, pleasure, degeneracy and domination are closely related. The Master has to relinquish these, and even the one who saves him with her devotion. Writing the novel keeps him alive, as do the ministrations of his lover, based on Bulgakov's third wife Yelena Sergeyevna, who rescued the manuscript of his masterpiece and restored its text. Late in life Bulgakov was banned, censored and understandably suffered depression, and was at the same time composing a novel about his fate: life and art were closely intertwined. He had struck a kind of bargain with the regime; he survived but without hope. He and wife were alone, out of life, ekeing out a low-key existence, and resigned to their fate. Trapped in an apartment room and suffering a terrible ostracism, Bulgakov wrote for the desk drawer. The latter parts of the novel are atmospherically autobiographical, capturing his move towards to a disembodied existence, broken in this world, a great feat of composition. Life is reduced to a perpetual limbo-like existence, vaguely tolerable but confined to a narrow space: 'He has not earned light, he has earned rest'. (p. 379) In 1939, with his own condition deteriorating, Bulgakov again contacted Stalin requesting to leave Russia, but this letter went unanswered. Bulgakov and the poet Mandelstam were both direct victims of Stalin, who personally and malignly intervened in both cases.

Takeover involves taking over people's souls as part of taking over a whole society – it's more than just a structural collapse. A feverish all-consuming fire arises, uprooting old mental habits. Under these pressures, familiar personality structures begin to wilt just as society does. Little remains to give people coherence and stability. 'The centre cannot hold', the unfamiliar becomes expected. Citizens are panicked into accepting ideas they would normally abhor. Human nature reveals itself as not fixed, but mutable under pressure. The takeover merchants take advantage of the atmosphere of fluid uncertainty they themselves have created in order to consolidate power. They want citizens to feel fearful and insecure, but at the same time emboldened by the new ideas. Some basic barrier has been broken down in the human personality.

Between the wars, a new type, a fellow traveller of destruction, appears in literature as well as in reality: the urban sociopath, a descendent and development of the superfluous man, now visible on the pavements rather than hidden in a basement; the unwanted have now endowed themselves with a mission. Loss of moral scruples and of internalized inhibitions is displayed by the speaker in Attila József's poem 'Innocent Song'. A sensitive young Hungarian poet of the inter-war years, József captures corrupted innocence, a feature of his disrupted times:

> I have no God, I have no King,
> My mother never wore a ring,
> I have no crib or funeral cover,
> I give no kiss, I take no lover.

It is a hard-edged world in which the social cement has crumbled; the previous values of religion, patriotism and family life, now corrupted, have evaporated, with no morality replacing them. Prematurely adult, having had no real childhood, the youthful speaker desires the role neither of victim nor survivor. Vagrants on the fringes of the criminal underworld turn into armed bohemians, the frightening foot soldiers of the new regime:

> Should there be none who wish to buy
> The devil's free to have a try:
> Then shall I use my common sense
> And rob and kill in innocence.

Sexuality, the wellspring of life and its continuity, has been polluted from cradle through marriage to the grave:

> Till, on a rope, they hang me high,
> And in the blessed earth I lie –
> And lust and poisoned grasses start
> Rank form my pure and simple heart.

This is an updated version of Blake's poem 'London', where

the harlot's curse 'blights with plagues the marriage hearse'. The streetwise vagrant, previously on the outskirts of society, has now moved closer to its centre.

For a time József joined the Communist Party. The déclassé individual goes along with the rising group, but without enthusiasm. He prostitutes himself to power, the new currency which takes over from love, family life and fruitful social connections. He couldn't care less, as his casual compact with destruction demonstrates. Innocence is enlisted in the cause of death and destruction, a strange misalliance. The disenfranchised become accomplices of the new dispensation. What results is not anarchy, but a tight unfreedom, the close grasp of the new order. A form of amorality now engulfs all. Gangs of sociopaths on the loose, the cannon fodder of the takeover merchants, constitute, with signals from above, a self-generated threat to order. Once they appear, the rank and poisoned grasses flourish without end. József's narrator has no ideological stance, he is essentially neither right nor left, but speaks with the detached, amoral tone common in much modern literature. Common decency has gone and in its stead ambition envy and grasping without limit prevail. This is a jungle, the battle of all against all, life reduced to a state of nature. Individuals are able to destroy but not to recreate themselves or society. József committed suicide in 1937 at the age of thirty-two, which does not surprise us, as no way out presented itself. The end of his poem ('Till, on a rope, they hang me high) anticipates the secret police strung up on poles by the populace during the Hungarian Revolution of 1956.

Bertolt Brecht's play *The Resistible Rise of Arturo Ui*, was written in the USA in 1941, published in German in 1957, and first staged in 1958. Dogsborough (based on the German President Hindenburg), who runs the Cauliflower Trust (Germany), is so entangled in corruption that he cannot escape its coils. Mrs Dullfeet (based on the wife of the murdered Austrian ruler Dollfuss), goes easy on Ui (the Hitler figure) on the mistaken grounds that one shouldn't resist him, as it will only provoke him to further atrocities. Ui and his gang use a mixture of beguilement and threats, one minute Ui is an injured innocent pathetic nobody, the next a powerful figure threatening revenge. Ui utilizes his pseudo-victim status to gain sympathy as one of the downtrodden, even though he is aggressively on the make. He has outbreaks of heightened craziness, then periods of calm rationality. The quick changes between meekness and aggression (similar to Koroviev's in Bulgakov's novel) psychologically break any opposition, which can't handle them. Brecht captured this contradictory variability in his poem 'The God of War':

> And without shame he talked on and presented himself as a great one for order. And he described how everywhere he put barns in order, by emptying them.
>
> And as one who throws crumbs to sparrows, he fed poor people with crusts of bread which he had taken away from poor people.
>
> His voice was no loud, now soft, but always hoarse.

Ui has the cheek to blame others for the mess what he himself has created, deploring people being murdered in the street without the protection of his own standover tactics. So his threats become a self-fulfilling prophecy, just as Hitler warned the Jews their actions would result in a world war in which they would be destroyed.

In Scene 10 Ui makes a speech in which he demands faith and trust from everyone:

> I'm a quiet man. But
> I won't be threatened. Either trust me blindly
> Or go your way. I owe you no accounting,
> Just do your duty, and do it to the full.
> The recompense is up to me, because
> Duty comes first and then the recompense.
> What I demand of you is trust.

A classic contradictory mixture of reasonableness and threat, because a demand is being made under the guise of tolerance. Trust is of its nature something that cannot be demanded. Ui goes on:

> You lack Faith, and where faith is lacking, all is lost.
> How do you think I got this far? By faith!
> Because of my fanatical, my unflinching
> Faith in the cause! With faith and nothing else
> I flung a challenge at this city and forced
> It to its knees. With faith I made my way
> To Dogsborough. With faith I climbed the steps
> Of City Hall, with nothing in my naked
> Hands but indomitable faith. (p.69)

These are typical destabilizing double-think totalitarian paradoxes, true on one level but not on another. Faith can't be fanatical. Ui calls for faith and trust, but these are the qualities he himself lacks towards his cronies and victims alike. He does have faith in himself, enormous will power, the ability to impose his desires on reality. The claim 'With nothing in my naked hands but indomitable faith' is a typical half truth, since he also has weapons in his supposedly naked hands. The play brilliantly exploits the double implication in every Ui claim: 'What irks me is to be misunderstood…as a fly-by-night adventurer' (p. 31); 'Dog can eat dog without a second thought/I call it chaos.' (p. 49) Everything Ui says about others applies even more to himself.

But Brecht diminishes the abnormality of Hitler's crimes, the totalitarian element, by reducing them to mafia-like violence. As a supporter of Stalinism, Brecht had an incentive to play down this aspect. Nor does Brecht show how ordinary people voluntarily collaborate with the Ui ideology; they are have to be cajoled and threatened into it. Brecht as a Marxist Communist couldn't bring himself to believe ordinary people could act voluntarily in this way; they had to be tricked. Brecht used the same duplicitous word games to justify his allegiance to Soviet Russia as those he exposed in his play.

Love, which involves fidelity, trust and self-sacrifice, is often viewed in political literature as an insufficient antidote to the present harsh world. The speaker in József's poem declares: 'I give no kiss, I take no lover'. Dostoievsky's Underground Man doesn't fall in love (except with himself), as he has moved beyond romantic passion to control strategies; even more, he is threatened by love and aims to destroy it. Similarly the love affairs in *Hedda Gabler* are destroyed by the power drives of Hedda and Brack. Belief in over-riding the necessity of politics, *politique d'abord*, became a defining feature of the 1930s. The Spanish Civil War is the background setting to two poems of the era, Sorley McLean's 'The Cry of Europe' and Yeats' 'Politics'. Both accept that love and politics have competing claims which demand acknowledgement, but how are they to be related and realized? McLean, a Communist, begins his poem:

> Girl of the yellow, heavy-yellow, gold-yellow hair,
> the song of your mouth and Europe's shivering cry,
> fair, heavy-haired, spirited, beautiful girl,
> the disgrace of our day would not be bitter in your kiss.
>
> Would your song and splendid beauty
> Take from me the dead loathsomeness of these ways,
> the brute and the brigand at the head of Europe
> and your mouth proud and red with the old song?

Confronted with the menace of Hitler, McLean admits the compulsions of love can seem as more pressing as those of politics. Yet, following Lenin, he rejects personal happiness and reluctantly admits:

> What would the kiss of your proud mouth be
> To each drop of the precious blood
> That fell on the frozen uplands
> Of Spanish mountains from a column of steel?[9]

He can make a beautiful song out of this tension, but can resolve it only by endorsing the pre-eminent claims of political activism.

---

9   Sorley Maclean *Spring Tide and Neap tide: Selected Poems 1932-72*, Canongate, Edinburgh, 1977, p. 12.

Thomas Mann wrote: 'In our time the destiny of man presents its meaning in political terms', a saying popularised as the epigraph to Yeats' poem 'Politics', which does not however fully endorse the sentiment. The beauty of a girl momentarily distracts the poet from present conflicts:

> How can I, that girl standing there,
> My attention fix
> On Roman or on Russian
> Or on Spanish politics?

Many commentators insist we focus on these political matters, but Yeats reluctantly concludes:

> And maybe what they say is true
> Of war and war's alarms,
> But O that I were young again
> And held her in my arms.

The poet comes down, just, on the non-political side of the tension. In *Rhinoceros, The Plague* and *Nineteen Eighty-Four* the heroes move beyond their love affairs, as larger demands call. Constantine Fitzgibbon wrote a political novel called *When The Kissing Had To Stop*.

During this period George Orwell noted many pacifists changed into supporters of war at the first sign of pressure. In Max Frisch's play *The Fire Raisers* the fire wardens become the arsonists. Apparently deferential, they divert attention from their activities. The locals eventually agree to aid them, just as Bukgakov's Bosoi rents out a flat to an intruder. How could people be so gullible? The fire raisers confound their antagonists by giving frank answers to worried questions, they admit they are arsonists, a form of chutzpah intended to be so shocking it takes their adversaries' breath away. The fire is already in people's minds. A series of escalating stratagems and salami tactics ratchets up the stakes. Ordinary people have been so compromised by their earlier weaknesses they can no longer call out the fire-raisers by the grand refusal of saying 'No!' By shifting reality to an absurd plane, Frisch demonstrates the absurdity of accustomed responses, like the bureaucrat in Bulgakov's novel who reacts normally to outlandish events.

Ionesco's play *Rhinoceros* can apply to any rapid takeover; he himself experienced Fascist takeovers in his native Romania and the activism of the pro-Communist left in post-war France. *Rhinoceros* is a comprehensive account of the dozen or so small stages by which people can induce in themselves compromising behaviour. Absurd imagery is deployed in a more protean way than in *The Fire Raisers*: the rhinos are inherently absurd, ugly, ferocious, thick-skinned, aggressive, ridiculous, unnatural, non-human, hunting in packs, and at home in swamps, perfect images from the animal world of takeover types. Here no higher level Big Brother tyrants exist, nor instigators advancing their own arguments, like the fire-raisers, to drive the change – ordinary people con themselves of their own volition. Their pathetically self-defeating responses threaten the community's existence by aligning it with radical change.

When a threat arises the first reaction, as the play shows, is often to deny its existence through applied amnesia. People are naturally reluctant to move out of their comfort zone. When this illusion becomes harder to maintain, various counter-political reactions wish it away: people don't want to be involved, they want to continue as before. This denial helps the virus to spread unchecked in its early stages. People try to downgrade extraordinary events. When the clerk Boeuf is late for work again, this time because he has become a rhino, the boss Papillon reacts ridiculously: 'Well! That's the last straw. This time he's fired for good'. (p. 61) The boss is still seeing things on his own outdated level of perception. His attempt at domesticating the threat naturally fails. People rationalize things away: 'I believe what I see with my own eyes' (p. 49), and 'There's a first time for everything'. (p. 54) Reacting incongruously to the abnormal fatally limits their responses.

When one rhinoceros appears, the people make a great fuss about it, which only gives it undeserved attention. Berenger, the unlikely hero, on the other hand ignores it at the beginning. Another diversion, common among thinkers, is to have long arguments about the threat's nature and origin, admirable in ordinary circumstances, but pointless, as the only need now is to admit the threat and act on it. The logician applies conventional reason and gets hopelessly lost. The argument over whether it is an African or Asian rhino is irrelevant, analogous to distinguishing between the Fascist and Communist varieties of totalitarianism. The essential point is they are both dangerous. The arguments advanced are hopeful self-comforting speculations that miss the point; heightened knowledge can be a hindrance. The logician unwittingly demonstrates Ionesco's point that formalized ways of thinking cannot cope with novel problems. All these rationalizations depend on the hope the worst won't happen.

The next reaction is to admit a problem exists, but to blame others (for example the city authorities) for not acting against it. And when the threat becomes a permanent part of the landscape a new phase occurs: what was once a threat begins to be accepted as normal. Formerly the old status quo was accepted, and now the new abnormal one is accepted just as readily. It is now argued that the perceived threat is minimal, and that it has been exaggerated, another delusional stage on the road to acceptance. A further stage is endorsement: the new phenomenon should be dialogued with and shown liberal tolerance, an example of how once admirable values are inappropriate in this new frightening context, which demands decisions, not the luxury of fence-sitting. These rationalizations take the form that what exists can be justified ('to understand all is to forgive all') which confuses empathy with endorsement. The citizens argue we must look at things from the rhino's point of view, they too are beautiful by their own standards of beauty, perhaps even superior to us human beings because they are so free, spontaneous and natural. To those who adopt this new compliant perspective, these specious arguments seem plausible. The exceptional is thereby tamed.

The final part of the process is to internalize the new vogue and become an arsonist/rhino/takeover merchant too. Guilt abounds: the rhinos are more moral than us, and so on. This is the tendency to find fault with your own side, later known as the 'adversary culture'. Those who lack self-confidence in their own society are most likely to succumb. The arguments advanced are not objective accounts of reality, but conclusions convenient to the speaker. Things aren't as bad as they seem: 'People make mountains out of molehills.' (p. 50) The sequence of rationalizations is always one step behind the developing threat, so it is unable to effect or prevent anything. On the other hand exceptional figures like Berenger (who speaks for the author) argue simply that a threat does exist, admit it, understand that is objectionable and must therefore be actively opposed. In a disturbed atmosphere people are liable to panic, changing suddenly from one view to its opposite. George Orwell noted in the 1930s that people made the 'swing-over from "War is hell" to "War is glorious" not only with no sense of incongruity but almost without any intervening stage'.[10]

Berenger's girlfriend Daisy, who for much of the play has sensible reactions, finally succumbs, leaving him isolated. The central character Jean is in ordinary times an uncritical conformist towards normality, and when rhinos appear, he becomes an uncritical conformist towards the new, extraordinary situation. His attitude hasn't changed, but the situation has. At the beginning Berenger (the name is related to *étrange*, stranger, outsider) is an out-of-sorts bohemian, whereas Jean is a dutiful conformist. When a threat arises one might expect the conformist Jean to defend the status quo. But it is he who embraces the new normality, whereas Berenger, a non-conformist to the end, remains the sceptical outsider. This subverts our expectations. Ideas and movements can arise that are destructive and anti-human. To acknowledge the new developments as malign and to oppose them absolutely is a relatively simple matter, if one does not preen oneself with 'complex' arguments which have the effect of first denying and

---

10 George Orwell *Collected Essays, Journalism and Letters*, Vol. II, Secker & Warburg, London, 1968, p. 251.

then justifying any intrusion. The play operates as humorous satire; by putting the characters in an unusual situation, the ridiculous nature of their reactions is exposed.

Ionesco explained that his play *Rhinoceros* grew out of his experience of Fascism, and of wider 'serious collective diseases':

> *Rhinoceros* is certainly an anti-Nazi play, yet it is also and mainly an attack on collective hysteria and the epidemics that lurk beneath the surface of reason and ideas but are nonetheless passed off as ideologies. Suddenly people get caught up in some new religion or fanatical doctrine...then what takes place is really a mental mutation...when people no longer share your opinion you can no longer reach an understanding with them, you have the impression you are trying to get through to monsters. To rhinoceroses? For example, they have the same mixture of ingenuousness and ferocity. They would kill you without a qualm if you did not think as they do. And in the last quarter of this century history has given us clear proof that people transformed in this way are not just *like*, but truly *become* rhinoceroses.[11]

This happens to Jószef's protagonist and to Ui's gang, who become fellow-travellers of disruption not because of ideas which have some content, but because of immersion in the atmosphere of the times leads to 'mental mutations'. *The Master and Margarita* and *Rhinoceros* are standout literary works on the detailed intricacies of takeovers as they morph from the personal to the political, and from the benign to the malign.

Camus' *The Plague* has a number of different, though connected, levels of meaning. The first is the basic story of the rise and decline of a plague in the Algerian city of Oran. The novel must be plausible on this level if it is to succeed on its further levels. Secondly it is an allegorical representation of the German occupation of France in the second world war: the sanitation squads represent the resistance, the

---

11 Eugene Ionesco *Notes and Counter-notes,* John Calder, Grove Press, New York, 1964, pp. 206 & 212-3.

plague Nazism, the crematoria the gas chambers, and so on. Thirdly, on its widest level it applies to any situation where monstrous ideas and events are imposed on a society, forcing people to react in contrary ways. In the novel the petty criminal Cottard is, like József's speaker, depressed and at odds with society in normal times, since he can't bear normality. But he is energized by the levelling nature of the plague, welcomes it for psychological reasons, and thrives in its economy. Under the larger burden of the plague, his own smaller burden has been lifted from him. The proto-totalitarian welcomes any disruption from which he can benefit. In Brecht's *Arturo Ui*, for example, the character Bowl helps the new rulers get revenge on his former boss. Embracing the plague situation, he becomes a collaborator because he can profit from it, like French black-marketeers who thrived under the German occupation. For similar reasons Cottard fears the ending of the plague.

In William Golding's allegorical novel *Lord of the Flies* (1954) a group of children (or infantilized adults) marooned on an island foment an internally generated societal collapse, caused by differences in ambition rather than beliefs. Within the group an army-like subset, the power-seeking hunters, break away from agreed majority rule, thereby splitting a community already in danger. Many of the characters regress. The novel demonstrates how fragile the crust of civilized behaviour is, how it can disintegrate into barbarism under pressure when the props which undergird civilized behaviour are weakened. One aspect of totalitarian regimes is that they are not modern, as they present themselves, but succumb to dark tribal urges, awakened for example by the sinister, insistent drumming in Gunter Grass's novel *The Tin Drum*. It's not any explicit ideology, but the appeal to raw emotion that matters most. This was obvious in the case of the Nazis, but also of Communist regimes, in spite of their claim to be progressive – show trials were a contemporary form of medieval witch hunts.

Harold Pinter's play *The Caretaker* (1961) is a compelling account of the psychology of takeover, and also of successful resistance to it. The main character, a tramp who wants to rent a room (as in Bulgakov's novel) is adept at presenting himself as a mere downtrodden victim as a way of disarming the two owner brothers, and so of hoping to run the show. One brother ultimately says 'No!', which the Underground Man's school friends, Bulgakov's Bozoi and the characters in *Rhinoceros,* except Berenger, conspicuously fail to do. The apparently dumb, non-intellectualizing brother, Ashton, intuitively senses a threat. He understands the intruder's weak point, calls his bluff and gets rid of him when he overplays his hand. Takeover ploys on a personal plane are commonly depicted in modern literature, as are defences to them. Hedda Gabler in Ibsen's play and the caretaker in Pinter's play attempt permanent, though non-political, domination. Neither succeed because they work in a small compass, where alternative, autonomous arenas of action still exist. Society in these literary works exists on its own level, but larger political insights can be drawn from them.

Sylvia Plath's poem 'Mushrooms' provides an acute account of psychological mechanisms at play during an attempt at subtle domination. The poem exemplifies, but also widens, the strategies of Underground Man. Here the takeover is permanent and communal, not just individual. The mushrooms, like Pinter's caretaker, present themselves as considerate, but in reality they are adopting a victim posture as a power ploy. They insinuate themselves into the company of others they have little in common with. They do not appear as fearsome extremists, like old-fashioned tyrants who told their intended victims directly they were out to get them. On the contrary they are deferential and courteous – they are going to help you. Their bland manners are a blind which disarms their victims. They have a characteristic mixture of 'ingenuousness and ferocity' (Ionesco), like the carrot and stick brainwashing technique, a double-think paradox contained in the wonderfully evocative phrase 'soft fists':

> Nobody sees us,
> Stops us, betrays us;
> The small grains make room.

> Soft fists insist on
> Heaving the needles,
> The leafy bedding

The tone of the poem – quiet, whispered, discreet – captures this tactical approach. No demand is explicitly made ('asking little or nothing'), but in fact a very large demand, that they take up all our space, is being made. They are megalomaniacs asking for everything: complete domination by displacement of the original occupiers. They turn the Gospel notion on its head: the truly meek do not inherit the earth, only the pretend meek. Notice the cozening paradoxes, really contradictions. The mushrooms present themselves in liberal guise, but they mean to take our room to manoeuvre away from us. Individually the mushrooms are weak, but as a mass they are irresistible, endlessly proliferating, stopping at nothing, an unnatural foetus-like swarm, like plants growing in time-lapse photography:

> Nudgers and shovers
> In spite of ourselves.
> Our kind multiplies:
>
> We shall by morning
> Inherit the earth.
> Our foot's in the door.

They are blind, deaf and dumb, concentrating on one thing, oblivious to all others; you can't communicate with them, it's all one way. They multiply incrementally, smoothly – there is no one specific stage where they assert themselves, or when you can stop them. They 'diet', appearing abstemious and puritan, but they are in reality a famished mass which shall 'inherit the earth'. In contrast to their verbal cozening, there is no give nor compromise in their behaviour. They represent themselves as at one with their intended victims ('we are edible'), deceitfully suggesting the victims can be incorporated into the existing schema. The poem is written from the internalized point of view of the about-to-be-dominant group. Like Ionesco's rhinoceros epidemic and Camus' plague, they take over without the need of a Big Brother at their back. Unlike Ui in Brecht's play *The Resistible Rise of Arturo Ui,* they are irresistible, as no hope of stopping them is held out to their passive victims. Plath was drawn to the imagery of Nazis and extermination camps in poems such as 'Lady Lazarus' and 'Daddy'.

Brecht's solution to Fascism was to support a counter ideology, Communism. Ionesco believed on the contrary that once a belief becomes generally accepted, it can coalesce into an orthodoxy, and can itself become a tyranny. Ionesco realized: 'If I set up a ready-made ideology in opposition to other ready-made ideologies, which clutter up the brain, I should only be opposing one system of rhinoceric slogans to another'.[12] Berenger is immune from rhinoceritis because he is a constant self-doubter. Ionesco believed that when fanatical movements arise we should oppose them as such, which is *au fond* a simple and intellectually non-difficult matter, but requires a certain resilient moral insight and strength.

Camus came to a similar conclusion: convoluted intellectual paradoxes will get you into the mess. Towards the end of *The Plague* Tarrou states Camus' position with great clarity:

> All I maintain is that on this earth there are pestilences and there are victims, and it's up to us, as far as possible, not to join forces with the pestilences...I've heard such quantities of argument, which very nearly turned my head, and turned other people's heads enough to make them approve of murder; and I'd come to realize that all our troubles spring from our failure to use plain, clear-cut language...That's why I say there are pestilences and there are victims; no more than that. (pp. 207-8)

People may participate either as victims or supporters of the plague. Human beings can aid and abet the evil that is always potentially in the world. Simon in *The Lord of the Flies* concludes that evil comes from within us. Tarrou likewise believes that the plague isn't something external, imposed on us willy nilly. Tarrou has been the servant of a distorted ideology in his past life, believing, like

---

12 Eugene Ionesco *Notes and Counter-notes,* op. cit, p. 218.

Kirilov in *The Devils*, he could kill in order to bring a just society into being. His action in eventually combating the plague atones for his past life. Arthur Koestler believed the final battle would be between the Communists and the ex-Communists, between those who have experienced the plague and succumbed to it, and who have come out the other end. Camus' anti-hero, Dr Rieux, doesn't fully understand the nature of the plague, nor can he control it, yet he acts to resist it.

Camus believed that, in the face of chaos and evil actions, we act provisionally in the hope that some meaning will emerge in the course of our resistance. Berenger similarly will never become a rhino because he has experienced the temptation as a possibility and rejected it within himself. It's a great achievement to end the plague bacillus without spreading it in doing so. Berenger refuses to comply for reasons he cannot fully understand. Ionesco is revealing in Berenger a man who survives because he does have human frailties and doubts and doesn't have all the answers; he isn't a super hero who rests satisfied with his own pre-defined position. Berenger survives because he keeps believing, in the midst of threats, in his own self worth, which he is not prepared to surrender.

A new kind of hero, really an anti-hero, emerges in political literature at this stage: having been through it all (depression, world war, starvation, deprivation, the camps, absolute tyranny), he is detached and minimalist in his demands. He has experienced the virus he is resisting, while at the same time clinging to a few basic beliefs. He is a stoical survivor, involved as a necessity even though it goes against the grain of his personality. He is secular in relation to all large, preconceived belief systems, facing the modernist black hole unaided, learning as he goes, feeling his way, quizzical, breathing under water.[13] In this he is unlike the Romantic hero or the Socialist realist one, who surrender themselves to salvage a cause. Nor is he in the cynical, destructive mould of the Underground Man, nor of the street gangster bohemian, nor of the adversary thinker. Like Captain Vere (truth) in *Billy Budd* he gets no consolation from old beliefs nor

---

13   Terrence Des Pres *The Survivor* is a book length exposition of this stance.

from radical new ones. He has the wearying task of continuing alone in the dark without panic and with few ready-made guidelines. This view, which emerges in the ruins of the second world war and of the camps, acquires the generic name of existentialism, with Camus as its clearest spokesman.

4

TOTAL DOMINATION

In the public mind extermination camps which led to immediate death, and concentration camps, which led to 'death in life', are defining examples of totalitarian barbarity. Full-blown cases, which included genocide, are comparatively few, namely the regimes of Lenin, Hitler, Stalin, Mao and Pol Pot (the latter annihilated a quarter of his own population), with some others were not far behind. The camps happened in the regimes' early stages, after a revolutionary takeover initiated the rulers' grip. Extreme clampdowns were a sign of the dictators' inability to beguile their populations, so they had to employ heavy coercive doses. The complete domination of one group of human beings by another was unprecedented, as up till the twentieth century governments did not have the technical means nor the psychological insights to totally control populations. In this situation life itself was constantly threatened, almost no hope of relief presented itself, with survival the paramount aim. In addition to the camps, other forms of extreme punishment included imprisonment in harsh conditions, hard labour, routinized torture, brain-washing, total war, mass arrests and the transfer of populations. But even under the extraordinary cruelty imposed in the camps, political literature reveals familiar human relations, familiar hierarchies, and familiar tussles between oppressors and victims. Power was manipulated by dominant characters, and its victims succumbed, or acceded to it, or resisted it, or some mixture of these.

Among the best known examples of extermination/concentration camp literature are Tadeusz Borowski's *This Way to the Gas, Ladies and Gentlemen,* Primo Levi's *If This is A Man,* Alexander Solzhenitsyn's *One Day in the Life of Ivan Denisovich,* and Varlam Shalamov's *Kolyma Tales.* They have noticeable similarities in the experiences described, and in the perspective of the prisoner-authors. Borowski and Levi were imprisoned by the Nazi regime in the Auschwitz extermination camp, and Solzhenitsyn and Shalamov by the Soviet Communist regime in hard labour camps. Almost all concentration camp literature was written by inmates, as it was almost impossible to imagine from outside what the experience was like. Levi's account is directly autobiographical, and in the other three the narrator's experience closely mirrors the author's. Most camp literature was written close in time to the events it depicts.

Victims herded from the transport trains straight to the gas chambers were highest on the casualty list, with no room to manoeuvre – we hardly hear from them. Borowski's situation working as a herder at an extermination camp placed him at a crucial hinge in the process. The crematorium workers witnessed immediate death and faced it themselves, putting them at unbelievable strain. The situation of Levi, assigned to an adjacent work gang, was next worst off, as any physical decline meant being consigned to immediate death in the gas chambers. Solzhenistyn's *Ivan Denisovich* does not describe an extermination camp, though many died; its narrator is in a remote Soviet hard labour gang where death came frequently from exhaustion and starvation as well from more direct killing. The nominal aim was to improve the regime's productivity through slave labour, but another was to eliminate those surplus to requirements, aims which neatly dovetailed; an overall aim was to totally subjugate human will. In all types of camp a shaky balance existed between living and dying. The fate of prisoners was to a minor but important extent in their own hands. And if things were bad in Solzhenitsyn's labour camp, how much worse were they in the Arctic concentration camps. Shalamov was imprisoned in a Siberian *taiga* (snow forest) camp so isolated and lacking in provisions that chances of survival were even lower, with cold as much the guards playing the role of killer.

The Polish writer Tadeusz Borowski was born in 1922 in Ukraine. His parents were deported by the Soviets in the late 1930s. As a young man he opposed the Nazis in Poland, and published poetry and fiction in the underground press. Arrested by the Germans, he was sent to the Auschwitz concentration camp in 1943 and later to Dachau, in both of which he behaved very courageously and miraculously survived. He published his book *This Way for the Gas* in 1949, soon after the events, and a further book, *The World of Stone*, on his time in displaced persons camps in Germany. His poetry and short stories were admired in Poland after the war, but after rejecting one form of totalitarianism, his nihilism and ideological frame of mind led him (somewhat like Brecht) to partly align himself with another form, Stalinism. It is unclear how much he believed in it. He worked for the ruling Polish Communist Party as a political journalist, but when his friends began to be arrested by the regime the strain became too great, and in 1951 he committed suicide by gassing himself, a fate he had been lucky to avoid in Auschwitz. Borowski appears under the name of 'Beta' in Czeslaw Milosz's *The Captive Mind*.

Primo Levi, born in 1919, was an Italian Jewish writer who like Solzhenitsyn had scientific as well as literary interests. He had difficulty finding employment because of Mussolini's racial laws, and took to the mountains north of Turin in 1943 as part of an anti-Fascist partisan group, but was arrested by the Germans in December of that year, and deported to Auschwitz, where he survived for almost a year, living on his bread ration and smuggled soup. Levi eventually secured a job as a laboratory assistant, a better position than being in a crematorium unit or in an outdoor work gang. He was liberated by the Red Army in January 1945, one of few Italian Jews still alive in the camps, and returned to Italy by a circuitous route. He later had a distinguished career in chemistry and writing, being most famous for his camp autobiography and reflections *If This Is a Man*, published in 1947. He died in 1987, whether by suicide or accident is not clear.

Alexander Solzhenitsyn was born in 1918 to a family of Russian rural landowners in Ukraine. From an early age he became a writer and mathematician. By the time of the second world war, in which he served as an artillery captain and was twice decorated, he had long discarded the momentary Communist sympathies of his youth. He was exceptional in being sent to camp for directly criticizing Stalin in a letter in 1945. Solzhenitsyn's labour camp life in Kazakhstan during his eight year term is recreated in *One Day in the Life of Ivan Denisovich* (first published in *Novy Mir* in 1961). He was then moved to a less severe confinement in a scientific research facility at Mavrino, recreated in *The First Circle*, after which he went into internal exile. He became the Soviet Union's most famous dissident for his writings, beginning with *Ivan Denisovich* and continuing with his exhaustive exposé of the Soviet concentration camp empire in *The Gulag Archipelago*. He was awarded the Nobel Prize for literature in 1970, but was expelled from the Soviet Union in 1974, after which he lived in the United States until he returned to Russia in 1994 after the collapse of Communism. He died in 2008.

Varlam Shalamov was born in 1907 to a father who was an Orthodox priest. Early on he became a writer and dissident (like the other three), being arrested in 1929 as a Trotskyite and released after three years. He was rearrested in 1937 as a counter-revolutionary and sent for two long sentences in extreme conditions at Kolyma in the Magadan area in remote eastern Siberia. Like Solzhenitsyn and Borowski his family life was ruined as a consequence of his imprisonment. After his release in 1951 and amnesty after Stalin's death in 1953 he returned to live near Moscow, working on his camp tales and poetry over subsequent decades. During this period he became acquainted with fellow dissident authors such as Solzhenitsyn, Boris Pasternak and Nadezhda Mandelstam. Shalamov's first book was smuggled abroad and published in translation in the West in 1966, with its first Russian publication in 1987 during Gorbachev's thaw and after the author's death in 1982 aged 75.

All four writers were untypical in being regime opponents before being sent to the camps. The vast majority of inmates in Hitler's and Stalin's camps were there for no personal reason at all, except for the tyrants' desire to suborn whole classes of people. Borowski and Shamalov wrote short pieces, usually centered on a single incident and deliberately lacking larger narrative drive, from which the narrator and the reader can draw insights. Borowski and Levi published their books soon after they were liberated, as the Nazis had been totally defeated in 1945. But Soviet Communists continued to curtail freedoms. Solzhenitsyn was extremely lucky to get *Ivan Denisovich* published in 1961 during Khrushchev's short thaw; the curtain soon descended again. The four accounts reveal the difference in ideological worldview and behaviour between Nazism and Communism was not crucial – the two regimes acted in similar ways. These books raise many troubling questions. Was power totally imposed from above? Was survival the only aim of the prisoners? Were the inmates pure victims, with no other roles?

Though concentration camp literature is characterized by total terror passed down from above through a hierarchical system, we can detect even here a subtle psychology whereby victims respond to their situation in different ways. They are not just inert 'living corpses', but have at times some room, however small, for manoeuvre. The camps were in one sense orderly places among the dissolution caused by the constant threat of death. As Terence Des Pres understands: 'The conditions of life-in-death forced a terrible paradox on survivors. They stayed alive by helping the run the camps'.[14] They did the dirty work, literally and metaphorically. The regime forced inmates to both co-operate and compete with each other at the same time. As Solzhenitsyn notes in *One Day*: 'You might well ask why a prisoner worked so hard for ten years in a camp…In the camps they had these gangs to make the prisoners keep each other on their toes. So the fellows at the top did not have to worry'.

The prisoners on whom Borowski focusses are themselves organized into a roughly graded hierarchy. Above them were the SS men who superintended the camp and were all-powerful. Then came the *kapos*, favoured prisoners with 'cushy' jobs, sometimes former

---

14   Terence Des Pres *The Survivor,* Oxford University Press, New York, 1976, p. 116.

criminals who had survived many crises. The *kapo* of each group faced both ways, identifying with the guards above (the Stockholm syndrome), and both ruling and protecting those below, thus transmitting the control mechanism, which became to an extent self-generating. He was a lynchpin of camp 'order'. Through the *kapos*, who took on lead roles, commands were passed down from the higher ups in a pecking order; at each level the individual was a receiver of commands and also a transmitter of them. As Solzhenitsyn wrote: '[Ivan Denisovich] had no dealings with the camp commandant or... with foremen or engineers – that was the team leader's job. He'd protect him with his own chest of steel. In return [the team leader] had only to lift an eye brow or beckon with finger – and you ran and did what he wanted.' (p. 40)

The *Sonderkommando* (of which Borowski's narrator was one) were work units of prisoners assisting in the extermination process in order to keep the camp processes functioning. They constituted an intermediate group, a platoon of useful, relatively healthy males who did the crucial jobs, for example herding prisoners from trains straight to the showers, then to the gas chambers to instant death, and then removing the corpses to the crematoria. Lower down came the sicker prisoners and *Musselmänn*, those who had lost the will to survive.[15] These lowest-rung groups lived in fear of being 'selected', that is, being deemed useless and sent to the gas chambers they were supposed to be servicing. Unlike Borowski and Levi, Solzhenitsyn and Shalamov had no one below them, which made their situation a little less complex. In Solzhenitsyn's and Shalamov's tales a hierarchy of domination passed down from the guards and replicated among the prisoners existed, but was not quite as crucial, as both groups were located in an environment which was itself an equal or even greater agent of elimination. Cold and isolation, which the guards themselves also had to endure, were common causes of suffering and death.

The drive to take over everybody, a mentality evident in

---

15 Those who gave up were called *Musselmänn* (Muslims), in the (incorrect) belief that the Muslim faith required utter resignation to life's setbacks.

oppressive regimes, did not cease the moment somebody submitted to power. Domination was reapplied time and time again to maintain control, as in a permanent revolution. Positive acquiescence and active propagation of the control virus were constantly required, not just resignation to the status quo. At Auschwitz there were two types of camp: a concentration camp and an adjacent extermination camp, which give Borowski's and Levi's accounts a terrible extra dimension. The prisoners who perform these tasks are the focal point since they combine the roles of oppressors and victims; they sometimes take it out on those below them even more than the system demands, as Borowski understands: 'The ramp exhausts you, you rebel – and the easiest way to relieve your hate is to turn against someone weaker.' (p. 40).

The SS had so successfully caused the mechanisms of control to be internalized in those below them that they themselves had to carry out fewer overt acts of terror. Borowski understands it was in the *Sonderkommando's* interest, as well as the SS's, to have people from the transports detrained, undressed and taken to the gas chambers without any outbreak of disorder. Any such disturbance threatened the *Sonderkommando* who might be attacked by the prisoners, or blamed by the SS. Of course this orderliness was in the guards' but not in the victims' interests; Borowski's narrator understands: 'Surely you realize, my friend, that to unload a transport, to see that everyone gets undressed and then to drive them inside the gas chambers, is hard work which requires, if I may say so, a great deal of tact.' (p. 144) The victims' fate had to be kept from them. Those about to be murdered were treated with a certain deceptive civility (hence the title of Borowski's book *This Way to the Gas, Ladies and Gentlemen*). Their fears were allayed to avoid a disorderly panic. In this way the *Sonderkommandos* were implicated in the SS's plans. This was forced on them as the price they paid for staying alive. They not only suffered 'normal' privations as Ivan Denisovich did, but they were in addition sullied by their daily job. There were beneficial and negative aspects of this situation: such prisoners had some room to manoeuvre, but they kept the whole evil thing going and could if they wished mistreat those below them (which Ivan Denisovich and Shalamov couldn't). Concentration camp literature is mostly written from the perspective of the lowest rung in the pile, as with Solzhenitsyn's and Shalamov's narrators. Borowski's and Levi's narrators are slightly higher up. Both understood how at all levels the prisoners retained some slight ability to refuse consent, how the privileged oppressed the underprivileged, and how even the masters were themselves ultimately slaves to the whole system.

The camps were orderly and directed, yet because irrational beings ran them, they were at the same time random and arbitrary. The latter characteristic was the most fearful of all, since anything could happen at any time for no reason, and couldn't be prepared for. Goodness or badness, smartness or blindness, were often not the final arbiters of survival. Nonetheless, the utmost precautions had to be taken to act in an orderly way. Intense focus had to be directed at the means of survival; every other concern faded away. Elemental things loomed large and mattered most: having food, water, heat, sleep and rest, and also if possible avoiding overwork, tensions, beatings, solitary confinement, starvation, illness, punishment and death. Ivan Denisovich chews a morsel of bread slowly and deliberately, to suck every bit of energy and satisfaction he can get out of it. So with every moment, every action, every thought, an intense concentration was necessary to get it right. This caused an enormous stress on the body and on a personality struggling to remain intact.

You had to keep your head down and be inconspicuous. There was always an immense series of little decisions to perform correctly. It was not a question of one 'grand refusal' or commitment, like sacrificing yourself for a cause. Heroics were neither fruitful nor even possible. You had to garner great willpower, discipline and self-control, especially hard when you are permanently tired. This involved suppressing the desires of the ego, including one's natural emotions. Personal wants had to be foregone as dangerous, as they could prevent you seeing things objectively. Nostalgia was out, since daydreaming or thinking about the past or indulging your imagination could weaken your grip on the present. Lower rank prisoners largely lost interest in sex. To dwell on the future could equally be a distraction, but could also act as a tonic presaging hope. Imprisonment was not an event, but a duration, as time had little structure or meaning, every day was the same, future and past were cut off, with space similarly denied.

Prisoners also had to dampen down their normal interest in ideas and ideologies. In Borowski's story 'The People Who Walked On', a Jew who is interested in acquiring eggs is praised more than those who ask (normally valuable questions) like 'Is there life after death?' or 'Will these crimes be punished?' Of course strong beliefs, like those of the Baptist Aloysha and the Jehovah's Witnesses (who believed Hitler was literally the anti-Christ) were greatly helpful to survival. Those who lacked beliefs soon collapsed into a *Musselmänner* state. In Shalamov's tales life is stripped down to bare essentials:

> We'd all learned meekness and had forgotten how to be surprised. We had no pride, vanity or ambition, and jealousy and passions seemed as alien to us as Mars, and trivial in addition. It was much more important to learn to button your pants in the forest. Grown men cried if they weren't able to do that. We understood that death was no worse than life, and we feared neither. We were overwhelmed by indifference...We realized that life, even the worst life, consists of an alternation of joys and sorrows, success and failures, and there was no need to fear the failures more than the successes. (p. 57 – Shalamov 2)[16]

Each Shalamov short story (of either success or failure) is itself stripped down in style, told in a detached tone by the inmate-narrator. Each episode is self-contained, the tales, like prison life itself, don't add up, the prisoner's actions are not directed by any specific meaning, and the story line does not advance. In this sense there is no narrative drive. The prisoners' words and thoughts are elicited with great strain. Shalamov realized that 'each came with difficulty; each appeared suddenly and separately. Thoughts and words didn't appear in streams. Each retuned alone, unaccompanied by the watchful guards of familiar words. Each appeared first on the tongue and only later

---

16   Shalamov page references are to one of his four texts.

in the mind.' (p. 76 – Shalamov 2). It was an existence deprived of context, and was thus one of reduced expectations and consciousness: 'We realized we were at the end of our rope, and we simply let matters take their course. Nothing bothered us any more…Our spiritual calm, achieved by a dulling of the senses, was reminiscent of the 'dungeon's supreme freedom', and Tolstoy's non-resistance to evil. Our spiritual calm was always guarded by our subordination to another's will'. (pp. 63-4 – Shalamov 2) This strange upending of the normal deprivation/ freedom polarity was an antidote to ever present strain.

Shamalov survived because he accepted there was no overall rationale for the camps: "What for?' was a question that did not arise' like Levi's 'there is no why here.' (p. 389 – Shalamov 4), One learnt little but how to endure suffering. In introducing Shalamov's tales Alissa Valles's understands they 'refuse to provide any variety of redemptive narrative'. His stay was so long and brutal that an end was never in sight, and eventually came from an external factor, the general amnesty after Stalin's death. It had been a marathon. History was in this case was not written by the winners, but by the last man standing: 'whoever writes last is right'. (p. 171 – Shalamov 4) Shalamov explained: 'I'd have died a long time ago if it weren't for the songs.' (p. 126 – Shalamov 4). He and other prisoners were sustained by the hymns and songs they sang, and by communal recitals at night of poetry and oral narratives, a memory of a more flourishing existence which refreshed them: 'Everything is equal in the face of memory, as of death' (p. 156 – Shalamov 4). Shalamov himself composed poems and stories at the time; some pieces he wrote on scraps of paper, but poems were committed memory as a safer option. Memory was important, but just as important was blotting out terrible experiences, which exhaustion helped you achieve: 'here the past was the other side of the wall…nobody remembered anything.' (p. 150 –Shalamov 4). Living and literature merged in the camp experience: 'it's impossible to draw a boundary between art and life'. (p. 84 – Shalamov 4). But the inmate could be 'deceived by literature and by a thousand widely believed legends', which made life in the underworld appear too romantic, glamorous and too easily explained. (p. 8 – Shalamov 4). There was a danger in fictionalizing one's memory as much as in remembering.

In *Ivan Denisovich* the inmates can survive to live another day if they put all their ingenuity into the constant struggle against the cold, the lack of food and the brutality of the guards. Like Robinson Crusoe, the victims of this camp inhabit a world where life has been reduced to basics. As one of the novel's Russian critics, V.I. Lakshin, puts it: 'In conditions reminiscent of the primitive struggle for existence, the value of the simplest 'material' elements in life – food, clothing, footwear, a roof over one's head – is discovered anew. An extra ration of bread becomes the subject of the highest poetry'.[17] Survival depends on successfully carrying out everyday needs that in our normal lives would be considered mundane. It is Ivan Denisovich who puts the most sustained energy and effort into survival. Until sleep comes at the day's and the novel's close, his vigilance is never relaxed. The effect of such concentration is registered through the intense strain on him we feel all the time. This wariness caused a mental exhaustion to equal one's physical exhaustion. If you cracked, you were gone. But on the other hand you couldn't overtly resist. This balancing act required great discipline and staying power. It was a dual track existence: you had to keep two opposite drives, to submit and yet be resistant, in your consciousness at the same time. Both were needed to survive. This feature Des Pres calls 'double vision' or 'duality of behaviour': 'The survivor must act on two levels, 'be 'with and against'', as Eugen Kogon says'. (pp. 99-100). One had to look both ways, to acknowledge two different realities as the same time. The paradoxical, contradictory, double-think life created by totalitarian regimes required a response in which nominal opposites (for example, individualism and community) are satisfactorily held together in a new coherent whole.

The ego was diminished by undergoing a kind of purification through suffering. You became a new person, stoic, inured, lean,

---

17 Mihajlo Mihajlov 'Dostoyevsky's and Solzhenitsyn's House of the Dead', *Quadrant*, Vol. X, No. 2, March-April, 1966, p.50.

carrying no excess burdens nor emotional baggage. Ivan Denisovich retains a consciousness resolutely determined on physical survival which defends itself utterly against any invasion of the self. His means of survival is to concentrate solely on what is immediate and present to him. He lives without props. He can't even afford to argue about political evils in the Soviet Union. This is graphically shown in one of the most quoted incidents in the novel, an argument in an office over whether the Russian film-maker Eisenstein was a toady of the Soviet system. Throughout the scene Ivan Denisovich remains silent, worrying only about whether he will get another bowl of *kasha*. (pp. 70-71) The successful inmate becomes an unillusioned existentialist, working out his position at every moment without a preconceived viewpoint and without hope. But he is not an autonomous individual, not one hermetically sealed and self-sufficient; he needs his community. The prisoners have to set up a mutual self-help society with its own morality, a human space with all the healthy qualities of normal communal living. Though in harsh conditions, the inmates in the four authors' writings instinctively create a warm camp camaraderie, with kindness, mutual support, resilience, jokes, linguistic inventiveness, meal rituals and so on, in other words something approaching full normal flourishing life. They are forming oases, a civil society of their own, little platoons at the centre of the maelstrom. This bonding is the glue which keeps them going. The prisoner's dilemma is on the one hand to absolutely protect himself. But unlike Robinson Crusoe, each prisoner lives in a community of human beings who endure the same deprivations and the same strain, which gives each an additional responsibility. Each has to constantly ensure he doesn't by his self-preserving behavior ruin the chances of his fellow inmates, who are not enemies nor rivals, but a necessary component of his own survival. As Levi puts it: 'He fights for his life but still remains everybody's friend.' (p. 63) This fact is shown with great force in the only extended episode in the novel *One Day in the Life of Ivan Denisovich*, the incident when a Moldavian prisoner is discovered missing from roll-call (pp. 94-109). This is a 'matter of life or death' for them all.

The system tried to make the prisoners compete for survival in order to keep the wheels of their hell running. This attitude can be seen in the first bit of advice that Ivan Denisovich gets: 'Here, lads, we live by the law of taiga. But even people manage to live. D'you know who are the ones the camps finish off? Those who lick other men's leftovers, those who set store by the doctors, and those who peach on their mates.' (p. 8) The law of the jungle, where there was no honour, pitted all against all, even among thieves. Were they to act with total self-interest, every man for himself, mimicking the repressive system, or were they to act with some self-imposed restraints? Not all prisoners accepted the logic imposed on them. Self-interested behaviour, where everything is sacrificed to personal survival, could lead to the cycle described in Borowski: 'We said that there is no crime that a man will not commit in order to save himself. And, having saved himself, he will commit crimes for increasingly trivial reasons; he will commit them first out of duty, then from habit, and finally – for pleasure.' (p. 168) The insane logic of this drive is summed up in one Borowski story from Auschwitz: 'And in the midst of the mounting tide of atavism stand men from a different world, men who conspire in order to end conspiracies among people, men who steal so that there will be no more stealing in the world, men who kill so that people will cease to murder one another.' (p. 119) Dostoievsky, through the character of Shigalyov, anatomized this anomalous drive in *The Devils*.

In Borowski's stories there are some restrictions, or at least limits, on behaviour. The reader is appalled by the actions of Becker who has his own son killed for stealing food. (p. 54) Likewise we may not agree with the act of a starving prisoner, who gleefully eats the brains of executed Russians in the story 'The Supper'. The four authors believe group survival is all – you could cheat the system but not you fellow *zek*. Each man in turn owes his life to his comrades. You can't just look after yourself: 'The wolfhound is right but the cannibal is wrong', as a character in Solzhenitsyn's *The First Circle* proclaims. Morality coincides with survival, but self-interest doesn't.

The prisoner was not a completely helpless victim; some choices remained open to him. To survive was not just a matter of outright defiance on the one extreme or outright assimilation on the other. To survive the prisoner had to know how to adapt to the rules of the camp, but at the same time to be spiritually outside it all, in order to preserve a sphere of separateness. In the risky camp underworld in which he was immersed he needed to get around the rules in countless small and dangerous ways. In the camps normal forms of economic exchange existed. Bread, shirts and tobacco were valuable commodities, whose price varied according to the laws of supply and demand. Theft among the SS officers was considered normal, but among the prisoners themselves was severely punished.

The aim of totalitarian regimes had always been to have their populations in spiritual thrall to them by internalizing the regime's mentality. This was demonstrated by the extraordinary concentration camp paradox that those who unsuccessfully attempted suicide were punished with immediate execution. They had shown by their action they were defiant internal emigres, who wished for total escape, the worse possible insult to the regime. They had preferred death to spiritual surrender, the ultimate heresy, they were not amenable to conversion by any means. So by an internally logical but insane form of thinking they were punished by death. The regime desired the annihilation of their personalities, and if they didn't offer this they were not allowed to continue existing. As the poet W. H. Auden understood about those who capitulated: 'Their shame/Was all the worst could wish; they lost their pride/And died as men before their bodies died.' Levi wisely noted that 'our personality is fragile, much more in danger than our life' (p. 61), and the importance of 'the power to refuse our consent…to remain alive, not to begin to die' (p. 47).

Among the prisoners Ivan Denisovich is outstanding. Relative to him, the others in his camp range in a spectrum from those who have given up to those who can accommodate themselves to camp life to those who most clearly attract the author's sympathy, like the Baptist Alyosha who prays: 'Give us this day our daily bread'. (p. 138). Yet Ivan Denisovich is also realistic. He understands his persecutors have devised a system that makes physical revolt impossible, and acts accordingly. Of his own trial and sentence the narrator records: 'he reckoned simply. If he didn't sign he'd be shot. If he signed he'd still get a chance to live. So he signed.' (p. 59) This may be a compromise, but more importantly it is common sense. Ivan Denisovich's philosophy of camp life is clearly stated: '(He) complained of nothing: neither about the length of his stretch, nor about the length of the day, nor about their filching another Sunday. This was all he thought about now: we'll survive. We'll stick it out, God grant, till it's over'. (p. 121). This attitude should not be confused with quietism.

Even after his camp period, Solzhenitsyn, in his relations with the Soviet government from the publication of *One Day* in 1961 to his expulsion in 1974, maintained the same attitude. From a position of weakness, without power and not in control, he played a subtle cat-and-mouse game of compromise and resistance with the regime, a tightrope walk of knowing when to object and when to deal. He was not the absolutist figure, a fundamentalist *refusnik* so often ascribed to him in the West. Nor was this a dissident attitude like the adversary culture of the west; it was not so much a question of opposing an authority system as creating an alternative one, as Solidarity in Poland later demonstrated. You had to become attached to nothing, which gave you freedom; when you had little, you slept in peace. This required an ability to see everything with complete objectivity, to be outside your own desires. The prisoners saw themselves as objects. Borowski particularly captures this quality in his narrator. As Levi put it: 'Man's capacity to dig himself in, to secrete a shell, to build around himself a tenuous barrier of defence, even in apparently desperate circumstances, is astonishing'. (p. 62)

The events themselves were so monstrous that the difficulty was simply to record them. The author does not have to point out the meaning of events; that is evident enough once they have been recounted. It's not the creative faculty that is uppermost, but understanding and recall. So the narrator, though recording apocalyptic events, becomes unexpectedly distanced, seemingly uninvolved and unaffected. He employs minimalist techniques: the smallest things possible, a tiny canvas, one person, during one 'normal' day, not thousands undergoing unbearable torments (which neither he nor the reader couldn't digest). He does not moralize nor even comment. It's reminds one of Orwell's clear, factual, non-panicky cast of mind. Nature is one element which provides a relief from humanity's barbarism. In Levi's book the prisoners look forward to the appearance of spring. In Shalamov's Siberian world the dwarf cedars of the *taiga* bend over to survive the winter snowfall, and then spring back to life, heralding a new season and giving the prisoners some consolation and hope.

In totalitarian regimes the possibility of effective dissent is deliberately eliminated or a least minimized. In these circumstances should one try to resist? Rebellion was almost pointless, as it would be instantly quashed with death resulting. But the alternative, resignation to the camp regime, was equally unsatisfactory. In Borowski's view there is no simple 'yes' or 'no' answer to this dilemma. He keeps raising the dilemma subtly, but not answering it directly, in a number of different guises to reveal its full complexity. One instance is in the story 'The Man With the Package'. An old sick Jew, condemned to the crematorium, takes a package of his possessions with him. He knows very well it will be taken from him, and that camp life is about not being attached to one's desires. He could have given it to someone else. Yet the narrator, and his interlocutor, a doctor, agree with this touching last action: 'It would be like holding someone's hand, you see'. This is a small example of the worthwhileness of some apparently useless action. The story ends on this note: 'I don't know why, but it was said later around the camp that the Jews who were driven to the gas chambers sang soul-stirring Hebrew songs which nobody could understand'. (p. 151) Their precise content was not the point. In 'The January Offensive' the dilemma is raised and answered in a different way. The action of a Russian woman soldier, who soon after giving birth goes on to contribute to a military offensive against the Germans, privileges effective action over self-interest. A character raises the problem in another way: 'Is it better for a man locked inside the ghetto to sacrifice his life, or is it better for him to escape from the ghetto to the Aryan side, to save his life and this be able to read Pindar's *Epinicae*?' (p. 172) There are no cut-and-dried answer to these questions.

Borowski describes three different incidents involving women prisoners about to be killed, from which he lets us draw our own conclusions. On one occasion, a guard notices a young girl who begs to know what they will do to her. Instinctively touched by her plight, he tells her to be brave and not to look, and gently leads her forward to execution. This is in the circumstances an act of mercy. (p. 96) On another occasion a blonde girl appears, different from the rest and immediately noticeable. She exudes, in Solzhenitsyn's words on another occasion, 'the unaccountable spiritual superiority of certain human beings'. She is above it all, displaying a profound disdain for her terrible situation, as she enquires: 'Listen, tell me where they are taking us', she is 'a girl with a wise, mature look in her eyes. Here she stands waiting. And over there in the gas chamber: communal death, disgusting and ugly'. She has 'a lovely gold watch on her delicate wrist', useless but a symbol of something higher. The guard won't tell her:

> 'I know,' she says with a shade of proud contempt in her voice, tossing her head. She walks off resolutely in the direction of the trucks. Someone tries to stop her; she boldly pushes him aside and runs up the steps. In the distance I can only catch a glimpse of her blond hair flying in the breeze. (p. 44)

This is proud contempt, a sovereign gesture of superiority, transcending the scene; even if not effective, it is ultimately worthwhile, like the Jew's package, or the Hebrew songs, a memory the narrator has etched on his mind.

The third case is one of actual rebellion. A sadistic SS man, Sergeant Schillinger, takes a fancy to a beautiful Jewish girl about to be gassed. As he walks up to take her hand she suddenly throws a handful of gravel in his face. Crying out in pain he drops his revolver, which she grabs and fires several shots into his abdomen. The dying Schillinger, quickly changing roles and seeing himself as the victim, cries out: 'My God, what have I done to deserve such punishment?' He ludicrously identifies himself with Christ's suffering and death on the Cross ('why hast thou forsaken me?'), a Christian murdered by a Jew. The narrator comments: 'That man didn't understand to the very end'. The woman's action, though ultimately ineffective, is worthwhile, as she was about to die anyway. It momentarily disrupts the order which the SS relies on, breaking for a moment the spell by which small numbers can peacefully herd large numbers to their deaths. This incident may have a factual basis. It is surprisingly similar to an incident recounted by Bruno Bettelheim, who like Borowski was in Auschwitz, but perhaps earlier: 'Once, a group of naked prisoners about to enter the gas chamber stood lined up in front of it. In some way one of the commanding SS officers learned that one of the women had been a dancer. So he ordered her to dance for him. She did, and as she danced, she approached him, seized his gun and shot him. She too was immediately shot to death.' But, just in case one's hopes are lifted too high by such incidents, any easy conclusion is undercut by the frank, brutal postscript to the Borowski story: 'When, shortly before the camp was evacuated, the same *Sonderkommando* staged a revolt in the crematoria, several SS guards turned the machine guns on them and killed every one – without exception'. (pp. 145-6)

In some camps a contrast was evident between the everyday life of the guards (soccer, musical concerts, nature, sunny days) and the incomprehensible slaughter going on nearby. It was like being in another world; the narrator cannot connect the two. One passage in Borowski's account claims the concentration camp is a paradigm of all life: 'We told them with much relish about our difficult, patient, concentration-camp existence which had taught us that the whole world is really like the concentration camp; the weak work for the strong, and if they have no strength or will to work – then let them steal, or let them die.' (p. 168) In this view the world is ruled by absolute power. Yet the whole tenor of Borowski's writings seems to deny this, and to suggest on the contrary that the death camps were an unprecedented occurrence. In the story 'Silence' an innocent US soldier at the end of the war tells the surviving camp inmates things have returned to normal and not to exact vengeance. The inmates pretend to agree, then immediately after the soldier leaves they trample to death a captured camp guard. (p. 163) This reveals the unbridgeable gap between the abnormal world and the other.

Outsiders found it too difficult to summon up the imagination needed to comprehend camp life. It wasn't an imaginative faculty that was needed, it was the ability to recreate in words the actual experience. In the camps the great feat was to concentrate intensely on the moment, rather than to indulge the imagination, which could be a life-threatening distraction. In *Ivan Denisovich* Solzhenitsyn doesn't pile on the horrors or point out great evils. It is all the more effective because his approach is calm, almost remote. The tone of voice of the other three narrators mirrors this. They are absolutely detached and matter-of-fact, even in the midst of horrific events. This is itself a survival technique. It may seem inappropriate, as the expected reaction would be to be outraged by the inhumanity of it all. The author, like the prisoner, must see things with absolute truth and clarity. Al Alvarez wrote: 'The judgments are there by omission'. Around Borowski's stories 'there is a kind of moral silence, like the pause which follows a scream.'[18] The author, like his hero, is not interested in large statements and interpretations. The feelings he wants to convey are fiercely present in the barest recital of events. He doesn't lash out at evil. The author's impact comes precisely from his compression and restraint. The impression that lingers is of a controlled indignation that such things could be.

The standard creative mind, oriented to highlights, invention, empathy, emotional renderings, significance, narrative sequence, dramatic effects and shaping the material, and so on no longer fitted. There were no neat endings, no closure, only dead ends, literally, in the camps. There was no need for effects, the material at hand did that itself. Quite new techniques were needed; in *Ivan Denisovich* there is

---

18 Al Alvarez 'The Literature of the Holocaust', *Commentary*, November, 1964.

just one day, one camp, one prisoner, with survival just possible. The perspective is sparse and limited, the scale is restricted, with no spare room to expand. There was no need for context or wider horizons or to point out meaning: it didn't exist, there was no why. There is no narrative, no larger explanation, no need for larger statements. The experience tells its own story. All is boiled down to the smallest residue. The author is subservient and not in control of events, others are. Drama and novels are lesser forms here; only short stories and short poems fit the bill, being small in scale and without a story line. This has something in common with modernist literature, which is detached and hard-edged. Emotions have been evacuated, so the world is looked at clinically, out there, quite apart from the consciousness of the author. This is the opposite of the pathetic fallacy, an author's sympathetic identification with events. Descriptions are often clear and tangible precisely because objects and events have no inner meaning; under pressure they have been emptied of all resonances and associations. For these reasons camp life was a counter literary experience.

For some camp victims the determination to record their experiences was the drive that kept them going. After release some prisoners had a burning desire to record the experiences, in order to redeem those who did not survive, to remember them so they would not be forgotten, and to warn future generations to take heed. The rest of humanity wouldn't believe it, the experience was so unimaginable. Milan Kundera believed that overcoming totalitarianism was a battle of memory over forgetting. Such sentiments were in the forefront of Solzhenitsyn's mind. As one of those who had come back from the land of the dead, he felt under an enormous obligation to speak on behalf of all those fellow inmates who had perished in the camps. He wrote in his Introduction to the *Gulag Archipelago*: 'I dedicate this to all those who did not live to tell it'. He adds that 'everything will be told…on behalf of those who have perished'. In addition he states that the Gulag Archipelago still exists as he writes, it's not just something in the past. Solzhenitsyn gives utterance to the previously silent, so that justice might finally be done and their wrongful fate acknowledged.

In retrospectively writing up the experience the great feat was to recall it precisely; there was no need to gild the lily. The survivor author had to make another enormous effort, to suffer it all over again by endowing it with a new existence in print. This was to repeat his experiences in a different form, but also to be relieved of them. Composing a text acted as a purgative, as Shalamov reflected: 'Even if you can't get something published, it's easier to bear a thing if you write it down. Once you've done that, you can forget...' (p. 151 – Shalamov 2) By this means the experience had at last been externalized, which released pressure. Solzhenitsyn had set his milder camp in the *First Circle* of Hell. Shalamov understood very well the uniqueness of his fate, by placing his icy gulag in the last, frozen circle of Hell in Dante's *Inferno*:

> Our tools are primitive
>   and simple:
>   a rouble's worth of paper,
>   a hurrying pencil
>
> That's all we require
>   to build a castle –
> high in the air –
>   above the world's bustle.
>
> Dante needed nothing else
>   to build gates
> into that Hell hole
>   founded on ice.[19]

For the Soviet population, whether in the camps or not, the decades of the 1930s and 1940s were a horror period. The middle sections of *The Plague* and *The Tin Drum* reveal whole societies under similar Nazi pressures. The atmosphere of death from the camps wafted

---

19 Robert Chandler 'This purple honey: The poetry of Varlam Shalamov', *Times Literary Supplement*, 7 March, 2014, p. 15.

over the whole of Europe, putting normal life in lockdown, as Anna Akhmatova expressed in one of her finest poems:

> Wild honey smells of open air,
> Dust of sun's ray,
> Girl's mouth of violets –
> And gold of nothing. Mignonette smells of water,
> Love of apples.
> But – one lesson we shall no forget –
> Bloods smells of blood alone.
>
> And in vain did Rome's Viceroy
> Wash his hands before the whole people
> To Mob's malign yells;
> And Scotland's Queen
> In vain from narrow palms
> Rinsed crimson spurts
> In stifling gloom of royal palace.[20]

Other things have fruitful associations, but not gold or blood which wipe out everything else. Blood leads to terror alone, in an atmosphere of all pervading gloom. Akhmatova refers, like Bulgakov, to Pontius Pilate as show trial judge, and to Shakespeare's portrait of rulers like Macbeth besmirched in blood: 'my hand will rather/the multitudinous seas incarnadine,/making the green one red'. Marina Tsvetayeva and Osip Mandelstam completed, with Akhamtova and Pasternak, the quartet of outstanding but tragic Russian poets living diminished lives during the Stalin era. On one occasion in a restaurant Mandelstam impulsively snatched out of the hands of a secret policeman a list of designated victims and tore it up. Another crazy-brave action of his was more dangerous, an ode written in 1933 mocking Stalin:

> Ringed with a scum of chicken-necked bosses

---

20 Ronald Hingley *Nightingale Fever: Russian Poets in Revolution*, Weidenfeld and Nicolson, London, 1982, p. 185.

> He toys with the tributes of half-men...
> He forges decrees in a line like horseshoes,
> One for the groin, one the forehead, temple, eye.

This poem sealed his fate. Out of the blue Stalin phoned Pasternak and asked if Mandelstam was really a creative genius. Stalin considered himself a creative genius, so his query implied that Russia could not accommodate two. Caught off guard Pasternak gave an unsatisfactory reply, which he ever afterwards regretted. Mandelstam was arrested but was firstly allowed to live in a kind of suspended animation in the city of Voronezh with his wife Nadezhda: 'Our lives no longer feel ground under them./At ten paces you can't hear our words'. Akhmatova wrote similarly of the unreality of life in 'Voronezh':

> You walk on permafrost
> in these streets
> The town's silly and heavy
> like a glass paperweight
> stuck on a desk...
> Judas and the Word
> Are stalking each other
> Through this scraggy town
> Where every line has three stresses
> And only one word, *dark*.

With the lines 'Judas and the Word/Are stalking each other' Akhmatova picks up a key a theme in Bulgakov's novel. At the same time Bulgakov and his wife were enduring the suspended animation of internal exile. Mandelstam was rearrested and died in 1938, two years before Bulgakov, in terrible circumstances on a train taking him to a Siberian camp. In an earlier poem Mandelstam had foreseen his own death and resurrection:

> Mounds of human heads are wandering into the distance.

> I dwindle among them. Nobody sees me. But in books
> Much loved, and in children's games I shall rise
> From the dead to say the sun is shining. [21]

This came to pass, but much later. Mandelstam's and Bulgakov's wives preserved their memories and their manuscripts in the hope of giving them an afterlife. The reconstructed manuscript of *The Master and Margarita* survived beyond the life span of Stalin, creativity painfully triumphing over destruction in the long run. In the late 1960s, decades after her husband's death, Nadezhda Mandelstam published her remarkable volumes of autobiographical reminiscence, *Hope Against Hope* and *Hope Abandoned*. In the same period Mandelstam's collected poems and Bulgakov's masterpiece *The Master and Margarita* first saw the light of day.

---

[21] Osip Mandelstam *Selected Poems*, trans. Clarence Brown & W.S. Merwin, OUP, London, 1973, pp. 69-70 & 84.

5

ENDLESS DOMINATION

> In paradise the work week is fixed at thirty hours
> salaries are higher prices are steadily going down
> manual labor is not tiring (because of reduced gravity)
> chopping wood is no harder than typing
> the social system is stable and the rulers are wise
> really in paradise one is better off than in whatever country

In his 'Report from paradise' the Polish poet Zbigniew Herbert is satirizing a strange new form of domination: everyday life under a regime which has 'normalized' itself after an earlier terror phase, but retains its grip through low-level bribery and complicity. The ugly means by which power was gained in the past is no longer an issue, either forgotten or suppressed. An anodyne lifestyle is offered to the populace as a reward for acquiescence. All hopes of terminating the regime have been eliminated. The rulers have to keep winning the hearts and minds of their subjects, a necessity if the regime is to perpetuate itself. Ideological drive, including persuasion, mass propaganda and mind games, become the preferred means of control. The regime hopes these will provide a new societal glue, replacing the solid civil structures of the past. Up till this juncture, totalitarian and normal Western governments had been the two commonly imagined forms of rule. Now some intermediate middle ground seemed a possibility.

Historically this situation existed under Communism after the deaths of Stalin and Mao. Nazi Germany had only a brief 'normalized' period in the 1930s. It was George Orwell's great genius that he recreated routinized totalitarian rule in its milder form in *Nineteen Eighty-Four* (1949), so his novel was prophetic, though he himself described it as a warning not a prophecy. *Nineteen Eighty-Four* is set in the future, about 60 years after the regime of Big Brother had been set up. (The Soviet Union was 67 years old in 1984.) The novel depicts the shabby reality of everyday life as an accepted, endless condition. The uniqueness of the totalitarian mentality made it extremely difficult to understand from afar. Orwell once wrote: 'There is almost no English writer who happened to see totalitarianism from the inside...England is lacking, therefore, in what one might call concentration camp literature. To understand such things one has to be able to imagine oneself as the victim.'[22] There are certain gains and certain losses in employing imagination as a substitute for gaps in one's experience. One has to imagine oneself not just as a victim, but also as part of the ruling class, and more importantly as a middle level citizen transmitting the domination/victim control virus as well as assimilating it.

The Soviet Union under Bolshevik rule was the first totalitarian state, so it is no surprise that two Russian authors were the first to base their novels on this development. The Russian naval engineer Yevgeny Zamyatin (1884-1937) lived at the same time as the Russian doctor Mikhail Bulgakov (1891-1940), with many parallels in their lives and writing careers. Both were among other things satirists, an extremely dangerous occupation in the high-terror interwar years dominated by Lenin's and Stalin's forced state building. Both mention the manuscripts of their own novels in *We* and *The Master and Margarita* respectively, as the mere existence of these caused fraught lives for their authors. Both appealed to Stalin to leave the Soviet Union who took a personal interest in their cases. Both had their works banned in Russia, and died prematurely in distressed circumstances around the age of fifty. Both adapted insights learnt from Dostoievsky; Bulgakov

---

22 George Orwell *The Collected Essays,* Vol. III, p. 235.

believed the Soviet system was metaphysically evil, as suggested in *The Devils*.

Zamyatin's critique of totalitarianism is derived in part from Dostoievsky's horror, in *Notes From Underground*, of an anthill society, a metaphor for a new intense form of 'lowest common denominator' control. Zamyatin's anti-utopian novel, *We*, was first published abroad in 1924 in a English translation. The title of novel is better rendered in French as *Nous Autres* (*We Others*). In it the rebel group is called the Mephi, after Mephistopheles, the Devil's offsider in the Faust legend; Bulgakov's novel also highlights demonic possession, as in the Walpurgis Night ball scene. The hero's suffering and fate is paralleled with that of Christ in both the author's novels. Zamyatin was censored by the Tsarist authorities for his satirical writings, as well as later by the Bolshevik regime; his work was repressed and he lost his literary posts. In 1931 his request to Stalin that he move abroad, made two years after Bulgakov's was rejected, was unexpectedly granted, and he lived in Paris until his death in 1937.

In *We,* written in 1919-1921, the inhabitants live dull, atomized and regimented lives, rendered anonymous and less than human by them being allocated numbers (like later concentration camp inmates) instead of personal names, thus becoming ciphers rather than citizens. Natural social cohesion has been replaced by a totally mechanized, grey society, where technical progress and morality have become separated, science as nightmare. Scientific planning and social engineering are the regime's mainstays, with people constantly watched and coerced into submission. Human emotions are replaced by drug-induced apathy. The oppressive supreme ruler of the One State, who enforces total control, has the ironic double-think name of the Benefactor; his rule is backed by the Guardians (another euphemism), his secret police. With the endless prospect of the same conditions stretching into the future, there is scant memory of an earlier, more benign form of social organization, the period before the new rulers came to power a millennium ago after a Two Hundred Years' War. There is no memory of how the new regime installed itself, nor any inkling of how it might end. Both past and future have been blocked off.

Unlike the variegated classes of past eras, society in *We* is divided into two sharp categories: the party, a minority but an all powerful establishment, and the vast large undifferentiated masses. This division is enforced by keeping ordinary citizens outside the physical centre of society. The latter are quarantined in a primitive state of nature outside a Green Wall, where, having not undergone the 'benefit' of mind-altering treatments, they are left to stew in their own primeval backwardness. After visiting a museum known as the House of Antiquity, the novel's central character, the conformist D-503, suspects against the grain that olden times must have had some vital quality now missing. Ostensible praise of the present regime is therefore undermined by a vague, subterranean yearning for freedom. As a result *We* operates on two different levels: the narrator, D-503, is to all appearances in favor of the new regime, but keeps having atavistic lapses, which the author (and the reader) silently endorse. This split consciousness gives the novel its tension and its irony.

The narrator/hero hopes his love for a woman, O-90, offers a solution to his present disquiet. Love is described as a subversive activity, 'the other sovereign of the universe', in a world in which the regime strives to eliminate the last vestiges of the soul, of the imagination and of alternative forms of sovereignty. Zamyatin, like Bulgakov, contemplates but eventually rejects the consolation that personal relations can be a successful antidote to the regime's repressions. A woman friend, I-330, who is more emancipated in spirit than the main character, inveigles him into joining a rebellion, led by the secret opposition group, the Mephi. But a medical procedure surgically removes the hero D-503's capacity for independent thought, rendering his putative rebellion nugatory. Later in the novel D-503, in concert with I-330, hopes against hope that the regime will ultimately collapse: 'there is no ultimate revolution – revolutions are infinite in number.' (p. 169) No existing regime can successfully proclaim the end of history.

A sharp distinction between elite and masses, which Orwell later utilized, was an important Zamyatin innovation. It reflects the *pays réel* and *pays légal* separation (the actual as opposed to the formal nation) made by the right-wing French political thinker Charles Maurras during the same period. The later use of the term *nomenklatura* to describe the Communist Party monopoly roughly corresponds to the *pays légal*.[23] One potential weakness in the novel is the physical separation of the elite and the masses by a Green Wall. In totalitarian societies party members are actually embedded in normal society to enforce the rulers' desires. A gulf between the ruling class and its subjects was noticeable in past centuries in Europe, but it wasn't marked by a geographic separation. The equalizing doctrines of the Enlightenment and French Revolution lessened the gap, whereas the shakeout caused by the Industrial Revolution increased it. But society remained stratified, not totally divided, with each layer connected with those above and below it.

Both Huxley's *Brave New World* (1932) and Orwell's *1984* (1949) are patterned on Zamyatin's *We*, though Huxley claimed not to have read it. These three anti-utopian novels are intended as criticisms of the present world by extrapolating contemporary tendencies, feared by the author, to their logical conclusions. There exist in *Brave New World*, as in *We*, a few people in the superior society in whom the atavistic desire for freedom (what Zamyatin called 'that wild simian echo') has not yet been entirely extinguished. They have somehow resisted the state's attempts to amputate their imaginations. They act gratuitously, they are unhappy, and refuse to be totally processed. In such a 'perfect' society, these attitudes constitute rebellion: they are flaws in the system which have to be removed. In these novels the dissidents are brought into contact with the rulers, who explain how the system works, in order to brand the rebels as a dangerous opposition.

Anti-utopian novels end on a characteristically pessimistic note,

---

23 In Western societies today an analogous division is sometimes caused by minority elites contending with a majority of 'reprehensibles' (Hilary Clinton's phrase).

with the rebels doomed to defeat. Societal stability comes first; freedom and happiness are incompatible. The savage outside the Green Wall prefers to be unhappy but free; to have both is impossible. Jonathon Swift achieved something similar in creating the Struldbruggs in *Gulliver's Travels*. People believe that a wonderful life would result if we could lift ourselves above the mortal limitations of existence. In their fictions Swift and Zamyatin create such a life to show how horrible it would in reality be.

Anti-utopian novels are unusual in not satisfying many of the expectations of the reader. Of their nature they can't have highly developed plots or characters. As Irving Howe put it: 'The human relations which the ordinary novel takes as its premise become the possibilities towards which the anti-utopian novel strives'. What these novels demand is ingenuity in creating the details of life in a controlled universe, which is one of their strengths. Huxley however made many aspects of his world genuinely attractive (sex, drugs and modes of transport, for instance), and he often writes with that witty, cocktail party brilliance characteristic of the 1920s. This leads us to wonder just how severely Huxley rejects the Brave New World he so enjoys creating and, as a self-confessed 'amused aesthete', just how much he feels himself seriously menaced by it. The regime in *Brave New World* is much less frightening than those in Zamyatin's and Orwell's novels. Regimentation seems in Huxley's view to bring not an increase in terror but low-grade pleasure. There is not much horrific domination from above, with the regime resorting to drugs and hedonism rather than coercion as control mechanisms.

The question readers ask about anti-utopian fictions is whether they are coming true or not: will 1984 be like *1984* or like *Brave New World* or neither? On this criterion Aldous Huxley's work has not enjoyed a good reputation. It was often believed in the immediate post-war period that George Orwell's nightmare of totalitarian rule, obsessed with power and enforced by cruelty, was far more likely than the soft, purposeless pleasures of *Brave New World*. Even Huxley himself, in his forward written in 1946, was rather apologetic about the predictive accuracy of his book. Orwell wrote of Huxley's novel in 1940:

> Here the hedonistic principle is pushed to the utmost, the whole world has turned into a Riviera hotel. But though *Brave New World* was a brilliant caricature of the present (the present of 1930) it probably casts no light on the future. No society of that kind would last more than a couple of generations, because a ruling class which thought principally in terms of a 'good time' would soon lose its vitality. A ruling class has got to have a strict morality, a quasi-religious belief in itself, a mystique.[24]

However the situation in the Western world is now considerably different from the dark days of the 1940s when these comments were made. The possibility we face today in the West is not of apocalyptic political terror thrust upon us from above overnight. Relaxed rulers of the Bill Clinton and Silvio Berlusconi 'good time' type are now par for the course. Travel guides reveal how much of world 'has turned into a Riviera hotel'. Leaders have learnt to govern without defined morality or religious beliefs. Many ruling classes now encourage their citizenry, and themselves, to make self-satisfaction their prime goal. Dramatic breakthroughs in genetics, biology and the bio-medical sciences, such as the fabrication of the DNA molecule, *in vitro* fertilization and designer babies, give credence to some of Huxley's predictions.

Another aspect of Huxley's vision which is important today is his belief that changing the consciousness of people (or mind-bending) rather than imposing new political restrictions is the way to control society and to achieve universal human happiness. Huxley was himself an early experimenter with drugs like mescalin and LSD. The following eulogy by the controller Mustapha Mond of the 'drugs and hedonism' way of life could easily describe the attitude of many alternative groups in the USA:

> If ever, by some unlucky chance, anything unpleasant should somehow happen, why, there's always SOMA to give you a holiday from the facts. In the past you could only accomplish these things by making a great effort and after years of hard moral training...anyone can be virtuous now...Christianity without tears.

---

24   Orwell, George *The Collected Essays,* Vol. II, p. 31.

Hebert Marcuse and his colleagues from the Frankfurt School believed Western ruling elites dulled the innate revolutionary aspirations of their citizens by a diet of drugs, sex, consumer goods and mass entertainment. So parts of *Brave New World* do seem much more pertinent now than when Huxley wrote his foreword seven decades ago. The question remains whether this style of life is admirable or not.

Orwell's *Nineteen Eighty-Four* is original in the way it portrays the physical streetscapes of the new 'utopia'. It is not the 'glittering antiseptic world of glass and steel and snow white concrete' (p. 153) we expect from futuristic utopias like *We* and *Brave New World*. Reality is the seedy, decaying suburbia of aging tenements, with grimy, crowded streets and the peeling masonry of the deceptively named Victory Mansions. It is a life of spam meat, poor gin, bad health, pink slops and low quality goods. Scenes of tawdry daily existence reveal a disconnect with the triumphalist rhetoric of the regime, and remind us of daily life in Eastern Europe under Communist rule.

The Victory Mansions scenes are based in part on the London of Orwell's flat life. He did not set his futurist novel in continental Europe, but he did extend his imaginative gaze, adding together his reading knowledge of Germany and Russia under repressive regimes, Koestler's account in *Darkness at Noon,* and his own experiences in the Spanish civil war and briefly in devastated Germany in 1945. His wartime experience at the BBC gave him insights into modern propaganda techniques.[25] This geographical montage was a natural move, since he believed that 'totalitarian ideas have taken root in the minds of intellectuals everywhere',[26] and that a range of countries might in the future exhibit similar characteristics. Orwell did not believe the West was already totalitarian. *Nineteen Eight-Four* was intended to reveal what could happen if developments already noticeable by the end of the war were extended to their logical conclusion. The novel

---

25 The diverse sources and experiences out of which Orwell assembled his novel are laid out in William Steinhoff *The Road to 1984,* Weidenfeld and Nicolson, London, 1975.
26 George Orwell *The Collected Essays,* Vol. IV, p. 502.

was prescient in many ways: Goldstein's manual dividing the world up into three power blocs was an amazingly accurate foretaste of the political shape of the post-war world.

Orwell comes close to showing how a totalitarian regime elicits support. Confected emotions can be elicited by government media blitzes permeating populations with moral panic and other mental mutations. Orwell understood that for such a regime the techniques of the takeover phase never end. Endless change and switching of targets prevent incipient opposition group coagulating. During the Two Minutes Hate sessions, mass indignation can be turned on and off at will and towards contrary targets; today's hero can become tomorrow's villain. Mind manipulation is reflected in language manipulation. The mind in this view is a blank space on to which anything can be imprinted: 'an abstract, undirected emotion that could be switched from one object to another like the flames of a blow lamp' (p. 15). Society is pulverized so that no small platoons, the building blocks of civil society, can form. No solidarity either personal or organizational is possible. The two minutes' hate sessions produce a negative, manufactured sense of community. A combination of such pressures are applied to Winston, an outsider/dissident, to make him conform and love Big Brother. Endless obeisance, renewed tokens of enthusiasm and involvement must be shown, and he eventually succumbs. In this sense the distinction between big picture *grand mal* and local *petit mal* totalitarianism has been convincingly blurred.

War is Peace, Freedom is Slavery, the Ministry of Love spews out hate. These paradoxes, really contradictions, hold opposing concepts in one's mind at the same time, double think. Orwell tries to show how Winston is affected by the Two Minutes Hate, when he has images of raping and killing a naked Julia, but this sudden sadism is not convincing. Newspeak stops people thinking outside the regime's thought patterns. Thought Crime and the Thought Police play mind games with you, trying to get inside your being, so you can't even formulate dissenting thoughts, much less carry them out. Power has become an end in itself, not just a means. The basic goal is more than just class or race divisions or professed ideologies like Communism or Fascism – it is the endless imposition of control.

The means by which a regime entangles a citizen is evident in the episode of the revolutionary Brotherhood. Winston joins because he is a dissident, and is shown the Goldstein document, which, unlike regime propaganda, is close to reality. But the opposition is also part of the regime; both sides need the other as a focus of hate and love, a mirror image: 'Judas and the Word/are staking each other'. The Bolsheviks, who had once been revolutionary dissidents themselves and never wholly relinquished this stance, understood the attractions of subversion. Whether the Brotherhood exists or not is not the issue: the party needs it, as Stalin needed the reviled Trotsky and other 'traitors' for his show trials. The individual is lost in this maze of circling deceptions. Cynical party members like O'Brien can, by employing double-think, encompass both Goldstein's dissident ideas and party propaganda at the same time. O'Brien instinctively dominates Winston because he can read his mind and understand his motives. Like the Underground Man both have a potential dissident, and a potential power broker, in them. In this way dissent is co-opted, as there is no clear line between it and collaboration. This is a much more convincing mechanism of co-option than torture alone. But the use, or at least the possibility, of both is necessary.

There is historical evidence of a Brotherhood organization, a fake opposition to trap heretics, as described by the British intelligence officer Peter Wright:

> Strategic deception...has a long and potent history. The "Trust" operations of the GPU and OGPU in the early years of the Bolshevik regime are a powerful reminder to any KGB recruit of the role these organizations can play. At a time when the Bolshevik regime was threatened by several million White Russian émigrés in the 1920s, Felix Dzerzinsky, the legendary founder of the modern Russian Intelligence Services, masterminded the creation of a fake organization inside Russia dedicated to the overthrow of the Bolshevik regime. The Trust attracted the support of White Russian émigré groups abroad, and the Intelligence Services of the

West, particularly MI6. In fact, the Trust was totally controlled by the OGPU, and they were able to neutralize most émigré and hostile intelligence activity...the Trust persuaded the British not to attack the Soviet Government because it would be done by internal forces.[27]

The Zamyatin/Huxley origins of *Nineteen Eighty-Four* give it a clear and therefore misleading division between the oppressors and the victims. In the past as long as citizens kept their heads down and didn't actively revolt, they could survive. But in Orwell's novel the gap characteristic of former authoritarian regimes still exists. There are rulers (like O'Brien) and the ruled (like Winston Smith), with the connections pretty tenuous, rather than a sliding scale or spectrum of entanglement. The extent to which Winston transmits the regime's virus is minimal, as is the extent to which O'Brien is himself a victim of the regime's wiles. Power is still imposed mainly from on high, as in past. What is missing in *Nineteen Eighty-Four* is a hero who is not a cleanskin rebel remote from the sources of control, like Winston, but one who is entangled in the mindset of the society he also opposes, who receives and transmits the virus down the line.

What is also missing in anti-utopian literature is the creation of the multiform layers which exist in any society: the rulers, the various intermediate institutions in society and the citizenry itself, and the natural (or in this case artificial) connections between them. Orwell does try in Part One to show Winston and his peers (Parsons, Ampleforth and so on) in an intermediate position in the regime structure, part going along and part disgruntled. But we need to see how they manipulate each other in the regime's direction in day-to-day mind games and power struggles. There is little manoeuvring, envy, ambition and lack of trust between party members. The techniques by which intermediate organs in society organically transmit the virus both ways are not clearly shown, as they were in later East European literature.

In totalitarian societies the intermediate organs have been perme-

---

27 Peter Wright *Spycatcher*, Viking, New York, 1987, p. 206; see also Christopher Andrew *The Secret World*, Penguin, UK, 2019, pp. 575 sqq. on this deception.

ated by the regime to do its work – they can't act autonomously. In this case everyone can become an oppressor as well as a victim; one partakes in both as a seamless whole. Interestingly in his early novels Orwell did provide such examples in ordinary social relations, but in *Nineteen Eighty-Four* he doesn't. He is perceptive on the technical mechanisms of domination, but not on the more subtle modes of acquiescence. Compare Camus' *The Plague* where by contrast all share and transmit the virus. Totalitarianism is not just a political pecking order, a rational descending hierarchy, as much as horizontal self-torturing porridge. Of course Orwell was writing just as these things were first being understood, and he did not have the 'benefit' of living on the continent under a Nazi or Communist regime, as Camus and Solzhenitsyn did. Orwell understood that to appreciate such things one has to be able to imagine oneself as the victim. This was admirable in Orwell and other writers, in contrast to those who sided with the oppressors.

Another of Orwell's achievements was to create a battery of devices with which the regime dominates its citizens from above. These include The Ministry of Information, where the past is continually reshaped and reality confined to the memory hole, an idea originating from Orwell's Spanish and BBC experiences. If reports of battles were falsified by a regime in total control, its citizenry was rendered powerless by its lack of contrary information. It was thereby deprived of a true picture of the past. But for Orwell as a novelist some problems remained. Winston takes us on a tour of the mechanical instruments of oppression in Part One, but it could be *anyone* taking us around. He's not part of the mentality; in fact, he is outside and against it. Orwell needs a part-oppressor, part-victim figure who 'believes' (in a double-think kind of way) in what he is doing when he rewrites history. In *Eichmann In Jerusalem,* Hannah Arendt provides a portrait of a totalitarian functionary for whom rearranging the past had become an internalized necessity. Arendt accounts for Eichmann's 'sense of elation in the present' by noting that a person like Eichmann could 'afford to face reality because his crime had become part and parcel of it...these lies changed from year to year and frequently contradicted each other...the practice of self-deception had become so common, almost a normal pre-requisite for survival.'[28] Some creation of this kind is needed in the novel, a middle level apparatchik who himself has become part of the system of rearranging the past, not Winston explaining but not believing in it. Winston after his treatment in Room 101 would be a candidate.

The thought control devices are imposed from above as a job lot in the novel; they aren't convincingly integrated into the behaviors of everyday life. Orwell is at home with the domestic victims and with the world O'Brien inhabits. It's when he tries to connect them he falters. The novel recreates everyday life in a relatively benign time, but his examples of imposed terror come from the heightened phase of totalitarianism. The regime should be able to elicit voluntary internalization of its beliefs. The Goldstein passages and the Newspeak appendix, wonderful as they are, are not integrated into the fabric of daily life in the novel. If Orwell wished to fully convey the uniqueness and horror of the new system he had to create someone like the Underground Man who recognizes and manipulates all psychic states, both in his own mind and in others, and the connections between them. The two Minute Hate sessions do not generate belief horizontally among citizens; they are imposed unwillingly on Winston. This structural weakness forces Winston into the role of the traditional rebel, who believes he can remain entirely uncontaminated by his milieu, and spiritually sustained by his 'grand refusal'. A full portrait of O'Brien from the inside the party apparatus and with its normal moral ambiguities is needed, not just his explanatory speeches. In *The Book of Laughter and Forgetting*, the Czech novelist Milan Kundera achieves this by showing how public moves are aligned with the personalities of the actors. These structural weaknesses in *Nineteen Eighty-Four* should not lead us to deny how pioneering the novel was. Samizdat writers in Russia and East Europe were amazed that Orwell had got it so right. Orwell did not have the advantage of the later analyses of Hannah Arendt and the post-war Russian and East European experiences on these matters.

---

28 Hannah Arendt *Eichmann In Jerusalem*, Faber and Faber, London, 1963, p. 47.

Because oppression is imposed from above in the novel, and no effective counter pressure can arise from below, Winston has no hope. The novel is pessimistic; there is no way out by rebellion. Orwell understood how effective shutting down of dissent could be when employed in a hermetically sealed system. In this pessimistic frame of mind Orwell wanted to show all possible escape routes – love, freedom, the past, nature, rebellion – had been closed off. For Winston and Julia, sex is 'a political act' (p. 104): 'She had torn her clothes off, and when we flung them aside it was with that same magnificent gesture by which a whole civilization seemed to be annihilated.' (p.103) But sex as rebellion is not strong enough, as Bulgakov and Zamyatin understood. Both characters are broken and repudiate each other. The natural world also offers some hope: 'Truisms are true, hold on to that! The solid world exists, its laws do not change. Stones are hard, water is wet, objects unsupported fall towards the earth's center.' (p. 68) The lovers hear a thrush singing, magnificently, for no reason, just the sheer pleasure of singing. Like the Jew's package in Borowski, this is an image of something unable to be manipulated, something which exists purely for its own sake, admirable even if ineffective, beyond the reach of propaganda. But just as the past can be manipulated, so can the laws of the natural world: two and two can be tweaked to equal five.

But Orwell did allow one outlet. Like Zamyatin's, his novel is structured with a minority of the population within the system, and with the masses, the ordinary people, called the proles, uneducated and without political consciousness, outside the system and thereby rendered impotent. This always seemed a strange feature of Orwell's novel, as the system wasn't total at all. Winston has the heterodox habit of wandering among the proles, as Orwell himself habitually did, as recorded in *Down And Out In London And Paris* and *The Road to Wigan Pier*. The proles are in a Huxleyian/Marcusian situation of being so stupefied by beer, films, sex and so on, that their rebellious instincts are dulled. 'Hope lay in the proles'. This is an unexpected assertion in the novel, since most people believed that in East Europe and the Soviet Union rebellion would come from dissent within the ruling group, or from other New Class groupings. Orwell suggested through the Goldstein document four ways by which such regimes might be overthrown:

> Either it is conquered from without, or it governs so inefficiently that the masses are stirred to revolt, or it allows a strong and discontented middle group to come into being, or it loses its self-confidence and willingness to govern. These causes do not operate singly, and as a rule all four of them are present to some degree. A ruling class which could guard against all of them would remain in power permanently. Ultimately the determining factor is the mental attitude of the ruling class itself. (p. 166)

This is an acute prophecy of the reasons why Communism eventually collapsed in the late 1980s. Before Communism disintegrated, it was the most unlikely group, the proles in Poland, who first undermined it by being 'stirred to revolt'. Solidarity in Poland, stirred to revolt by the inefficiencies of the regime, was composed of ordinary Polish people who, left outside the power structure, united for communal ends by forming new intermediate organs which restored civil society within the carapace of the decaying Communist system. They were joined by other unionists and by a middle level group of dissenters (such as KOR). Under this pressure the Party did lose its will to rule: '(The Party) allows a strong and discontented middle group to come into being, or it loses its self-confidence and willingness to govern'. Orwell was proved prophetically correct.

Goldstein's division of the post-war world into three power blocks, with sporadic warfare on the edges of their spheres of influence, also turned out to be prophetic: 'Between the frontiers of the superstates, and not permanently in the possession of any of them, lies a rough quadrilateral with it corners at Tangiers, Brazzaville, Darwin and Hong Kong, containing within it about a fifth of the population of the earth.' (p.152) Like continental plate theory, the big powers brush against each other with tensions and wars at their edges, but with their heartlands remaining relatively inert. Orwell understood the importance of developments like small wars fought with helicopter gunships (as in Vietnam). The way Goldstein describes the big powers changing sides has eventuated. Russia and China were aligned against the USA in the Cold War period, until the USA-China alliance of the 1970s changed the power dynamic, just as Eurasia, Eastasia and Oceania keep swapping alliances with each other in *Nineteen Eighty-Four.*

Solzhenitsyn was able to build on Orwell's pioneering account. His great political novel on the Soviet Union, *The First Circle* (1968), is, like Orwell's two decades before, focused on a repressive regime past in its inaugural total terror phase and seemingly without beginning or end. The novel overcomes Orwell's limitations by its use of circular imagery, on the analogy of the layers of an onion, rather than on stratified groupings. This device diminishes the gulf between oppressors and victims, and the simple oppositional choices available in *Nineteen Eighty-Four*. The reference in the title of Solzhenitsyn's novel is to the outer layer of the underworld in Dante's *Divine Comedy*, where the sages of antiquity endure their punishments. The Mavrino prison, the setting of the novel, is the least worst example of a concentration camp; the prisoners there are on the first/outer circle, the one closest to being free, like life on the outside.

The title also indicates something important about the novel's structure. There exist two centres, or circles from which influence radiates in the novel. One circle has Stalin at its centre, the circle of the all-pervading State system, a network of investigation, suspicion, fear, mistrust and oppression which Stalin superintends, like an horrendous spider controlling its web, as the critic Helen Muchnic observed. Near the centre of the other circle are those who are spiritually free, refusing to be caught up in the regime's atmosphere. These circles have different centres, yet they overlap, like hemispheres partly imposed on each other. Each character is within the magnetic field of both circles, and so is tugged in contrary directions. There are no pure tyrants and no pure victims, with everyone potentially partaking of both.

The crucial thing is not whether you are physically imprisoned or not, it is whether you are spiritually free. Some of the prisoners are free in their minds, though in prison. In many senses they are freer than people outside, like, for example, those at the State Prosecutor Makarygin's party. To know what to legitimately adapt to, and what to refuse, ensures the survival of one's personality. Such decisions take place, as Solzhenitsyn shows, on an infinite number of small occasions, not in one overwhelming choice. Within each character this tightrope walk produces a tense and wearying personal struggle. Everyone has the chance to manipulate as well as to act properly, with characters shown in various states of entanglement and freedom. Prisoners like Nerzhin, Bobynin and Spiridon are free from the possessions, ambitions and responsibilities which make others vulnerable. This is most clearly stated in the passage where Bobynin is talking to the Minister:

> I've got nothing, see? Nothing! You can't touch my wife and child – they were killed by a bomb. My parents are dead. I own nothing in the world except a handkerchief...You took my freedom away a long time ago and you can't give it back to me because you haven't got it yourself...You only have power over people so long as you don't take everything away from them. But when you've robbed a man of everything he's no longer in you power – he's free again. (pp. 106-7)

One can admire Bobynin here without necessarily agreeing with all he says, nor can one assume that he is purely a mouthpiece for the author's views. Freedom of dispossession and detachment isn't the only freedom. Bobynin and his fellow prisoners are obviously being kept unfree in many ways; and there is something else the regime can take away from them – life.

In such passages Solzhenitsyn creates a feeling of vitality, exuberance, fearlessness and resolution in his characters in contrast to the regime and its officials. The prisoners at Mavrino, while acknowledging the enormous disabilities under which they live, are, like the *zeks* in *Ivan Denisovich* growing, thinking, inquiring people who are exercising all the attributes which create life and distinguish men and women. Bobynin's 'superiors' defer to him, since as Solzhenitsyn notes: 'One can build the Empire State Building, discipline the Prussian army, make a state hierarchy mightier than God, yet fail to overcome the unaccountable spiritual superiority of certain human beings.' (p.71) This reminds us of Borowski's blond woman prisoner who exudes the same quality. Characters like Bobynin give the novel its dominant tone. The novel focusses on them, so that by the end Stalin seems in some ways a peripheral figure. This is what makes *The First Circle* a far from grim or depressing novel.

Another dimension of life which thwarts the regime's attempts to control everything is the physical reality of the universe and the laws by which it operates. The regime can bend men's minds and break their bodies but it can't do the same to the laws of physics. The childish way the regime tries to schedule the scrambler and clipper programs, and their angry frustration when the limitations of electronics are forced on them, illustrates this: two and two still make four. Bobynin explains this in a key speech which begins: 'What d'you think science is – a magic wand that you just have to wave to get what you want.' (pp. 108-9)

The closer one comes to the centre of the Stalin circle, the more one feels, not the strength, but the vulnerability and precariousness of power. The thoughts which run through the Soviet official Yakonov's mind after his second interview with his Minister best convey the anxiety and fear which the system generates among its powerbrokers:

> They had started the usual murderous game and it was approaching its climax. Yakonov knew all there was to know about this kind of lunatic scramble – it was more than flesh and blood could bear to be hopelessly caught up in impossible, grotesque, crippling schedules. You were trapped and held in a deadly grip. The system crushed you, driving you harder and faster all the time, demanding more and more, setting inhuman time limits. This was why buildings and bridges collapsed, why crops rotted in the fields or never came up at all. But until it dawned on someone that people were only human, there was no way out of this vicious circle for those involved, except by falling ill, getting caught in a machine or having some other kind of accident. (p. 150)

In *The First Circle* we can't make a simple division between the oppressors and the oppressed. Everyone is oppressed in this 'vicious circle', but who is free? Solzhenitsyn's own focus, as well as his sympathy, coincides with the prisoners' circle, though he does not exactly identify with any one of them, and he is able to 'sympathetically' portray Stalin from the inside. The ability of the prisoners' circle of influence to break the 'cunningly wrought chain' of State control is more potential than actual; its successes in the novel are random and fitful. But its importance lies in being an alternative source of values. This is one meaning of the most quoted sentence in the novel: 'For a country to have a great writer is like having an another government'. (p. 436)

Everyone in the novel is a victim of Stalin's system, including Stalin himself. For the first hundred pages the movement of the novel is inward towards the centre of the State system, from the prisoners to laboratory chiefs to the Minister of State Security, Abakumov, and finally from Abakumov to Stalin himself. All are caught up in the regime's sinister game: the prisoners, their wives, the 'free workers' at Mavrino, the guests at Makarygin's party, and the party officials. Chapters 18 to 21 on Stalin are the greatest sustained feat of the novel. Everyone in it is a victim of Stalin's system, including Stalin himself. He is portrayed primarily as a man who is feeling on his own body and in his own soul the disintegrating effects of the atmosphere he himself has created: weariness, suspicion, isolation, tension, and friendlessness (he trusted only Hitler and was let down). He is constantly gnawed at by a vague terrifying feeling that perhaps everything in the world can't be controlled. Fearful, hypochondriac, bored, he is enervated by having to keep on feeding this monstrous system, which now has a momentum of its own. Its appetites are consuming him, its main originator and contributor. Thus the brilliance of Solzhenitsyn's parody of Stalin's desire for longevity is enhanced by the substratum of truth which underlines his wry comment: 'Now that he had decided to live to 90, Stalin reflected gloomily that this would give him no personal pleasure and that he would just have to suffer another 20 years for the sake of mankind.' (p. 111) Stalin is not created as a visibly demonic monster, like a modern day Genghis Khan. Solzhenitsyn's 'sympathetic' portrait of Stalin doesn't lessen the feeling of evil about him; the fact that it is now so automatically internalized in everyone makes it all the more terrifying, and convincing. All are caught up in it. Similarly in Brecht's poem 'The Mask of Evil' a Hitler-like tyrant is suffering under the pressure he has imposed on himself: 'On my wall hangs a Japanese carving,/The mask of an evil demon, decorated with gold lacquer./Sympathetically I observe/The swollen veins of the forehead, indicating/What a strain it is to be evil.' [29]

In *The First Circle* the novelist Galakhov cannot compose freely because he always imagines a censor standing over him as he writes. He has so internalized the mentality of the regime that he doesn't need overt compulsion to make him confirm. He is in this sense less free than those in prison. The system gets its fearsomeness not merely because orders are passed down in a form of pecking order. Fear has its own momentum and is distributed automatically by those who compromise with the system. Thus the imagery in the novel is not so much hierarchical and vertical, as circular and lateral. The principal character Nerzhin, like all others, is pulled in both directions, and finally chooses peace of mind, but at the cost of enduring more lack of freedom. His friend Rubin is a fundamentally decent person but with ideological blindspots. With these mixed portraits, Solzhenitsyn approaches the complexity of daily life under such a regime.

Solzhenitsyn believed in the transformative power of the personal sphere, as Orwell did with the proles. The regime in *The First Circle* is subverted by those instinctive gestures of human generosity and affection which happen quite unpredictably in life. An example is love between men and women: 'For the first time in her life a man had kissed her. In this way the cunningly wrought chain broke at the link formed by a woman's heart'. (p. 42). The imagery here is again circular. The action of the whole novel hinges on an act of this kind. An apparently small gesture by the diplomat Volodin in warning a professor shows that even one impulsive act of decency can shake a whole system, and

---

29   Alan Bold ed. *The Penguin Book of Socialist Verse,* Penguin Books, Harmondsworth, 1970, p. 239.

endanger the power of tyranny and unfreedom. As Volodin reads in his mother's notebooks: 'Compassion is the spontaneous movement of the human heart'. (p. 418) Volodin (whose first name is Innokenty, and whose surname means free will) gradually becomes a free man during the novel. As he loses his physical freedom on being arrested, he moves at the same time from the centre of the oppressive circle towards the centre of the opposite one. Like Matryona in Solzhenitsyn's short story 'Matryona's Home', the influence of his action eddies out into the whole society: 'We all lived beside her and did not understand that she was that just person without whom according to the proverb, the village could not endure. Nor the city. Nor all our land.'

6

COMING OUT ABRUPTLY

In *Nineteen Eighty-Four* Orwell nominated a number of ways a totalitarian regime might end. One was being conquered from without, which happened to Nazi Germany, terminated artificially in 1945 by an invasion of allied military forces, though by that stage it was also collapsing internally. It wasn't that the inhabitants overthrew the regime from below, or from within their own hearts. Germans were therefore suddenly in a new situation, a drastic break from their immediate past, *Stund Null*, year zero. Eastern and south-eastern Europe were relieved of Nazi atrocities at the end of the war, only a few years later to undergo another takeover phase when Communist rule, similar to the recent Nazi one, was imposed on them. Orwell's third and fourth cases, that an opposition group might coalesce while a regime lost its self-confidence, eventually applied to the Soviet Union and Eastern Europe around 1990.

Stalin's post-war policy was extreme. Returning soldiers were imprisoned in large numbers, and he was planning new purges. After his death in 1953, Russia and East Europe gradually came out of their extreme terror period, but not to freedom. The Communist regime in the Soviet Union survived Stalin's death, meaning its mentality had been to some degree internalized, whereas Nazism did not survive Hitler. The totalitarian mentality was not as fully internalized in the newly conquered satellites of Eastern Europe, which had recent memories of normal society, as it was in the Soviet Union, with its decades of heavy Communist rule. All came out from under gradually when

Communism disintegrated in the later 1980s, internally and voluntarily, unlike Germany in 1945. The statelet of Communist East Germany was a unique case, part of a divided Germany, still atmospherically close to Europe, but like the rest of Eastern Europe under Soviet thrall. Much post-war literature consisted of bottled up survivor accounts of recent Communist and Nazi horrors, now able to be fully ventilated in the west after 1945. These often dealt with individual survival stories, rather than the reactions of whole societies. The last third of Camus' *The Plague* and Grass' *The Tin Drum* do however attempt a nation-wide perspective of the highly oppressive Nazi regime in its terminal phases and aftermath. Heinrich Böll's novel *The Clown* assessed the effects of the Nazi past on post-war Germany, and on consequent German guilt.

The eastern half of the continent was devastated, with massive involuntary movements of populations, widespread hunger, and millions of displaced people. Survivors had to change from the struggle of 'all against all' during war-time deprivation, to rudimentary forms of camaraderie and trust, as they moved towards re-forming normal societies. In both ex-Nazi and newly Communist countries, physical structures, personal psyches and even the meaning of words had been so utterly destroyed that people had to go back in their minds and in daily life to ground zero in order to start again. Everything both regimes touched had been denatured, so in response a new minimalist approach arose, with the simplest things acknowledged and described without any resonances whatsoever. This was not just a literary technique, but a necessary way people went about rebuilding their lives.

Authors in the past had often admired the natural world of birds and animals which, unburdened by a higher consciousness, does not panic like us. In the newly devastated landscape authors went even further, turning for consolation even to inanimate objects, which they praised as steadfast and unswayed by emotion, in comparison with human fervor. This literature is of necessity rudimentary, as it forgoes cross references and explanations. It never moves out of its own limited space or time frame; in this it has some similarities to concentration camp literature. These qualities are evident in the Polish poet Zbigniew Herbert's much admired poem 'The Pebble', acknowledged as a defining example of how one coped with the post-war situation. The pebble, modestly knowing its own limits, is resistant to takeover. The virus of over-heated fanaticism cannot disturb its calm, elemental existence. The poem is a catalogue of the traits needed to be proof against a disturbed condition:

> The pebble is a perfect creature
> equal to itself
> mindful of its limits

Nature has something that we are in danger of losing. The poem reverses our accustomed way of looking at things, derived from a vestigial romanticism, where warmth is favourable, and cold is not:

> I feel a heavy remorse
> when I hold it in my hand
> and its noble body
> is permeated by false warmth

We wrongly believe that, being warm, we are superior to inanimate nature. We have therefore a false warmth, whereas the pebble has a cold, undistracted serenity. It does not have an overheated consciousness, and so is not given to fretting over endless self-examination, or of being disoriented by outside influences. To be detached, limited and without personal desires were essential qualities, once scorned, in these present days. The pebble has evacuated itself of the personal indulgences which can be dangerous to us; its ardour consists of strength, not of desire. The pebble knows precisely what it is, and being secure in this, will not be manipulated into changing itself into something else, a temptation for us:

> Pebbles cannot be tamed
> to the end they will look at us
> with a calm and very clear eye

The pebble prizes stability in a fickle world. It is secure in its own basic identity, seeking nothing further. It is not blown this way and that by current fads, such as a desire for instant meaning or transcendence. Lacking an inflated ego, it is neither narcissistic nor megalomaniac, but recognizes limits and exercises self-restraint. It is proof against the traumas which had recently bedevilled Europe. It looks at possible intrusive forces 'with a calm and very clear eye'. This is the opposite of being opaque and devious, or of torturing oneself, or of satisfying oneself with conundrums and ambiguities. It refuses to play the power game, and in this it is resisting, not perpetuating, the takeover virus. It is not trying to engulf adjacent objects. The pebble is a precursor of the existentialist movement – when people no longer have unchanging essences, bare existence is prized.

The pebble's sustaining simplicity resists the manipulative and aggrandizing behaviour characteristic of the all-devouring mushrooms in Sylvia Plath's poem. It does not hunt in packs, does not take anyone over, but is itself impervious to conquest; it won't be swayed by the importunings of others. It's not just a matter of resisting. The pebble establishes its own firm identity; like Shalamov's arctic pines, it survives all conditions. This is not the effacement of identity, but the beginning, the precondition, of one. It means one is objective, not disoriented by the self's own distorting field. One has achieved self-restraint, and is therefore invulnerable to rapid personality change. Herbert's fellow Polish poet Czeslaw Milosz noted about this period that 'the sudden crumbling of all current notions and criteria is a rare occurrence and is characteristic only of the most stormy periods in history'. Language in its previous forms was unable to cope with this; current forms of expression hid the horror. Milosz understood that our normal hierarchy of needs dissolves under the impact of catastrophe: 'then to satisfy hunger is more important than finding food that suits one's taste.' Post-war poetry followed suit, with minimal technical devices and emotions. Milosz understood, as did many others at the time, that 'objects represent a stable reality, do not alter with reflexes of fear, love, or hate, and always 'behave' logically.'[30]

Words corrupted by the Nazi regime could hardly be used any

---

30 Czeslaw Milosz 'Ruins and Poetry', *The New York Review of Books*, March 17, 1983, pp. 20-4.

more after 1945 because of their indelible associations with recent political rhetoric. The past literary tradition had itself been debased. Günter Eich's exemplary poem 'Inventory' began the process of learning to speak again by compiling a list of basic words matching basic objects:

> A tin is my plate
> my mug
> I have scratched my name
> in the tinplate.

In an article summarizing these developments the German author Hans Magnus Enzenberger noted how 'fragments of everyday life, scraps of slang, words from the world of consumer goods, force their way into the poetic text'.[31] Enzenberger and Milosz describe identical reactions under German Nazism and Polish Communism.

The Russian word for stone is *kamen*, the title of books by Osip Mandelstam and Tadeusz Borowski. Stone can have two symbolic meanings: a favourable one of objectivity and unchangingness, and an unfavorable one of death and non-life. Concentration camp survivors had two contrary reactions towards their experiences, which align with the contrary associations of stone. One was that the camps had annulled belief and rendered everything arbitrary. As a result a natural reaction was meaningless hedonism: if no belief is worthwhile then enjoy yourself, devour the time left to you, satisfy yourself and act self-interestedly as everyone else does, like for example the citizens of Oran at the end of *The Plague*. The opposite reaction was to retreat into a quiet, detached, almost mystical state of world-weariness, moving towards the 'oceanic feeling' associated with Eastern religions. One becomes stoical and impassive; having seen everything, including the worst, where people behaved in inhuman ways, life is evacuated of meaning, with every experience rendered random and arbitrary. Believing in little, one becomes comatose, withdrawn, depressed and stone-like. The life has been drained out of life. (Life

---

31 Hans Magnus Enzenberger 'In Search of the Lost Language', *Encounter*, September, 1963, p. 49.

evacuated of meaning also became, for less extreme reasons, a feature of much modernist literature, such as *Waiting For Godot*).

These two reactions are comparable to the competing dispositions foregrounded by medieval preachers as *carpe diem* (seize the day) and *vanitas vanitatum* (the vanity of human endeavor). Such reactions were the extreme ends of the spectrum; not everyone went as far as them. Some could accommodate both. These attitudes expressed in their different ways the meaninglessness of existence in and after the camps. Both could lead to depression and suicide, as experienced by Borowski and (perhaps) Levi, and by the poets Attila József, Alexander Wat and Sylvia Plath, who in some of her late poems became focused on Holocaust-induced self-recrimination. Arthur Koestler noticed in the post-war period a transfer from identifying with the political commissar (representing change from without, revolution, and the radical reorganization of society) to the mystical yogi (change from within, non-violence, and surrender to the 'oceanic feeling').

Borowski captures some of these features in his story of post-war reactions 'The World of Stone'. The narrator moves through a bombed-out city in Poland. People have resumed their normal daily tasks with some purposefulness, but he is utterly remote from them, as though looking at them through a glass screen. The world seems to have become so attenuated, so without substance that he imagines it floating upwards, or exploding into nothingness. The 'physical sensibilities have coagulated and stiffened within me like resin'; he feels 'a total indifference', even to erotic sensations. He has no stimuli response, no emotional reactions, an 'irreverence bordering almost on contempt', and a 'terrible disenchantment', as though in deep depression. He tries to 'relate the deliberate senselessness of my own fate to that of the Universe'. But the world of life, of hot summer afternoons and the 'stale, crumbling dry dust of the ruins', like his mood, does not respond. (p. 178). This was a reaction common at the time. Borowski was numbed by his concentration camp experience into a kind of detached stoicism, so that afterwards nothing much had value. In *The Captive Mind* Czelaw Milosz wrote of Borowki: 'his nihilism results from an ethical passion, from disappointed *love* of the world and of humanity...The human species is *naked* in his stories, stripped of those tendencies towards good which last only so long as the habit of civilization lasts'. (p. 122). Borowski had the decency to see that the new Polish Communist regime, like the Nazi one, was malign, and came to oppose it.

An unchanging, diffident world chiselled out of stone is also created in Anna Akhmatova's poem 'Verdict':

> Today I have much work to do:
> I must finally kill my memory,
> I must, so my soul can turn to stone,
> I must learn to live again.

Once again the desiccated and the living commingle, the depressed narrator deadening herself by trying to elide her past, but life, 'the hot summer rustle', goes on. The world returns no signals to her – a condition of continued life is suppressed animation. In the last stanza of her poem a terrible conjunction of meaning and nothingness, 'the bright day and the empty house', unavoidably confronts her. Each reinforces the incommunicable world of its other, each absolute makes its opposite worse.

Alexander Wat was a Polish poet and short story writer who, influenced between the wars by the futurist movement, became sympathetic to Marxist ideas and Communist groupings. Despite this he was arrested (like a fellow sympathizer Solzhenitsyn) by the Soviet NKVD police in 1940 and exiled to Kazakhstan in 1941; this experience understandably turned him against Communism. His writings were censored in post-war Communist Poland, causing him to emigrate in 1959 and to settle in Berkeley, California, near his fellow Polish poet Czeslaw Milosz. His 'Stone Poem' follows the line of thought of similar poems. A movement towards a detached calmness, in contrast to the frenzied chaos of the present world (the 'pulsating turning of the sun'), makes life bearable:

> Retreating into
> > the depths of myself, stone,
> motionless, silent; growing cold;
> > present through a waning
> > > of presence – in the cold
> attractions of the moon.

Though diminished the speaker maintains an unchangeable oneness in comparison with the fluctuating, process-obsessed world outside.

> Thus I shall be submitted
> Only to the rhythms of day and
> > night. But –
> no dance in them. No whirling, no
> > frenzy: only
> > > monastic rule and silence.

Like other *kamen* poets he cherishes stillness and existence over change: 'They do not become, they are'. Only this retreat, with all its deficiencies, keeps him going. The Jewish Wat converted to Catholicism late in life. His account of his literary and political endeavours, *My Century,* is one of the outstanding memoirs of the period. Stricken by a painful, incurable illness, he suicided in 1967.

Nature poetry survived, but as Brecht wrote:

> What times are these when a conversation
> About trees is almost a crime
> Because I included a silence about so many misdeeds!

The German political philosopher Adorno believed that to continue to write lyric poetry in this age was barbaric. In his poem, 'Apocalypse', the English poet D.J. Enright opposed the attempt to forget the horrors of the past, and to believe that things would now return to normal. His poem was occasioned by a sentence in a German Tourist brochure: 'By the early summer of 1945, strains of sweet music floated on the air again. While the town still reeked of smoke, charred buildings and the stench of smoke, the Philharmonic Orchestra bestowed the everlasting and imperishable joy which music never fails to give':

> It sooths the savage doubts.
> One Bach outweighs ten Belsens. If 200,000 people
> Were remaindered at Hiroshima, the sales of So-and So's
> New novel reached a higher figure in as short a time…

The world of genocide and the normal world cannot be understood in terms of each other. In the poem the survivors believe: 'All, in a sense, goes on. All is in order.' They can't realize how everything has changed.

The designation 'year zero' was obviously necessary for many who had to start life anew from under the ashes, but it also less helpfully implied a clean break from the recent terrible past, as though it could be annulled. An opposite, and equally futile reaction, was to believe you could return to the same life as before, as though nothing had changed. Camus described the reaction of the inhabitants of Oran at the end of *The Plague*: 'Calmly they denied, in the teeth of the evidence, that we had ever known a crazy world in which men were killed off like flies, or that precise savagery, that calculated frenzy of the plague, which instilled an odious freedom as to all that was not the Here and Now; or those charnel-house stenches which stupefied whom they did not kill.' (pp. 242-3) Applied amnesia is part of the *petit mal* totalitarian equipment: a fluctuating identity and a memory-hole approach enabled people to elide anything in the past inconvenient to the present. The people of Oran in the novel are in this way still displaying the effects of the plague virus even as they, ironically, rejoice in its going.

Monstrous events created by humans don't just disappear of their own volition. When the plague ends, people believe the horror is all over. But in one sense it never ends: "The fire in the crematorium has been extinguished, but the smoke has not yet settled', as Camus put it.

(p. 149). The effect of these events lives long after them and can never be wholly atoned for. At the end of the plague: 'These ecstatic couples, locked together, hardly speaking, proclaimed in the midst of the tumult of rejoicing, with the proud egoism and injustice of happy people, that the plague was over, the reign of terror ended.' (p. 242) But in fact, as the narrator, the novel's main character Dr Rieux and Camus himself understand, the opposite is the case: the survivors deny the meaning of the world from which they have recently emerged.

Many works of political literature insist that the domination virus does not necessarily disappear with the demise of a regime, such as Hitler's going in 1945, or Stalin's or Mao's death, or with Communism's demise. The effect may continue in different and less overt ways. Something quite new has entered the world. As the Roman poet Horace put it: *Et semel emissum volat irrevocabile verbum* 'Once a word has been allowed to escape, it cannot be recalled'. (Epistles I. xvii, 35) The past, unlike ourselves, is steadfast. Should collaboration be punished, justice imposed for crimes, revenge undertaken for the injured, or would these responses lead to another round of crime and punishment? In *Notes From Underground* it is said that 'vengeance will hurt itself a hundred times more than it will hurt the one against whom it is directed.' (p. 97) The guilty are punished more by their own consciences, by having to live with what they did or failed to do, than by tribunals later set up by governments. Can a wrong ever be avenged? The tough-minded Austrian satirist Karl Kraus believed a monument to a young girl killed in Vienna was misguided, since the deed could not be changed, and the monument only helped to assuage the guilt of later generations, and so diminish the scope of the atrocity. A crime, like a word, once out in the open could never be fully retracted.

Another, different meaning of the phrase 'The plague has not yet ended' is that, now the secret is out, anyone in the future is empowered to start it up afresh. Rulers like Mao and Pol Pot learnt fast: the plague can break out in previously uninfected and unexpected places. We shouldn't pride ourselves on it being perpetually somewhere else, over there. Orwell, believing the totalitarian virus was potentially alive in thinkers and activists everywhere, set *Nineteen Eighty-Four* in Oceania, his native England.

The Russian Yevgeny Yevtushenko's poem, 'The Heirs of Stalin', has similar strengths and weaknesses to Brecht's output:

> Some heirs cut roses in retirement,
> but secretly believe,
> that this retirement is temporary.
> Some,
> even criticize Stalin from the rostrum,
> and at night
> they
> yearn for the old time.

'The Heirs of Stalin' was written during the late 1950s thaw, when it was acceptable to criticize Stalin and contemporary Soviet society. Yevtushenko subsequently followed the twists of the regime's line, writing a socialist realist paean 'Bratsk Station' to Soviet construction projects, and supporting the jailing of his fellow writers, the Russian dissidents Daniel and Sinyavsky, thus encouraging the same heirs of Stalin he had denounced in his earlier poem. He was, like Jean in *Rhinoceros*, consistent: he followed the regime's line both when it condemned Stalin and when it reinstituted his oppressive practices. Yevtushenko was unable to acknowledge that the plague had not yet ended in the Soviet Union. The plague's effects can start up again at any time, as Brecht warned at the end of *Arturo Ui*: 'The bitch that bore him is on heat again.' Brecht most likely meant the alleged rise of Fascist tendencies in the West. But the bitch on heat again after 1945 was in reality East European Communism, which Brecht dallied with in his usual ambiguous way by returning to East Germany.

Thomas Mann's statement 'In modern times the destiny of man presents itself in political terms' recognized the 1930s as an era of *politique d'abord*, politics above all else. Brecht wrote: 'History to the defeated/may say alas but cannot help or pardon', for him a strangely resigned attitude. In his longer autobiographical poem 'To Posterity' he replicated Attila József's dire situation of the street apparatchik, but with more self-aggrandizement:

> I ate my food between massacres.
> The shadow of murder lay upon my sleep.
> And when I loved, I loved with indifference.
> I looked upon nature with impatience...
>
> In my time streets led to the quicksand.
> Speech betrayed me to the slaughterer.
> There was little I could do. But without me,
> The rulers would have been more secure...

To overcome his impotence he resorts to a life of political commitment. Those who like Brecht were spared had a mixture of compassion, compromise and guilt. The apogee of *politique d'abord* was Auden's poem 'Spain':

> Today the deliberate increase in the chances of death,
> The conscious acceptance of guilt in the necessary murder;
>   Today the expending of powers
> On the flat ephemeral pamphlet and the boring meeting.

Unlike Brecht, Auden repudiated these sentiments. The fashionable madmen of the 1930s and the 1940s raised their pedantic boring cries in favour of regimes which, believing in politics above all else, dragged every activity into the public realm. Was political involvement truly a cry of compassion for the downtrodden, or was it just sloganeering to get your target group to go along with the new order. Or both? It can itself be a takeover technique, promoted by those who wish to hurl you into the whirlpool, and render you a pawn in other's agendas rather than a free actor. As a Marxist Communist Brecht opposed one form of political ideology, Fascism, with a counter ideological commitment. His plays were meant to arouse passion against injustice, not just as a safety valve through which the audience, by vicariously experiencing the action, is purged and moves on. This is the meaning of his Epilogue to *Arturo Ui*, which paraphrases Marx's dictum: 'Philosophers have variously interpreted the world; the job now is to change it':

> Therefore learn to see and not to gape.
> To act instead of talking all day long
> The world was almost won by such an ape!

Brecht attempted a *post hoc facto* rationalization of his *politique d'abord* in his poem 'To Posterity'. The resigned, quietest advice of past ages is not for him:

> I would gladly be wise.
> The old books tell us what wisdom is.
> Avoid the strife of the world, live out your little time
> Fearing no one
> Using no violence
> Returning good for evil –
> Not fulfilment of desire but forgetfulness
> Passes for wisdom.
> I can do none of this:
> Indeed I live in the dark ages!

This is an acute account of the weakness of quietism in politics, but also slyly self-serving. Our choices are not confined to the two opposite possibilities of resignation or political activism, as Brecht suggests. In this poem he has his own dilemmas in mind, not the travails of the victims of beliefs like his own. Brecht's problem is that you can become a mirror-image of your adversaries, reinforcing the mentality you started out to eliminate. Brecht 'concedes' this in his characteristically ambiguous way but still insists on the reader's sympathy:

> For we know only too well:
> Even the hatred of squalor
> Makes the brow grow stern.

> Even anger against injustice
> Makes the voice grow harsh. Alas, we
> Who wished to lay the foundation of kindness
> Could not ourselves be kind
>
> But you, when it comes to pass,
> That man can help his fellow man.
> Do not judge us
> Too harshly.

Some sort of confession of wrong surfaces in these lines, but as always with Brecht qualified by the appearance of honesty. But in reality only a person like Berenger, a stranger to all ideologies who fights this tendency, is on the right track.

Asked if he thought the victims of Stalin's show trials were really guilty, Brecht dodged implicating Stalin by neatly replying: 'The more innocent they are, the more they deserve to die', hoping this duplicitous blaming of the victims of the trials would get him off the hook. His remark avoided him either condemning or praising the trials. In fact it made his complicity worse. In his play *The Measures Taken* he justified the use of any stratagem to gain one's ends. He employed a love of paradox and slight of wording to lift himself above questions of conscience. Brecht had a manipulative personality, being a master of double bluffing. He was a self-interested hedonist, a Baal-like guru to whom anything was allowed. He treated others in a selfish way. He tried to manipulate the East German regime in the same way, but with only limited success. Being a larger version of himself, it was too powerful for him to have much effect on it.

After the war a new and understandable mood of disillusioned realism set in in Europe. People were devastated, left with little or nothing, with the political fervour of ideologies on both sides discredited. Wary of worldviews, mass movements and mass frenzies, the individual was on his own, an outsider, detached, ironic, reduced to living for the moment and with no larger horizons. People wished to remain untrammeled, anxious not to be contaminated, in order to retain an identity, no matter how reduced. The world no longer returned reassuring answers. One could no longer believe that beliefs, or human personalities, had discrete unchanging essences which could provide reassurance. A chasm opened up between the shibboleths of the articulate classes and life lived on the ground. Events lacked coherence and meaning; as a result they often seemed to follow a strange, illogical course. If a writer foregrounded the inherent absurdity of events, their true underlying reality, or unreality, would more likely be revealed. This new mentality, based on a sense of the absurd, came to be known as 'existentialism'.

In this development Albert Camus soon became a key figure. He believed we should face the world *provisionally*. We often did not have full knowledge, so our reactions were necessarily tentative. But we could not let this dire situation become an excuse for fatalism or premature commitment. At any moment we have to make qualified judgments, in our state of imperfect comprehension, while being open to adjusting our stance in the light of changing events and of our changing understandings of them. This attitude is discernible in his early essays such as 'Summer in Algiers'. It was crystallized in his break-through novel *L'Etranger* (*The Outsider*) (1942) which opens with the off-hand statement: 'Mother died today. Or, maybe, yesterday; I can't be sure', whose seeming nonchalance subverts expected responses. It was a new way of looking at things. The new attitude can be felt explicitly in Camus' extended study *The Myth of Sisyphus*:

> I can negate everything of that part of me that lives on vague nostalgia, except this desire for unity, this longing to solve, that need for clarity and cohesion...I don't know whether this world has a meaning that transcends it...What I touch, what resists me – that is what I understand. And these two certainties – my appetite for the absolute and for unity, and the impossibility of reducing this world to a rational and reasonable principle – I also know that I cannot reconcile them. (p. 51)

Samuel Becket's tramps 'on the far side of despair' similarly grope towards meaning, not fully accepting their situation, but striving for understanding even when floundering. In this reduced condition people can gain sustenance from nature, which sustains itself even in the worst conditions. When at a low ebb during the Spanish Civil War because of political infighting, and having been shot in the throat, Orwell quietly reflected in *Homage to Catalonia*: 'The leaves of the silver poplars, which, in places, fringed our trenches brushed against my face; I thought what a good thing it was to be alive in a world where silver poplars grow'. (p. 179) In *The Rebel* Camus argues that an act of rebellion against one's condition constitutes an essential form of self-definition in these dark times. Writers like Brecht, and Sartre in his long manifesto 'What is Literature?' took a different path to Camus, continuing with the previous vogue of direct ideological commitment.

In the last parts of his novel *The Tin Drum* the German Nobel Prize winning novelist Gunter Grass does not let his fellow countrymen off the hook. He parodies through his character Schmuh the distinctive German mix of civilization and brutality, and of retrospective apologias:

> Schmuh was a good marksman and perhaps a good man as well; for when Schmuh went sparrow-shooting, he kept ammunition in the left-hand pocket of his coat, but his right hand pocket was full of bird food, which he distributed among the sparrows with a generous sweeping movement, not before, but after he had done his shooting, and he never shot more than twelve birds in an afternoon. (p. 519)

The Germans didn't let their charitable hand know what their shooting hand was doing. In the same chapter 'In the Onion Cellar' post-war Germans, emotionally constipated, need onions to release their guilt, and to induce a feeling of remorse: 'These people wanted to talk, to unburden themselves, but they couldn't seem to get started; despite all their efforts, they left the essential unsaid, talked around it.' (p. 523) So they cut up onions to artificially induce weeping:

> Schmuh's guests had stopped looking, they could see nothing more, because their eyes were running over and not because their

heart were full; for it is not true that when the heart is full the eyes necessarily overflow, some people can never manage it, especially in our century, which in spite of all the suffering and sorrow will surely be known as the tearless century...what did the onion juice do? It did what the world and the sorrows of the world could not do: it brought forth a round human tear. It made them cry. At last they were able to cry again. To cry properly, without restraint, to cry like mad. The tears flowed and washed everything away. The rain came. The dew. Oskar has a vision of floodgates opening. Of dams bursting in the spring floods. (p.525)

It's a pathetically inadequate form of lustration.

The Nobel Prize winning German novelist, Heinrich Böll's *The Clown* (1963), takes its form from the existential style novel pioneered by Camus' *The Outsider*, with a close family resemblance as an apparently self-justifying monologue stretching back to *Notes From Underground*, and forward to Bellow's *Herzog*, with its apparent frank confession. The central character of *The Clown*, the entertainer and clown Hans Schnier, is an anti-hero, who does not accept conventional morality, either personally or socially. His luck has run out, his girlfriend Marie has left him, he drinks too much. The role of the sad, humorous clown embodied a new widespread view of life. No coherent view of things, by which Schnier can interpret events, is available to him. He is in a downward spiral which he attempts to halt by badgering his acquaintances. The clown represents one segment of post-war Germany, by turns depressed, unsure of itself, angry, guilty, and blaming others.

The novel consists of the clown's thoughts as they course through his mind in a stream of consciousness: 'I fall victim to my own imagination.' (p. 2). He treats everything with a certain disturbed detachment, as though toying with those he has deemed his sparring partners. He gets angrily worked up against society. The clown is adversary by nature, having many of the characteristics of the Underground Man: heightened consciousness, a sensitive artistic soul, asocial attitudes, and obsessive daily routines. He wants to be noticed, but also to be slighted, while regarding himself as morally purer than others. Though a home-grown nihilist, he is not as far gone in disillusionment as the speaker in Borowski's 'A World of Stone'. Nor is he like Camus' Dr Rieux, since he cannot formulate a set of plausible, though temporary, beliefs in order to rise above his fate.

To lift himself out of his pain the clown obsessively phones his acquaintances in order to put them on the spot, as part of his campaign of revenge on the world. An adept personal manipulator, the clown gets himself into a victim posture, poor, lost, a failure, then uses his friends' genuine human reactions to get a certain enjoyment out of it all; he is humiliating others as well as himself. Gaiety and icy control combine in his clown routine – he can readily slip between victim and standover postures. His interlocutors are forced to get involved in his elaborate games, and, as in the case of his father, are too incapacitated by guilt to resist. The clown opposes the state, the Catholics, his family, his former wife, his agent, and his own colleagues. He understands that parts of society have suppressed their complicity with their Nazi past, and uses this against them to great effect. But he also carries within himself the suppressing of his own past inadequacies. In the private sphere he acts, like the Underground Man, in a quasi-political way by trying to dominate others, akin to the way political activists manipulate the public realm. The clown is a proto-totalitarian personality now operating in the post-totalitarian world of post-war Europe, where people were more familiar with these tricks.

The clown never applies the same strict moral criteria to himself as he does to others. He lacks any mechanism of self-scrutiny, and the withering scorn he turns on society is a way of postponing an examination of his own decline. He is an obsessive personality; he keeps coming back to old grievances, such as Maria leaving him, like a dog unable to leave a bone alone. We, as eavesdroppers on his impassioned monologue, can see very well why Maria left him, but he himself is blind to his own weaknesses. He is not so much a hypocrite as a self-deceiver. Memories of disturbing events in his past keep returning to him, which he reinterprets to justify his present situation, a species of rationalization such as characters in *The Plague* and *Rhinoceros* conveniently undergo. Böll is deftly accomplishing two things here. He creates the clown's self-convincing double-think manoeuvres, at the same time indirectly revealing to the reader the unconvincingness of those rationalizations.

Böll makes the connection between private and public bargaining explicit:

> At the critical moment when he [the clown's father] was serving coffee, pouring it out, happy over his achievement, I ought to have said 'Let's have the money' or 'Hand over the money'. At the critical moment one always has to be primitive, barbaric. The one says: 'You get half of Poland, we get half of Rumania – and how about it, would you like two thirds of Silesia or only half. You get four ministerial seats, we get the Piggybank Company. I had been a fool to give way to my mood and his instead of just grabbing his wallet'. (p. 171)

The clown's father is satirized as representative of post-war, unreformed, bourgeois West Germany. The father has inherited a power-hungry state of mind, but so has the clown, as the above passage reveals. In a disturbed society, there are no innocents, as Józself's and Brecht's poems demonstrate. Everybody internalizes manipulative ways of behaving in a mean, tough, self-seeking way, when the normal decencies and voluntary renunciations of power do not flourish. The plague has not yet ended. There are no cleanskins, all are contaminated. The clown shouldn't consider himself, as he does, unpolluted. Similarly the behaviour of the character Brühl is unsatisfactory:

> When we turned in alarm to the window Brühl would ask us if we knew what it meant. By that time we knew: another deserter has been shot up there in the woods. 'That's what will happen to all those', said Brühl, 'who refuse to defend our sacred German soil from the Jewish Yankees'. (Not long ago I ran into him again; he is now old, and white-haired, a professor at a Teachers' Training College, and is said to be a man with a 'courageous political past', because he never joined the Party.) (p. 16)

People who in the past acted courageously paid the price; those who succumbed to the then current orthodoxy attach themselves to the current orthodoxy now, they haven't changed their behaviour:

> Although they were Hitler Youth leaders they were sent to the front because they 'didn't toe the line' and would have nothing to do with all that disgusting snooping. Kalick would never have been sent to the front, he toed the line then the way he toes the line today, a born conformist. (p.184)

Böll (through Schnier) shows how Protestants and Catholics, the right and left, the Christian Social Union and the Social Democratic Party, each view themselves as opposites, whereas all contribute to the prevailing unreality.

Many German writers became critical of post-war West German society. Germans had more reason that those in the United States to criticize – after all their government had an appalling past. Grass and Böll, like Yevtushenko in the Soviet Union, were from a younger generation who had experienced only the tail end of the terror period. They were determined to be dissidents in relation to post-war regimes which they saw as oppressive, on the lines of how one should have behaved under the wartime Nazi and Communist regimes. Such writers believed the plague had not yet ended, and that it persisted in their society. They thought ordinary Germans hadn't come to terms with their Nazi past. Some sections of society, they believed, had amnesia, some denied collaboration, some covered it up, and some had pseudo-repentance and contrition, as in 'In the Onion Cellar'. In other words, there had been in many cases no full break with the Nazi past. Though this was true in many cases, they took this position to apply comprehensively to post-war West German governments, to the new establishment, and to German society, all of which they believed to have a Nazi-like strand in them. These writers, admiring resistance to the Nazi, resisted in the same way the post-war regime. Are we supposed to admire the clown Schnier as a man of integrity and agree with him in his condemnation of post-war West German society, or do we view him as an unlikable, arrogant failure, satirized by Böll, or more likely, as a mixture of both?

Nazism in Germany had a shorter heyday than Communism in Russia. In spite of repeated scare stories of the likelihood of Nazi revanchism over the postwar decades, Fascism never materialized in West Germany again, but Communist revanchism persisted next door in East Germany and elsewhere in the east. West Germany by contrast witnessed an economic miracle, and in the long run conducted its own successful process of lustration: the nation eventually admitted its horrific past, in a way in which Russia has never done to this day. The extreme left revolutionary groupings which eventually led to the Baader-Meinhof gang in Germany, and to the Red Brigades in Italy, were the true inheritors of the totalitarian plague, not post-war German society whatever its faults. The clown is an example of the 'adversary culture', an outlook which admires the anti-societal alignment of the modern anti-hero, and as a result is constitutionally unable to come to terms with normal society. The adversary thinker must always oppose. He works things so that he is in a suffering posture, and is able to leverage advantage from this self-identified victim condition. Resistance to a government becomes the legitimizing paradigm.

7

INSIDE THE LEVIATHAN

Was endless Communist domination in Russia and East Europe a likely prospect? Could extremist regimes continue forever, or would they 'normalise' themselves without disintegrating? How did such countries fare in the less heightened times after Stalin's death in 1953, and what structures and habits evolved over the decades to keep intact governments which didn't seem to elicit a high degree of support from their citizenry? In other words, to what extent were these regimes a normal development of our times, and to what extent something exceptional?

A number of writers at the time, first in East Europe and then in Russia, recreated, like Orwell, the feeling of endless everyday life in countries which had acclimatised themselves to the non-apocalyptic but still repressive conditions of the Communist post-war decades, and which seemed an indefinite extension of the present. Some of the best known were the Czechs Milan Kundera, Ludvik Vaculic and Vaclav Havel, the Hungarians George Konrad and Miklós Haraszti, and the Poles Slawomir Mrozek and Tadeusz Konwicki. In Russia the satirists Vladimir Voinovich and Alexander Zinoviev were similarly prolific. Benedict Erofeev's *Moscow To The End Of The Line* and Sergei Dovlatov's *The Compromise* similarly exemplified the newly emerging literature, and Yuri Trifonov's *The House On The Embankment* added to the writing on ordinary life. These novels, which confirmed the political analyses of Zinoviev's *The Reality Of Communism*, and Konrad and Szelenyi's *The Intellectuals On The Road to Class Power*, represented a new development in literature.

The first wave of protest had appeared as a consequence of the Khrushchev thaw in the later 1950s after Stalin's death. Some loosening-up was evident, with those who asked for more freedom the first dissidents. But liberalisation took place only within strict limits – a threshold was soon reached beyond which you couldn't go. As George Konrad put it: 'The sheepfold may have grown in size, but we are still inside the fence.' In reaction to this bout of liberalization, the Communist regimes clamped down again. The high point of the first burst of liberalisation was the publication of Solzhenitsyn's *Ivan Denisovich* in 1962, and the beginning of the next clampdown was the search for the pseudonymous authors of *The Trial Begins* and *Moscow Speaking*, Tertz and Arzhak in the mid 1960s. These repressions were triggered by imaginative works which starkly laid bare the essence of Communist behaviour. Solzhenitsyn anatomized the Stalinist deformations which had become apparent, and Arzhak and Tertz (real names Yuli Daniel and Andrei Sinyavsky) showed how they had continued into the present. Compare the difference between the Lev Rubin of *The First Circle*, who believes Soviet Communism is reformable, and the later Lev Kopelev, on whom the Rubin character was based, who does not. The new writing was outside the regime's limits, so it was suppressed, as were its authors. The hopes raised by the thaw began to evaporate. The curtain was coming down again.

The trial of Daniel and Sinyavsky in 1966 in Russia, and the Soviet invasion of Czechoslovakia in 1968, began a period of tightening up from liberalisation, rather than a loosening-up from Stalinism. A new breed of internal émigrés now challenged Communist governments to abide by their own laws, constitutions and promises, and to lessen restrictions on freedoms. Writers and thinkers attempted an exposure dialogue with the regimes, which however, neither liberalised nor negotiated. Dissidence was a phenomenon caused by partial liberalisation. The new literature aimed to recreate (and expose) the inner workings of Communist societies without embellishment. Writers and thinkers in Czechoslovakia were in the forefront of the activity which led to the Prague Spring of the later 1960s. Writers acted as authors as much as political protestors. They were taking steps to write freely, whether they had been allowed that freedom or not. They were not just demanding the freedom to write, but exercising it.

In this new literature in the East the line between author, narrator and hero is blurred, so the novel is often presented as a form of autobiographical confession or self-revelation. The principal character, a single male living in a flat, is a self-liberated modern liberal, free, somewhat like the Western anti-hero, from traditional pieties. Though he presents himself as an iconoclastic free spirit, something sceptical and disillusioned in his demeanour hints that earlier enthusiasms have slowly been burned out of him. He combines in milder form the two divergent characteristics noticed in concentration camp victims, depression and hedonism. He has no long term and lasting relationships, nor is he part of a warm, natural web of life going on around him: the communal glue of civil society has been thinned out, the threads of life hang loose and tattered. Real privacy is difficult: visits from friends, for example, result in the same competitiveness and intrigues that go on at work.

Depressed and tatty flat conditions are mirrored in the urban wasteland through which the hero wanders. He passes through vaguely urinous stairwells in apartment blocks strung out along windblown streets. It is the grey, grim streetscape of a world subsiding into decay; masonry falls off buildings, doors don't fit. It's not the gleaming chromium world of *Brave New World*, but the seedy, jerry-built Victory Mansions of *Nineteen Eighty-Four*. A curious feature of many of these novels is their generalised descriptions of physical objects and locations: there are no close-ups, no long, lingering descriptions of detail, no accounts of the uniqueness of any chair, room, building or other object. There's no sense of attachment to any particular place; as in Borowski's stories the physical world does not resonate or evoke anything. This is partly because the hero is dislocated from his immediate world, sharing no intimacies with it, and partly because the monologue reflects the inner state of the hero, which has been evacuated of vibrant emotions. It also reflects the dismal, unimaginative urban planning imposed by the regimes.

As the main character goes down stairs, travels on buses, and stops at shops, cafeterias and cheap drinking houses, he has a number of chance meetings, encounters which are strung out in serial fashion: Dovlatov's journalistic assignments, Erofeev's railway stations, Zinoviev's speculations, the cases of Konrad's welfare officer, the queue in Konwicki's *The Polish Complex,* the activities of many Kundera protagonists. Small groups of people form random knots, momentarily coming together for warmth, talk and human comfort (like warming one's hands over a brazier on a cold night), and then dispersing again. This process of coagulating and dissolving is endlessly repeated. It is a poor substitute for natural communal life. No more complex set of relationships nor ongoing narrative develops. Every experience is new, but of the same kind. The picaresque mode is ideally suited to a society of atomised individuals.

Alternating with these passages of mundane reality are the interior monologues of the hero, who tries to suddenly rise above it all (sometimes through the use of alcohol), and to reach out for moments of sudden revelation. These are often dream, fantasy or hallucinatory sequences taking place in the hero's mind. The title of Konwicki's novel *A Minor Apocalypse* suggests this peculiar co-existence of the mundane and the transcendent (as does the name Winston Smith). The coalescence of these two states in the narrator/hero's mind often gives the novels a surreal or phantasmagoric feel. The principal character is usually a mind worker (journalist, writer, academic) of a scrutinising and reflective bent. He analyses every move and tries to find his way in and out of the traps and contradictions. The regime's *modus operandi* is depicted through the strain it causes on the hero's being, more than directly through the instruments of State control. The hero is constantly on the alert – he can never relax and let down his guard. His aim is survival from day to day, not any long-term solution to the regime's domination. He is a modern ranging and raging ego, unable to satisfy himself, and part of no larger belief system. It is a lone battle with no fellowship in cerebral suffering. He is self-torturing, worried, recriminating. All this goes against his naturally free-spirited personality. The tension between the two is enervating, and over time he is gradually being dragged down. In Zinoviev's novels the two alternating states are coalesced; no event is seen directly, only through the prism of endless speculation about it. Voinovich's Chonkin novels however do not fit this pattern. They follow the Solzhenitsyn model of presenting a wide range of more traditional characters, rather than a single modernist hero. Voinovich's novels (like Solzhenitsyn's) are as a consequence not as depressing or pessimistic as many of the East European and Soviet ones.

In *Nineteen Eighty-Four* Winston Smith is an object of the regime's attentions, but only parts of it brush off on him. In the new literature, however, all characters are immersed in the system and they imperceptibly contribute to it as well as being controlled by it. They combine the roles of victor and victim. The author/narrator/hero is not, like Winston, a cleanskin: he has sometimes had a period of mild belief in Communism during Stalin's time, and a certain mixture of repulsion and soiled guiltiness marks his actions. All characters are submerged in life's daily strains, and the more they struggle, the more they enmesh themselves. The narrator in *The Radiant Future* reflects on the all-encompassing ideological framework of life: 'This apparatus works in imperceptible ways to weave a delicate net within human consciousness, a net in which the newborn human 'I' struggles in vain. And when this 'I' matures, it is too late. It is completely imprisoned by this invisible ideological net.' (pp. 209-210)

In Kundera's *The Joke* the victim Ludvik wishes to get even with the man, Zemanek, who put him away. Ludvik attempts a complex process of outwitting his adversary, but he uses the regime's methods of intrigue and domination. His seduction of Zemanek's wife becomes a perpetuation of the regime's mentality, not, as he originally intended, an act of defiance. To get outside this mentality is hardly conceivable. A theme in many of the novels is how the system is designed to co-opt dissent. A character in Vaculic's *The Axe,* Slavek, says:

> you ought to admit that any kind of rebellion is useless. Look: all attempts to criticise social systems have had just one result, that the systems have adapted themselves, and they have also evolved for

themselves a wider immunity so that their control of people simply grows more and more elaborate and ingenious. Leaving barely a chink for escape.

These novels emphasise immersion in the system rather than breaking out of it. Novelists in the West, with its emphasis on individual freedom, concentrate on the latter, for example Donleavy's *The Ginger Man* and similar anti-heroes. Our standard image of the rebel against totalitarian regimes has been formed by people like Dietrich Bonhoeffer, Osip Mandelstam, Anton Schmied and Franz Jaegerstater, who resisted in dramatic individual ways, but they were exceptional. 'Normalised' regimes were designed to make such breakouts very difficult. An uncontaminated Winston Smith is not possible here.

On any issue that arises, an enormous number of possible reactions are canvassed, and an endless debate about them ensues, but with no clear-cut solution. Zinoviev's novels consist entirely of this. The endless argument about what is wrong with Ibansk (aka the Soviet Union) helps to keep it going. The spectrum of opinion ranges from support for the regime through various liberal positions to opposition and dissent, but it makes no difference. Pressures arise from all directions. In *The Ivankiad,* Voinovich is told by liberal friends that he is being provocative, getting others into trouble, unwilling to compromise, and so on. Those participating get caught up in this multi-faceted argument where it is easy to lose one's bearings. It's a torture cycle of innumerable arguments about motives. The participants gradually become players in the game, contributing to it whatever their actual 'position' is. In this elaborate dance, each becomes a mirror image of the others, with no-one able to break clear.

In these novels, beliefs (for example, in Communism and the party) are not very much in evidence. But it would be wrong to conclude that ideology should be disregarded. As Zinoviev expresses it in *The Radiant Future*: 'It is to be taken in by appearances to believe that our ideology leaves the souls of our people unaffected, or that it inspires in them scepticism or scorn. The ideological apparatus affects the minds of men quite independently of its content, by the very fact of its existence and its methods of operation.' (p. 209) In *The Joke* the character Zemanek changes his beliefs, but not his *modus operandi*. Ideology may have lost its content, but not its grip, and skilled wielders of words and concepts (the bureaucratic new class) play a leading role in propagating it and passing it along.

Characters in these novels, constantly faced with putting together varying responses of compromise and rejection, are forced into contradictory, double-think reactions of various kinds. Two cases from Voinovich's second Chonkin novel, *Pretender To The Throne*, illustrate how outbreaks of rejection can end up consolidating the regime. The prosecutor Evpraksein, when drunk, wants to make a clean break and act like a human being, but under pressure in court he goes to the other extreme and acts with unnecessary harshness to show that he is not a liberal. This mixture of private scorn and public approval eventually disintegrates his personality. Lieutenant Filippov, sent to catch the alleged German spy Hans, is plagued by anxieties and fear, even though he himself is the most feared person in the district, and eventually confesses to being the spy because of his inability to carry through the investigation. Like Stalin in *The First Circle*, Filippov is both most feared and most fearing. He combines the personalities of O'Brien and Winston Smith. Such figures transmit the control virus as much as being subjugated by it.

In a samizdat article on the Russian intelligentsia, O. Altaev has described this 'pervasive duality' in general terms:

> The intelligentsia does not accept the Soviet regime, it tends to shun it and at times even despises it. Yet, on the other hand, there is a symbiosis between them...The intelligentsia suffers because it is forced to live under Soviet rule, yet it strives toward prosperity. We have here a combination of the incombinable. It is not enough to call it conformism, for conformism is a completely legal compromise of interests by means of mutual concessions accepted in human society everywhere...It is servility but not of an ordinary kind, but an ostentatious servility with suffering, with 'a Dosto-

evskiian touch' to it. [32]

In discussing these contradictory pressures Altaev demonstrates how 'double-think' works within the personality:

> While remaining insurmountable in the mind, the discord is, nevertheless, existentially overcome by a specific type of sceptical or cynical behaviour with a sequential transfer of consciousness from one plane to another and an extra-intensive suppressing of undesirable recollections. In this way the psyche becomes extremely mobile. The subject constantly moves from one dimension to another.

This was reflected on a large scale by the regime's sudden switches in policy, with its amnesia about past events (the memory hole), and on a personal level by individuals suppressing undesirable reactions and adopting others. A mobile psyche is double-think in action.

In Kundera's *The Book Of Laughter And Forgetting* a character connects private and public levels of suppression: 'He airbrushed her out of the picture in the same way the Party propaganda section airbrushed Clementis from the balcony where Gottwald gave his historic speech.' The personality becomes fluid, moving easily from one plane to another. This fluidity goes so far that we notice a strange attraction to opposites. In *Pretender To The Throne* Hitler and Stalin dream identical dreams about the glorious conquering hero, Chonkin-Golitsyn. In *Notes Of A Non-Conspirator,* Etkind notices how a man, who rose to be Deputy Minister of Culture by denouncing his colleagues, published a biography of Chekhov, and comments: 'Why on earth do these double-dyed villains feel the urge to write about Chekhov? Chekhov said: 'One must be intellectually clear, morally clean, and physically tidy.' Do they remember these words? Of course they do, but there is obviously an as yet unstudied type of masochism.'

People believe that anything is possible, and anything is permitted. They stand outside themselves and see how far they can go, like Ludvik in *The Joke* who enjoys watching how low and debased he

---

32   Quoted in Daniel Rancour-Laferriere *The Slave Soul of Russia*, New York University Press, New York, 1995, p. 60.

can get in seducing Helena. This is suffering with a Dostoevskyian touch, like the Underground Man with Liza. Similarly, intellectuals in Zinoviev's novels enjoy the piquancy of toying with more and more intricate and contradictory conceits. Voinovich writes of the typical Soviet bureaucrat in *The Ivankiad:*

> He is one character in many. He simultaneously speaks at a high rostrum and sits at a session of the Executive Committee, passes sentence on someone in court and writes a satirical article in the newspaper concerning the periodic intensification of the class struggle. But strangely enough, he fights against precisely what he himself strives for in all his designs. Parasite of parasites, in a loud voice that drowns out the others, he sings, 'Parasites, never!' He fights against manifestations of Philistine psychology, but who is more Philistine than he? He criticises the bourgeois way of life, doing everything he can to live precisely in a bourgeois manner. He exposes toadyism toward the West, but grabs at anything that bears a foreign label. They say ideology prevents him from changing. If only it were so! (pp. 112-3)

Like the Pardoner in Chaucer's *Canterbury Tales,* he lessens the strain of his own vices by publicly lashing out at them in others. This personality type has trained itself to understand all mental states from innocence to domination, to know every move and every motive, and to divine the potential victim and the potential oppressor in its own soul. Zinoviev writes that 'a normal man comprises every imaginable characteristic regardless of how such characteristics inter-relate'. Like a character in Kafka's *The Trial,* a person enmeshed in this system runs over in his mind all possible outcomes in a nightmarish fantasy. This is a trial or process to which he subjects himself before any official organs do, a form of self-interrogation which induces guilt, fear and submission in the participants as much as and before the regime does.

Few autonomous intermediate institutions existed in Communist societies, as the structure of civil society has been deliberately eroded. The basic unit of organisation and control was the local bureaucratic committee, or commune, which 'each separate self-contained institution (a factory, an institute, an office, a military unit, a school, and so on)' has. The aggregate of these communes forms what passes for a social structure. No violence, coercion or even direct orders from above need occur for the local commune to function to the regime's satisfaction, though the threat of external sanctions (if there is trouble) is an essential element. No Big Brother or even an O'Brien figure occur in many of these novels, since control works horizontally as much as vertically, and has become self-generating.

A specific mechanism of control is the 'personal case' or show trial, as explained in Voinovich's *Pretender To The Throne*: 'A personal case is when a large human group closes ranks in the course of an interspecific struggle, to suffocate one of its members, out of sheer foolishness, out of malice, or for no reason at all. A personal case is like an avalanche – if one falls on you, you can explain all you want, you're dead either way.' (p. 144) Examples of the personal case occur frequently in these novels. It happens to Ludvik in Kundera's *The Joke* and in the same author's short story 'Nobody Will Laugh' where the Ginger Man protagonist is bawled out by both his institute and his apartment commune. In Vaculic's *The Axe* the journalist hero is subjected to an extensive process over the suicide of a girl whose case he had been reporting. A district administrative committee conducts a number of personal cases in *Pretender to the Throne*. Zinoviev's novels discuss such events. Ultimately every character constitutes his own constant personal case. In *The Radiant Future* the plot, such as it is, hinges around the narrator's (eventually unsuccessful) candidature for the Academy. In Voinovich's *The Ivankiad* and Etkind's *Notes Of A Non-Conspirator,* actual cases endured by the authors are described and analysed. In most examples (an exception is *The Ivankiad)* the subject of the inquiry is segregated, humiliated and returned to the fold chastened.

The commune system evolved naturally (and unnaturally) over the decades, and through it submission is transmitted as part of a large seamless bureaucratic whole. The 'personal case' is a heightened and directed form of what is happening in everyday life. Every assignment by the journalist in Dovlatov's *The Compromise* is used by his editor to test his behaviour. A more formalised form of control occurs when whole bureaucratic empires act in this co-ordinated way, as they do in Zinoviev's novels. The Soviet Union did not develop discrete bureaucratic institutions so much as a total or sovereign bureaucracy. The heroes in most novels are lower-level functionaries whose adversary nature has been dulled by absorption into this bureaucratic web, as Konrad and Szelenyi demonstrate. As in *Nineteen Eighty-Four,* the great majority of ordinary people are hardly met in these novels, and when they are it is in a sort of Hades in which they live (like the proles in Zamyatin and Orwell). In *The Joke,* when Ludvik is expelled from both the Party and the university, it's as though he's been expelled from life itself.

A number of other related characteristics emerge repeatedly in the new literature. Life is full of fear, mistrust, envy, rudeness and petty spite. The instinctive renunciations on which civilisation rests have been supressed, and people act in a crudely selfish way. It's not just that mediocrity triumphs and the good are done over, but that the worst get on. Professional competence is not respected, and boundaries are blurred: Voinovich jokes that a saucepan could become a member of the Writers' Union, though it could not become a writer. Activities have no inherent aims or goals, except to keep the powerful in power. Everything goes on at the same level; any breakdown or advance is nullified, and in the end there are no winners. All is constantly in motion, but no change occurs: 'chaos without the dynamism of chaos', Konwicki calls it in *The Polish Complex.* (p. 17). People are condemned to an endless round of the same thing. Artificially induced fervour is common, but no real beliefs exist. Ideas are imposed on to reality, and words are used to distort rather than disclose it. As a result the ordinary person has no secure point of reference by which to orient himself. (Some similar features, designated as 'political correctness' have become noticeable in the West over recent decades.)

Orwell emphasised control from above, personified by O'Brien. These novels emphasise in contrast a self-generating totalitarianism from below, where ambition, personal nastiness, irrelevant grudges and denunciation are all motor forces in minor court-room dramas which human beings cannot resist. The narrator in Vaculic's *The Axe* describes his personal case as 'our self-governing terrorising of ourselves. Terrorizing ourselves so democratically that there's no one for us to assassinate'. (p.125) The narrator of Konwicki's *The Polish Complex* reflects: 'We ourselves support the regime and its agonised movements. Our peculiar desire to dominate those nearest us oils the notched gears, runs the drive belt, stokes the fire. Our regime has given the stupid a chance to rule the wise, permitted villains to humiliate the honest, commanded the strong to torture the weak.' (p. 137) The narrator in Konwicki's A *Minor Apocalypse* asks the rhetorical question: 'So we've taken ourselves prisoner and we're keeping ourselves behind bars, is that it?', and his interrogator replies: 'That's it. We've given the oppressor the slip. We've outwitted him. We are free because we have imposed our own slavery'. (p. 118). The character Schizophrenic writes in *The Yawning Heights:*

> The most moral citizens are subjected to persecution, the most talented and efficient are reduced to the lowest common denominator of mediocrity and muddle. It is not necessarily the authorities who achieve this. A person's own colleagues, friends, work-mates and neighbours bend all their efforts to deny a man of talent the possibility of developing his own individuality, or an industrious man the chance of advancement.

This form of domination which is largely self-inflicted by a citizenry has been called 'totalitarianism from below'. In an article on this phenomenon by Jan Gross,[33] the author examines Soviet rule in eastern Poland from 1939 to 1941. Even in these disturbed war times, the Russians did not simply impose their domination from above; instead at the local level they allowed petty feuds, traditional rivalries and personal enmities full rein in the vacuum the war situation had created. Local groups wreaked vengeance on each other, as the restraints of normal times were lifted. This was one important mechanism through which the Russians exercised their control, and it happened even dur-

---

33 Jan Gross: 'A Note on the Nature of Soviet Totalitarianism', *Soviet Studies*, Vol. XXXIV, No. 3, July 1982.

ing the apocalyptic phase of totalitarianism. In heightened times we usually focus on imposed terror (camps, secret police, torture, forced migrations) because of its high visibility. But it also works naturally from below, even in abnormal times. Normal times allow us to see this self-terrorising side more clearly, though once again both forms of control are reciprocally present. Totalitarianism has a continuity from its *grand mal* to its *petit mal* forms. The Czech writer Milan Simecka shows one way this is achieved:

> The totalitarian state has far more powerful weapons at its disposal [than violence]: all citizens are its employees and it is no problem to shift them up or down the scale of incentives – rewarding the good and punishing the bad. This capacity is a thoroughly modern weapon. It worked well, because it was brought into play only when existing socialism, in its infra-structures, most resembled a consumer society, i.e. when it had something to reward or punish with.[34]

We think of totalitarianism as invading and obliterating the private sphere. But Gross shows in his example that we can look at it in another way, as the loss of the public realm. No objective outside world, to which, one could appeal, existed:

> The real power of a totalitarian state results from its being at the disposal of every inhabitant, available for hire at a moment's notice. The absence of the rule of law in a totalitarian regime is also reflected in the fact that every citizen has direct access to the coercive apparatus of the state, unmediated by lengthy and complicated procedures. Everybody can use the political police against everybody else quickly, without delay or undue formalities.

It was this privatisation and destruction of the public realm, and its random quality, which generated fear and insecurity in ordinary people. As Gross concludes: 'It was a weird power, power to destroy but not to protect. Nobody was able to provide for their own security, while anybody was able to ruin anybody else'. This is the kind of society described in Zinoviev's *The Reality of Communism*.

---

34 Jacques Rupnik *The Other Europe,* Weidenfeld and Nicolson, London, 1988, p. 238.

A poignant literary account of this deformity is Yuri Trifonov's novel *The House On The Embankment* (1975), in which the principal character Glebov fails to defend his mentor Professor Ganchuk in the interests of his own advancement. Glebov's childhood years in pre-war Moscow set the pattern of a life of self-inflicted terror (in the manner described by Zinoviev). Glebov is raised in the nightmare world of the crowded slums of Moscow, where people scramble over one another in their desperate quest for improvement. Trust is totally lacking, and Glebov learns how to exercise power over his classmates, whom he at one stage informs on. Glebov is consumed by envy and resentment at the inequality around him, symbolised by the house on the embankment, whose superior status both oppresses and attracts him.[35] In this house lives a schoolmate Lev Shulepnikov, who wields a mysterious power partly through personal qualities and partly through family connections with the state apparatus. As the novel moves to its climax, Glebov betrays the Ganchuk family out of a kind of motiveless vacuity of character: he is a 'nothing person'. In the professor's personal case, nobody wins; all power is temporary. At the end, the leaden, sinking feeling which has always attended Glebov's reflections on inequality and envy returns to him. The dismissed professor Ganchuk reflects on Dostoevsky's *Crime And Punishment*:

> He said that the thought that had tormented Dostoyevsky – if a man's last refuge is nothing but a dark room full of spiders, then *all is permitted* – had hitherto been interpreted in a wholly simplistic, trivial sense...Today's Raskolnikovs did not murder old women moneylenders with an axe, but they were faced with the same agonising choice; to cross or not to cross the line. In any case, what was the difference between using an axe and any other method? What was the difference between murder and just giving the victim a slight push, provided that it removed him?...Nowadays people don't fully understand what they are doing. Hence the arguments within themselves...they are trying to convince themselves. (p. 343)

---

35 The house on the embankment, a large multi-story block of flats on the Moscow River built to accommodate the Soviet *nomenklatura*, is the subject of Yuri Slezkine's ground breaking study of the Soviet system, *The House of Government: A Saga of the Russian Revolution*, Princeton University Press, Princeton and Oxford, 2017.

In this type of literature writers convey a world that is absurd and demoralising at the same time. As Konwicki put it: 'In our country tragedy often walks hand in hand with buffoonery.' When Western absurd theatre was first shown in Prague, people realised that the daily life they were living was 'absurd' in the same sense. Imaginative literature was needed to recreate this strange world, and to lead people to understand it. Straightforward, rational analysis of such a society founders on the dialectic. How can you describe double-think in action, voices that are simultaneously cozening and hectoring, systems that are crazy but have a logic of their own? In addition, it was harder to show that the system remained inhuman when the visible signs of coercion were not to the fore. Society looked outwardly bland and even slack. Slavery was invisible because internalized. Daniel and Sinyavsky used fantasies to get under the surface, to reveal the psychopathology of everyday life in the post-Stalin era. Writers, following Bulgakov, used various mixtures of fantasy, satire, dream sequences and grotesque and absurd comedy to reveal both the inner emptiness and the terrifying pressures of ordinary existence. A highly organized repressive society is too large to cope with as a whole. The novelists approached the problem obliquely: they described one (representative) person, in a restricted milieu and engaged in a relatively benign milieu, in other words a least worst case.

In Voinovich's *Pretender To The Throne* the action takes place in a remote peasant village, and the incidents are pure burlesque (such as a cow's skull falling out of a coffin). The regime's instruments of coercion are as distant as the horrors of war. The action is separated from larger scale traumas precisely to reveal the basic rules of coercion still apply in this bumpkin situation. The hero, Chonkin, is a guileless holy fool. The regime's officials expect him to act in the way they do, that is, by becoming habituated to an intricate system of motive analysis to cope with every situation. He disarms the overcomplex interpretation the officials impose on him by acting with straight-forward selflessness. The officials cannot handle this. The result is simultaneously comic and devastating. Their initial misreading of Chonkin eddies out into a misreading of the whole war situation. Instead of the obvious explanation of his behaviour – that he is a non-malicious man – the local party is forced to invent more sinister and outlandish scenarios. Headquarters also sends down paranoid directions about a German spy, Hans, which, combined with local self-importance, leads to events getting out of hand. Both groups, impelled by their own crazy logic, keep upping the ante. The local organs, needing to impress Moscow, arrest the investigating officer, Filippov, as the 'real' Hans. Events move to their unstoppable climax as fantasy takes over from reality. Each actor must outdo the one before him. The prosecutor Evpraksein invents the unnecessary conclusion (not even in the script of the show trial) that Chonkin is really the White Russian Prince Golitsyn, a new Tsar. Stalin and Hitler, obsessed by their own roles, fear this mirror-image figure. All proceeds logically and plausibly but without a scrap of evidence. As Geoffrey Hosking comments 'Man's imaginings confront and enslave him'.

In the new literature, the hero, battered and disillusioned, does not exempt himself from the satire. He knows he is enmeshed in the system, but he is also self-scrutinizingly detached from it, a dual track approach. This enables the narrator and the reader to simultaneously feel the strain (which comes from being part of it) as well as anger and indignation (which comes from standing aside from it). Physical removal from the scene (by exile, expulsion, prison or death) is not likely. Traditional forms of release are to the countryside (as in Vaculic's *The Axe*, where chopping wood in the forest relieves the pressure), to the world of nature and animals (as in Vaculic's *The Guinea Pigs*), or to the past (as in Jiri Grusa's *The Questionnaire*). Authors are attracted to underground folklore which is an alternative culture, as in Solzhenitsyn, Sinyavsky, the Ukrainian Valentyn Moroz, and Kundera's *The Joke*. In Russian literature this may be combined with a move towards religious beliefs. But for the heroes of the Konwicki, Zinoviev, Erofeev and Dovlatov novels, none of these escape routes presents itself as a possible solution. Erofeev never gets to Petushki. In Irving Howe's words: 'After the satire and indignation have been exhausted, there remains the sadness of martyred countries.'

In *Nineteen Eighty-Four* sexual relations subvert for a time the regime's dominance, and open up an area of genuine privacy. But this is not the case in the new literature, where sexual relations are often rather gruesomely portrayed as just another aspect of manipulation. A character in Malcolm Bradbury's *Rates of Exchange* understands that in Eastern Europe 'sex is just politics with the clothes off.' In Voinovich's short story 'An Exchange of Letters' the hero is trapped by a woman whose 'method has something in common with the process by which the totalitarian state traps men in their own fantasies'. In *The Joke* sexual activity parallels the regime's mode of behaviour rather than providing an answer to it. In Dovlatov and Erofeev sex and drinking lead to disintegration more than Bohemian free-spiritedness. But this is not true of the Chonkin novels or *The First Circle,* where human love is seen as an antidote.

These novels have many similarities to the self-scrutinizing stream of consciousness ones in the West, but some differences. The characters in these Eastern novels are sorting out two problems, whose connection is not entirely clear. Firstly, they have to decide how far totalitarianism is in the ordinary run of things, a new form of social organisation, and how far it is an excrescence. Like Solzhenitsyn's characters, they are making complicated choices of adaptation and resistance all the time. The hero easily sloughs off false transcendence (the claim to explain the meaning of life) offered by official propaganda. He has to establish his own identity against the all-pervading pressures around him. But when he does this he feels terribly alone. He now faces the problems of the Western modernist hero who is an isolated ego, neurotically trapped in his own musings, and hoping he has within himself the resources necessary to transcend his present condition. He may feel this in an even more intense way, because the atomisation is more severe in the East. Kundera moved from Prague to Paris, with his novels exhibiting a gradual shift in emphasis from the first to the second dilemma.

These problems cause great strain, pressing the individual to look for some realm larger than himself into which he can be subsumed.

In *Beyond Socialist Realism* Geoffrey Hosking detected in contemporary Russian literature a desire to merge with the mythic collective of one's ancestral spirits, providing examples of pre-Christian animism, pantheism, absorption in nature and other attempts at supra-personal immortality. In the West it is the absence of any shared venture which is most felt. Zinoviev explained in his interview with George Urban:

> I live in intellectual segregation, as most Frenchmen and Americans and Germans do too...each in his overheated, overfurnished, personal ghetto...each fighting the depressions and despair that comes from satiety, isolation, and the lack of a higher collective purpose...Fish can live only in water, birds only in the sky. I'm a fish, and I belong to the Soviet pool. I cannot be a bird, try as I might. You may use all your power of persuasion telling me: 'Fly with us! Look at these wonderful skies, enjoy the sunshine!' I could not do it because I'm not a bird. [36]

Zinoviev and some other novelists believed that totalitarianism has normalised itself, that it's the next stage in social organisation, and that some species of it are going to come to the West.

These pessimistic novels should not be looked at uncritically: there was a possibility of breakout, by individuals (like Solzhenitsyn) and by nations (like Poland). Both created alternative systems of beliefs. Moreover, things could happen unexpectedly, due to the weakness of the Soviet system, for example, those excoriated in Andrei Amalrik in *Will The Soviet Union Survive Until 1984*. Acceptance of the Zinoviev case can lead to shoulder-shrugging fatalism – there's nothing they or we can do about apparently endless domination. Finally, these literary works vindicate earlier writings like Arendt's on totalitarianism, Orwell's *Nineteen Eighty-Four*, Solzhenitsyn's works, and the protests of the dissidents in Russia and East Europe. These more recent authors, having the benefit of long experience from inside and under, supplement the original picture rather than undermining it.

---

[36] George Urban 'A Dissenter as a Soviet Man: A Conversation with Alexander Zinoviev', *Encounter*, May 1984, p.35.

8

THE ADVERSARY CULTURE

Since the Enlightenment thinkers and writers have, in the name of liberty, seen it as a pre-eminent task to criticise the oppressive tendencies of their rulers, who often in the past denied their citizens material and spiritual freedoms. The defining role of thinkers came to be a dissenting opposition – I criticise, therefore I am. The romantic and the avant-garde movements reinforced this supposed antagonism between thinker and society. But changes in the world have outpaced this kind of analysis. The role of thinkers is not just to criticise, but more to understand the present alignment of forces, which sometimes means criticising and sometimes affirming, and usually some mixture of both. Post-war societies in the West were peculiarly difficult to analyze by accepted methods, being relatively monochrome and predictable. They lacked obvious symbols and turning points which analysts could latch on to. But many analysts remain automatically antagonistic to present society. The valuable tradition of liberal critique of tyranny can, if continued as unthinking dissent, turn full circle and erode the freedoms it was inaugurated to protect. Lack of perspective makes it hard to realize how special our position is. Our societies are unusual in that they are normal.

In most past cultures, particularly tribal ones, people strongly identified with their own family, their own clan, and their own nation, to such an extent that it provided them with a basic identity, the ground of their being. But in more recent times, with the breakdown in traditional values identified by Edmund Burke and others, the reverse has occurred. It is now common for people to denigrate their own culture and to admire the *other*. This first became apparent between the wars with rise of fellow travellers, those in the West who admired the distant regimes of Stalin and Hitler, and who felt ashamed that their own nations were not advancing in the way these new types of regimes appeared to be. After the war, when these regimes were discredited, the other side of the same coin, those who constantly bag their own countries, came to the fore, as Lionel Trilling was one of the first to notice.

A Europe wrecked by ideologies necessitated withdrawal to a personal, uncommitted position, which discarded outworn rules. In this view it was the isolated individual consciousness, extremely aware of itself, which was the key rather than society, which was relegated to the role of duelling partner. The sudden moodswings, tensions, phobias, inner turmoil, associative connections and imaginative leaps of the anti-hero between meaning and blankness constitute the narrative. We are expected to admire this feat of apparent self-exposure. The modern artist/hero believes he is self-sufficient. Society, and others to whom he feels superior, offer him little. He (the voice and personality characteristics of modernism are often male) has greater insights and sensitivities than other people. His consciousness has been raised to a heightened state, and the constant anguish this causes makes it a burden to its possessor.

This was the attitude of the 'outsider', the new culture hero of the post war decades. The defining attitudes of this era were evident in novels such as J.P. Dunleavy's *The Ginger Man* (1955) and Joseph Heller's *Catch-22* (1961), both of which enjoyed cult-like status. The hero, having disentangled himself from convention, lives for the present. The central characters of Hesse's *Steppenwolf* (1927), Camus' *The Outsider* (1942), and Böll's *The Clown* (1963) likewise feel alienated. These novels consist of a monologue of the disjointed insights of the hero-narrator, as he processes information coming in from an unfriendly world outside. These attitudes were the base on which emerging socio-political forces, variously labelled as the counter culture, the permissive society, the adversary culture and protest movement, formed themselves from the 1960s onwards.

The hero of J.P. Donleavy's *The Ginger Man* (1956), Sebastian Dangerfield, a Dublin layabout, is manipulative, but at the same time cool and relaxed, not taking himself entirely seriously, enjoying his predicament rather than working himself up into a lather against it. He is sub-political, on the edges of society, not fighting against its larger forces, relaxed in his role as local conman, and knowingly gaming his acquaintances, whom he treats as victims of himself more than opponents. The Gingerman is a trickster, like Böll's clown, a loner sending up his immediate world, manoeuvring between the gaps and looking after himself, while taking others for a ride in a gentle way. *Look Back in Anger* and *Lucky Jim* were approximate English equivalents at the time. Those who set themselves up as activists in the West took this stance further, replacing bohemian slackness with commitment.

This initial attitude amounted to gentle indirect social satire, revealing weaknesses in society's structure not by looking at the whole scenario, but only at the hero's reactions to his immediate milieu. The Gingerman feels superior; he tortures his wife psychologically, prevailing over her through cynical moves. He uses his girlfriends, pretending interest in them to disguise his self-interest. He unfairly asks poor Miss Frost, who senses she has a bleak future, what she wants out of life, which makes her feel worse. It's a question he never asks himself. (The Underground Man raised the dismal prospects of the prostitute Lisa in the same cruel way.) The Gingerman is unhappy in himself but won't admit it, instead projecting it on to others. His fantasy life of wealth and success contrasts with his unadmitted present failure, where sex is employed as an instant but unsuccessful balm for all hurts. Early readers of the novel identified with its hero and admired him, but half a century later, having seen the outcome of such attitudes, we are not so sure. Is he a culture hero, or an example of the vacuity of the counter culture? He is an adversary figure to his friends, to society and ultimately to himself.

Joseph Heller's *Catch-22* (1955) is also not directly about politics or society; it's foremost a satire on bureaucracy, and on the absurdity of war. Catch-22 is the trap modern life's self-defeating nature entangles us in. In this case the hero Yossarian apparently goes crazy and refuses to fly bombing missions, but this is a sane reaction, which ironically reveals he is not crazy and so fit to fly, a typically circular absurd situation. In another instance, the more alfalfa a farmer doesn't grow, the bigger the government compensation he receives. The novel is a litany of such contradictory situations. Another example: 'The country was in peril; he was jeopardizing his traditional rights of freedom and independence by daring to exercise them.' (p. 414) Counter-productive actions are the only beneficial ones. War is Peace. Freedom is Slavery. George Orwell understood that things can turn into the opposite of themselves at the first touch of reality.

The novel ridicules a distorted wartime social pyramid. The needs of the bomber crews, who constantly risk their lives, should be the priority, with all others there to assist them. But the ground controller colonels, superior to the flight crews in the power grid, put their unimportant needs first, while they fight pathetic turf wars with bureaucratic generals over promotions and position. Process becomes all. Higher up and unseen are the military command and government which are directing the war. On one level the novel is a satire on government bureaucracy, where most actors are opportunists looking after themselves, and where administrators triumph over those actually doing the fighting, a typical anomaly. But the deeper satirical context here is war and death, very close to the bone, which means that actions we would normally describe with derision may now become criminally immoral. Death hangs over all, sobering and real – the rest is flummery. The bomber crews, unlike the others, are under immense strain at all times, especially as the causes of death are so arbitrary. In this upside down world your own side's behaviour threatens you as much as the enemy's. The central character Yossarion wages his private war against the military set-up, which he considers irresponsibly stupid. Heller, even more than Dunleavy, is deadly serious, satirizing the absurdities of war, and the military authorities in their forlorn attempts at imposing rationality on the inherently messy nature of armed conflict. The hero cannot be a cleanskin as he is necessarily ensnared in this madness.

The main activity in the novel is talk, which consists of a bewildering mixture of rationalization and realism. Talk is used to fend off reality, to deny it, and to twist it into shapes convenient to the speaker. Administrative experts at double-think contradictions confuse and dominate others, as in Voinovich's novel *The Ivankiad* and in Zinoviev's novels about the Soviet Union. A few like Yossarian see through it, and expose the absurdity for what it is: 'Every victim was a culprit, every culprit a victim, and someone had to stand up sometime to try to break the loony chain of inherited habit that was imperilling them all. (p. 414) Like Volodin in *The First Circle,* Yossarian's defiance breaks the chain, the circle which binds them all. The actors hope for affection and sex as possible solutions, or at least as respites, but these, as in most political novels, are not sufficient. Existentialist novelists and absurdist playwrights had already dealt with individuals navigating their way out of personal entrapment. Heller expanded their perspectives by locating such stances in wider political and military realms, which fitted the mood of the times.

Steppenwolf was an earlier, more romantic and darker work. The Weimar period in Germany had some similarities with the counter-culture period in the US – in both the spirit of Dionysius was abroad – which explains the revival of *Steppenwolf's* popularity in the 1960s. Hesse's main character is lonely, unsociable, an outsider, who finds normal life a flat, stale and unprofitable exercise; nothing excites his weary spirit. He is old and wise to the world's ways, he's been through a real hell, unlike the self-imposed tribulations of the younger anti-heroes of novels like those of Donleavy. Hermann Hesse himself understood this difference. Appending a new author's preface to a reissue of *Steppenwolf* in 1961, over three decades after it had first appeared, Hesse wrote that of all his novels this one was 'more violently misunderstood than any other, and frequently it is actually the affirmative and enthusiastic readers, rather than those who rejected the book, who have reacted to it oddly'. The novel's new younger US readers identified strongly with the Steppenwolf's descent into chaos, but not with his later redemption. They neglected, Hesse believed, the 'second, higher, indestructible world beyond the Steppenwolf and his problematic life…the story of the Steppenwolf pictures a disease and crisis – but not one leading to death and destruction, on the contrary: to healing.' (pp. 5-6).

Philip Roth is best known for novels like *Portnoy's Complaint* flaunting the transgressions of the sexual revolution of the 1970s. In a different mood in later life he wrote a trilogy of socio-political novels covering the turbulent decades from the 1940s to the 1980s. He had been in the 1970s an anti-Vietnam war left liberal, and he wanted in these novels to recapture the political enthusiasms of his earlier life, and to come to terms with them. His novel *I Married A Communist* (1998), set in the 1940s and 1950s, provides an explanatory prologue to later events. The great depression and the second world war have made life tough for people trying to improve their lot. Actual political events form the background to the novel's action, from the Truman Presidency and the recovery from the war, through the Democratic Party's division over Henry Wallace's candidacy in the 1948 election, to the anti-Communist McCarthy episode in the Eisenhower years of the 1950s. The novel is a *Bildungsroman,* a tale of how the narrator Nathan Zuckerman, Roth's *alter ego*, learns about himself and his role in the world as he grows up. Zuckerman, a generation younger than the main characters, also learns from his role model, his school teacher Murray Ringold, who narrates much of the story through Zuckerman. Murray's brother Ira Ringold, who has taken the name Iron Rinn, is the hero of the novel. Zuckerman also learns from a student friend Leo Gluksman, an aesthete diametrically opposed to Rinn's activist views. Zuckerman's role is to tell, half a century after the events, the version of Rinn's story as remembered by his brother Murray. Roth is giving the reader the flavour of the times, with the progressive left sympathetically portrayed.

The House of UnAmerican Activities Committee is seeking to

expose Soviet and Wallace sympathizers like the Ringolds. Murray Ringold loses his teaching position for some years and his brother Iron Rinn, once a unionist and Communist party agitator, now a popular actor playing President Lincoln in plays and speeches, is under similar pressure from the activist right. Rinn is married to a famous Hollywood actress, Eva Frame, shown as devious, showy, and hiding her true self. Her daughter from a previous marriage, Sylphid, a harpist, controls her mother. Rinn, formed in the rough and tough 1930s, is straight forward and self-educated, and opposite to the charming and socially adept Eva who directs his upward social mobility. To the young narrator the atmosphere at Rinn and Eva's townhouse is liberating: books, music, high culture and informed discussion, a sophistication rare in 1940s USA. Sylphid provides an extra dimension; with her cynical, destructive witty 'amused contempt' (p. 521) she sends up the house's guests. Rinn eventually has affairs with his daughter's friend and with his masseuse. The marriage between Rinn and Eva deteriorates, just as their pro-Communist left stance falls apart. People ditch their erstwhile friends out of a 'motiveless malignity'. We are getting into Kundera territory here, where sex and politics intermingle and clash. Parallels are drawn between political and personal inconstancy, in this case during the McCarthy period:

> Not only does the pleasure of betraying replace the prohibition, but you transgress without giving up your moral authority. You retain your purity...at the same time as you are realizing a satisfaction that verges on the sexual with its ambiguous components of pleasure and weakness, of aggression and shame: the satisfaction of undermining. (p. 644)

'The satisfaction of undermining' describes the basis of the adversary culture. Eva's memoir exposes Rinn's dubious political past. (pp. 642-4)[37] Rinn is attacked from both sides: the Communists claim he has sold out, while at the same time the McCarthyists pursue him.

---

37 When Eva publishes her memoir, dumping on her former husband Ira, he is described in the novel as 'hell bent in getting his revenge'. (p. 512). Critics have seen the negative portrait of Eva Frame in the novel as Roth's own revenge on his former wife, the famous actress Claire Bloom, who portrayed Roth unfavourably in her memoir.

In the 1960 the new left attempts to rehabilitate him. In all this Roth takes a detached stance; writing in the 1990s he knew from Kundera and other east European writers that Communism has been exposed as hollow, but believed it worthwhile to capture the beliefs, atmosphere and rationalizations of his earlier years.

The 1960s and 1970s brought the permissive society to centre stage. One great cry was 'liberation' from all restraints. Liberation movements had flourished in Victorian England: socialists, free thinkers, homosexuals, nudists, vegetarians, and advocates of sexual freedoms all existed as marginalized groups straining to liberate themselves from what they saw as a repressive society. Their endeavours were successively held up by the depressions of the 1890s and 1930s and by the two world wars. When these liberation movements began to flourish as the counter culture in the 1960s they had been held up for a century. The cry for freedom from restraints derived from a form of demotic Freudianism, which laughed out of court all they deemed non-liberated as 'repressed', and therefore socially unacceptable nerds. Who is going to own up to being repressed? Combined with a vulgar Darwinism (we are all inevitably evolving towards a better world) and vulgar Marxism (capitalism is conspiracy imprisoning ordinary people), it was a siren cry which became the established truth of the new anti-establishment left, which soon morphed into a new establishment in its own right.

In the 1950s the United States was still recovering from the second world. The 1960s introduced a new mood. From 1914 to 1945 Europe had been traumatized by a succession of shocks: wars, depression, revolutions, dictatorships and mass slaughter. Unimaginable terrors were likely to occur at any time. But Western societies soon reverted towards normality, with stable economies and without external threats. Many people believed Dachau and Hiroshima exemplified, in intensified form, the essentials of the contemporary condition, but the precise connection eludes us. Both worlds, the extreme and the normal, have undoubtedly existed in living memory, and at different times people emphasized one or the other. But in the post war world decades the apocalyptic period in European naturally continued to attract attention. It was very hard to de-escalate quickly from this fevered, 'larger-than-life' condition, when meaning stared out at one from every incident. Commentators have a natural attraction to crisis situations brimming with 'significance'. Ingrained habits of thought persisted, long after the conditions which caused them to arise had subsided. Hence the yearning for 'crises', and for situations which rework the old familiar tropes of repression and dissent. Accustomed to being tolerant, we fall over backwards to understand the *other*, and to acknowledge its legitimacy, even at the cost of our own. As a result the dissident figure, wielding endless critique of his own locale, became the new culture hero. Admired above all were the bohemian artist, the political activist, the crusading journalist and the radical academic, thinkers who accosted society's mores, often setting themselves up as gurus.

From the 1960s onwards the novelists Roth, Mailer and Bellow and Lowell in poetry focused on these developments. During this period Roth was a partisan activist, but in *American Pastoral* (1997) the narrator Nathan Zuckerman is looking back in a more detached, even elegiac, mood at these protest decades. The main figure in the novel, Seymour Levov, is from a second generation US Jewish family. An all-American sports star in his youth, he inherits his father's successful business. The Levov family saga typifies the inter-generational conflicts of the period. The pioneering grandfather, Lou Levov, is a traditionalist, his son Seymour a liberal, and his granddaughter, Merry, has been radicalized by disdain for her father, for capitalism, and for America itself. The previous generation's desire for assimilation has been halted, replaced by contempt for a slack society: 'Once Jews ran away from repression; now they run away from non-oppression'. In the novel three ethnic groups face this dilemma: confident, long-standing WASP families like the Orcutts; Irish Catholics like the family of Dawn Dwyer, Seymour's wife; and the Jewish Levov family itself. Roth's imagination has a sociological stretch which effectively captures key social currents. Extended dialogues between Seymour Levov and his daughter Merry, and between Seymour and his brother

Jerry, recount both sides of the disputes roiling society at the time.

In the third generation Merry has been indulged as a young girl with horses to ride and all she wants. Then her revulsion against her way of life deepens: 'A vision from which she was willing, if not to kill, then cruelly abandon her own family, a vision having nothing to do with 'ideals'...blind antagonism and an infantile desire to menace – *those* were her ideals. In search always of something to hate.' (p. 193) Merry becomes radicalized in the Weatherman terrorist cult, where in the course of bombing a commercial premises a bystander is killed. After this episode she is forced to live underground, during which time three more people are murdered as a result of her faction's activities. This wrecks the life of her liberal parents and leads to the family's disintegration, shattering the immigrant's American dream of continual improvement. The US nation, social norms, communities, families and individuals are all broken by this sudden upheaval. All certainties vanish: 'People suddenly forced to make sense of madness. All that public display. The dropping of inhibitions. Authority powerless. The kids going crazy. Intimidating everybody. The adults don't know what to make of it'. (p. 66)

Zuckerman (and Roth) realize by the end that people are lost, having cracked under the strain. They don't know who they really are, with their outward performances belying their true, distraught state. Their identities they have formed are not enough, now the props are gone:

> She [Dawn] was nothing like the one he had imagined...How to penetrate to the interior of people was some skill or capacity he did not possess...What was *he*, stripped of all the signs he flashed? People were standing up everywhere, shouting This is me! This is me!...the truth of it was that they had no more idea of who or of what they were than he had. (p. 382)

The novel has certain loose resemblances to Bellow's *Herzog* which had appeared a few decades before. The same political events set the scene. The disturbed Seymour manically sends off letters of protest to public figures, 'telling off the state and President' to relieve his own anguish, as Herzog does. Both heroes live in rural locations in New England close to the coastal urban action, as both authors did at the time. The novel is called *American Pastoral*: in its later part the survivors of the sixties lick their wounds in rural tranquillity, in contrast to earlier scenes of ghastly industrialized Newark.

Norman Mailer's take on these events as they happened differed markedly from Roth's. Out of the cauldron of 1968, that disturbed year which saw the apogee of the protest struggle in the United States, came two new and typically manic works by Mailer, the novel *The Armies of the Night*, an account of the massive anti-war protest march on the Pentagon on October 21, 1967, and the documentary analysis *Chicago and the Siege of Miami*. Mailer was a Dionysian culture hero transferring his impulses to the political arena. A bohemian like Brecht he harked back to the regressive spirit of the god Baal and ancient times. Mailer let himself go by wholly embracing the frenzied spirit of the age, riding roughshod over deeply embedded mores. In this he was representative of a certain spirit of the age. Mailer's basic insight was that some public happenings are today so 'emotional, spiritual, psychical, moral, existential or supernatural' that history becomes an 'interior' thing, and the historian must make way for the novelist. (Kundera had a similar insight.) The march on the Pentagon was for Mailer such a defining experience that to capture its feel, one had to enter 'that world of strange lights and intuitive speculations that is the novel'. (p. 255) In his self-stimulating attempts to heighten the tension Mailer presents himself as the centre of attention. All experiences are available to him as he tests them out; there are no limits to his self-expansion. But Mailer was too wayward to be a convincing analyst of political power games.

The events of the weekend – the rallies, endless speeches, the draft card handing-in ceremony, the mobilization and demonstration itself, the arrests, detention and release – are superbly described, but the book is as much about Mailer himself, who appears in a dual role, not only as the intuitively speculating novelist, but also as the hero of the action out there, Mailer in the third person, affecting events themselves. He wants to be everybody and in everything – actor, participant, instigator, observer, victim, partisan, reporter and analyst. He presents himself not self-analytically nor even confessionally, but by infusing the action with his own psychic drives. The events release him; all that he has been thinking and worrying about, all that has stored up over past years comes pouring out in a flood of words. As in *Steppenwolf* it is an attempt, common in the 19th and 20th centuries, to redeem one's past life and its deficiencies by turning them into art. As Mailer puts it: "He was off on the Romantic's great military dream, which is: seize defeat, convert it into triumph'. (p. 31) Lionel Trilling identified this drive as a key element in modern literature: 'the idea of losing oneself up to the point of self-destruction, of surrendering oneself to experience without regard to self-interest or conventional morality, of escaping wholly from the societal bonds.'[38]

Mailer is only half serious, a *faux naif* in comparison to the real activists, who wish to impose on to reality a counter authority system, not his bohemian fantasies. He does not restrain himself, as he lacks internal resistance mechanisms. He vaguely realizes there is a problem here, being aware of the mixture of seriousness and farce, guerilla theatre, in it all. He can't make up his mind whether the march on the Pentagon is a military exercise or a media extravaganza, and keeps shunting between the two perspectives. He starts to build up a picture of the physical bravery and courage of 'these Crusaders going out to attack the hard core of technology land', and records Paul Goodman telling them that they confront 'the most dangerous body of men at the present in the world'. (p. 98) (This was the year the Soviet Union militarily invaded Czechoslovakia). Yet the strategic logic of the dissenters shows that they live in another world altogether, a world of symbols. The Pentagon is 'symbolic' of the 'military-industrial complex', which is in turn the servant of 'the corporation'. What is needed to 'confront' this enormity is obviously a 'symbolic' gesture, and what better than a 'symbolic' attack on the Pentagon, because this

---

38 Lionel Trilling 'The Modern Element in Modern Literature', *Beyond Culture*, Penguin, Books, Harmondsworth, 1967, p. 40.

means 'confronting' the military and police, whose innate brutality is 'symbolic' of the malevolent intentions of the authorities, and so on. Mailer's analytical abilities falter in the face of his sympathy with the dissenters: *tout comprendre c'est tout pardonner*.

A few militant Yippies think it's for real and try to storm the Pentagon (some penetrate the corridors). The academics in Mailer's entourage know it's all play-acting. Mailer and his mates, the New York literary-intellectual contingent, shunt between the two views and so end up looking slightly ludicrous. How can we take these 'revolutionaries-for-a-weekend' (Mailer's phrase) seriously, who negotiate beforehand with the enemy (the authorities), and have to try hard to get arrested (Mailer succeeds, Dr. Spock doesn't), and who know that arrest means a token detention and then release? Mailer's main worry is whether he will be released in time to fly back to New York for a party (he isn't). He has an eye all the time on what the mass media are saying about him – a BBC camera crew accompanies him through most of his adventures when in the authorities' hands. No wonder that East European rebels, who faced real dangers, had little time for such Western 'revolutionaries'.

Mailer is perceptive enough to see an element of Gingerman posing in it all; he admits that he is not very taken by liberal academics, Black Power militants and draft-card burners. But after listing his doubts, he ends: 'Still, he was going to be there'. Why? Because for Mailer style, image and atmosphere are everything, and the marchers have these and their opponents do not. They are therefore irresistible. Rational argument or the content of their propositions are secondary. This leaves Mailer, a person with basically decent instincts, in an impossible position, because he is forced to pass over slogans like "Hey, Hey, LBJ! How many kids did you slay today?', and songs like 'The Master of Hate', dedicated to LBJ:

>   Suicide is an evil thing
>   But at times it is good
>   If you've been where the master lives

I think you surely should.

Many of the marchers admired contemporary tyrants like Castro, Mao and Ho Chi Minh. In contrast excessive animus was directed to the rulers of their own society, as exemplars of awful modern capitalist repression.

The Chicago riot outside the Democratic Convention was more grounded in reality. Mailer's book *Miami and the Siege of Chicago* is subdued, since he was only observing events, not leading them. The ideas of the rioters turn out to be the predictable propaganda of the American Left, that anti-Communists are Cold Warriors, that the US is becoming a great, grey, air-conditioned, totalitarian nightmare, the standard rhetoric thrown in the face of the power elite to damn it. We meet the expected rogues gallery: Nixon, Wallace, Reagan, Humphrey, Agnew, and Mayor Daley of Chicago, who are said in *The Armies of the Night* to be turning the country into 'some sexo-technological variety of neo-fascism'. (p. 93)

Mailer doesn't advance a coherent argument on why the US should withdraw from Asia; instead he advances what he calls a 'sleeping thesis', that is, a hunch: Communism fragments when it expands, remains monolithic when it doesn't. Any power involved in Asia will break itself on the back of the impossibility of the whole Asian situation. Therefore, let's leave Asia to the Communists: 'To leave Asia would be precisely to gain the balance of power. In the expansion of Communism, was its own containment. The only force which could ever defeat Communism was Communism.' (p. 187) These are wonderful-sounding half-truths until we remember that the whole point of countervailing pressure was to prevent Communist expansion. Taking the pressure off Communism did not reform it. On the contrary local resistance to Communist expansion, aided by the West, in Malaysia, the Philippines and Indonesia (the attempted PKI coup in 1975 was a close-run thing) meant the big dominoes held firm till Communism itself collapsed a little time later on. Mailer is suggesting the best solution is defeat. This was a Romantic's great military dream, but in this case defeat was not going to be converted into triumph.

In the end, what we are mainly left with is a tour around Mailer's mind: he is trying to wring too much imaginative significance out of events which aren't up to them. One's psychedelic yearnings for an existential moment are not guaranteed in reality. Mailer's writing is not an analysis of the phenomenon, but part of the phenomenon itself, part of a semi-successful bid at political destabilization. In them Mailer is a man overwhelmed, who surrenders to the *zeitgeist*, and so becomes a contributor, but not a reliable analyst, to that special kind of dementia which seized American public life at the time.

'All is permitted' behaviour permeated much of the literature of the 1960s and 1970s. In this view the individual is an all-powerful, all-encompassing agent of self-transcendence. We live under no thrall, countenance no taboos, and acknowledge no domain outside our own resources. 'Doing your own thing' leads by logical extension to the belief that we have dominion over the conditions under which we live. Once we have sloughed off the obscurantist cloak of religious and other superstitions holding us back, we can emerge resplendent as controlling deities, remaking the world in our own image. This post-Enlightenment arrogance has over the centuries strangely eroded the human freedoms the Enlightenment itself proclaimed. In its communal strain, this engorging hubris led to the totalitarian state, which appropriated to itself all rights, achievements and controls. In a gross parody of religion, it claimed to provide people with meaning and transcendence. This was one (misguided) modernist reaction to meaninglessness and lack of coherence. It welcomed personal and public chaos, since the resulting anarchy provided fertile ground for a new dispensation.

With sensibilities attuned to the apocalyptic, people like Mailer felt let down by a society which provided none of this. Hence the need to create a heightened and frenetic situation in which they could act out their desires. Normal society, for example, produced few visible signs of oppression. The vogue word at the time 'meaningful' betrayed a yearning for events that yield plenty of meaning in a world short of these. Sensibilities attuned to great expectations found the everyday world even flatter than it really was. Something, they felt, was missing. There were no heroic challenges left to pit oneself against. Yeats lamented that the contemporary scene provided 'no second Troy' for Maud Gonne. Our kind of society doesn't provide moments of sudden insight, and it blocks off avenues of transcendence. But if a demonstration was staged, police breaking it up were a visible sign of oppression. Thus the argument that society was repressive became self-fulfilling. The normal role between reality and analysis of it was thus reversed. Analysis was imposed on reality to transform it so that reality would now live up to the protester's preconceived and unreal expectations of it. Resentment at ordinary life combined with attraction to the 'great days' of the recent past badly skewed contemporary analysis. Peace hath her victories no less renowned than war.

Mailer's *The Armies of the Night* is said to have done for prose what Robert Lowell's *Life Studies* did for poetry. Lowell, who marched with the Mailer contingent, becomes a bit player in *The Armies of the Night*. Mailer was too close and indulgent a participant in the anti-Vietnam marches to match the equanimity of judgement displayed in Lowell's poems. Lowell amalgamated his personal state with the dramatic public events unfolding around him, but in a different and more original way. He added a new dimension to our understanding of modern public life: it's not just a simple matter of getting excited by the day's news, it's the constant oscillation between quiescence and excitement which is the new norm. In poems like 'Waking Early Sunday Morning' Lowell is able to align his own manic-depressive condition with wider shifts in public opinion. It's waking time, it's early, it's Sunday, it's morning, all times when we are most relaxed, until our mood-swings kick in:

> Sing softer! But what if a new
> diminuendo brings no true
> tenderness, only restlessness,
> excess, the hunger for success,
> sanity or self-deception
> fixed and kicked by reckless caution,

while we listen to the bells –
anywhere, but somewhere else!

A low period ('diminuendo') triggers a hunger for vicarious public excitement 'anywhere but somewhere else'. Linking our mood to the public one is not a one-way street – it involves a constant, exhausting roller-coaster ride switching between lows and highs. A public figure, the US President (most likely Kennedy), moves in the opposite direction, shedding tense affairs of state by relaxing in a swimming pool:

O to break loose. All life's grandeur
is something with a girl in summer ...
elated as the President
girdled by his establishment
this Sunday morning, free to chaff
his own thoughts with his bear-cuffed staff,
swimming nude, unbuttoned, sick
of his ghost-written rhetoric!

The President privately unwinds as a counterpoint to the emotional escalation of the protesters. Two decades earlier during the second world war Lowell had himself been an agitated conscientious objector, as he famously recalled in a poem:

I was a fire-breathing Catholic C.O.,
And made my manic statement,
Telling off the state and president, and then
Sat waiting in the bull pen...

In the 1960s Lowell had declined to attend a reception for the cultural elite at President Lyndon Johnson's White House. He now participated in anti-Vietnam rallies, but from a quite different perspective from his earlier self, and from his fellow participants Norman Mailer, Dwight Macdonald, Paul Goodman and other radicals. He stood apart as an aristocratic bard, detached, dignified, revealing by his limp demeanour he was outside it all, low key, even sorrowful in looks, slyly guying himself and others, not hyping things up like Mailer. When asked to speak to a noisy packed audience who couldn't hear him clearly, he began in a slightly disdainful tone: 'I'll bellow but it won't do any good.' He didn't play up to his audience; it had to come around to his way of being. Protest was for him now a necessary but uncomfortable duty. At a demonstration next day he was described as 'tall, awkward, dishevelled, somewhat diffident, and gazing around him in what appeared to be a rather vague and absent way...He had turned a radical protest meeting into a poetry reading.' As Mailer wryly commented: 'His firmness, his distaste for the occasion, communicated some subtle but impressive sense of his superiority.' [39]

How do we explain those who bag their own country, who seek 'the satisfaction of undermining'? When the designs of utopian thinkers are thwarted, they often perform a role reversal: 'Self-hate is really the same thing as sheer egoism', as the Steppenwolf realizes. (p. 16) It was the contrary combination of negative, destructive beliefs with a passionate desire to bring about change which gave rise to radical disillusion. The economist and political philosopher Michael Polanyi outlined the contradictions peculiar to the 'adversary culture':

> A man looking at the world with complete skepticism can see no grounds for moral authority or transcendent moral obligations; there may seem to be no scope then for his moral perfectionism. Yet he can satisfy it by turning his skepticism against existing society, denouncing its morality as shoddy, artificial, hypocritical, and a mere mask for lust and exploitation. Though such a combination of his moral skepticism with his moral indignation is inconsistent, the two are in fact fused together by a joint attack on the same target...They unite the two opposites in a moral nihilism charged with moral fury. This paradoxical combination is new in history and deserves a new name; I have called it moral inversion. In public life moral inversion leads to totalitarianism.[40]

Orwell called this way of behaving 'double think'. There exists a feeling of generalized antagonism, there are plenty of targets, but no basic beliefs. Other authors came to a similar diagnosis. We are reminded of Ionesco's 'mixture of ingenuousness and ferocity' in the

---

39 These events are described Ian Hamilton *Robert Lowell: A Biography*, Faber & Faber, London, 1988, pp. 363 sqq.
40 Michael Polanyi *Personal Knowledge*, University of Chicago Press, Chicago, 1958, Ch 7, section 11

rhino herds, of Conrad's 'strange commingling of hate and desire' in *Heart of Darkness*, of Thomas Mann's 'state which excited and enervated at the same time' in *Death in Venice*, of Dostoievsky's 'apathy with intensity', and of Orwell's 'cynicism with fanaticism'. Because people no longer have fixed beliefs, this internally contradictory scorn moves easily from target to target. Orwell provided examples in *Nineteen Eighty-Four*: 'The rage one felt was an abstract, undirected emotion which could be switched from one object to another like the flame of a blow-lamp'. (p.15). Shatov diagnoses the shortcomings of any adversary culture in *The Devils*, which is based on a repugnance of one's own culture.

These 'moral inversion' ideas were transferred to the Anglosphere by the Frankfurt school of German Marxist/Freudian political philosophers, led by Max Horkheimer, Theodore Adorno and Herbert Marcuse, which moved from Munich to New York after Hitler's takeover. Beginning with a Marxist critique of capitalism, they interpreted the rise of Nazism as an intensification of capitalism's strangulation of society. As Communism's grip slipped, East Europe and the Soviet Union began facing the dispiriting experience of modernity, while the totalitarian temptations in our society, the Marcusian notion of 'friendly fascism', were said to be increasing. Life in the West was, it was argued, getting more regimented and less free, whereas with deStalinization and the 1960s thaw things were freeing up in the East, with the first green shoots of democratic behavior emerging. This was a dubious claim of political convergence between East and West. In *Miami and the Siege of Chicago* Mailer was misguided enough to comment about US dissidents: 'We can be certain that their counterparts in Eastern Europe and the Soviet were being attacked and imprisoned by all the Russian bureaucrats who look like Spiro Agnew, Dick Nixon and Hubert Humphrey'. (p. 123) Some thinkers in the East, such as Alexander Zinoviev, promulgated their own, different version of convergence theory, believing a species of 'normalized' bureaucratic totalitarianism was arising everywhere as a next stage of societal organization.

In the US the Frankfurt School highlighted the 'authoritarian personality' as a psychologically disturbed and infantilized syndrome dominant in late capitalist (that is Western) societies, which admired strong leaders and was incipiently fascist. The authoritarian personality was supposed, contrary to evidence, to exist only on the right side of politics. Marcuse claimed that United States authorities were suffocating its citizens not by overt political means, but by subliminal ones: sex, hedonism, popular culture, media, consumerism and so on, as predicted in *Brave New World.* Citizens were culturally conditioned, and worse, didn't know it, so they couldn't rebel. Their natural revolutionary instincts had been numbed and diverted by media and consumer saturation. The US was, Mailer and his ilk believed, a totalitarian society in that all was controlled by the complicity of its citizens. 'Repressive tolerance', a convenient double-think term popularized by Marcuse, dissolved the opposition between authority and dissent, making a standpoint outside 'the system' impossible. The authorities' pretense at 'tolerance' co-opted dissent, it was claimed, and was itself a tool of control. A series of paradoxes were set up on these lines. Bored housewives didn't know what they were missing; they appeared happy, which only revealed what they lacked. The capitalist authorities were too subtle to openly oppress people, who as a result developed the art of internalizing their own violence. Thus the very absence of visible violence in the West became a knockdown argument in favour of its existence.

Cultural commentators such Al Alvarez in *Under Pressure,* Connor Cruise O'Brien in *Writers and Politics,* and George Steiner in *Language and Silence*, argued that there were infringements on freedom in both Eastern and Western types of society, and therefore impediments to writers' creativity. In the East, it was argued, these were politically imposed by the authorities who took a great interest in writers, whereas Western societies let them wallow in their own isolation. Thus East European regimes ironically acknowledged the importance of literature, in contrast to the situation in the West where writers were marginalized. Such arguments perversely ended up giving some comfort to repressive rule in East Europe and Russia. They ignored the

Tarrou/Camus position in *The Plague* – always side with the victim – and used convoluted arguments to surreptitiously excuse a clampdown on literature. These arguments collapsed with the collapse of Communism in 1990.

A natural reaction after 1945 had been to identify with the victims of extreme oppression. But as the war's horrors receded into the distance, other attitudes emerged. The victor-victim distinction diminished to be replaced by a morally undiscriminating desire to undergo the experience of persecution in some surrogate form, in the belief that it was more 'real' than our own mundane lives. What was sought was the transcendence that experience provided. We can witness a movement in this direction in the later poetry of Sylvia Plath. She yearned to undergo a great experience of death and rebirth, believing she had found this by identifying herself with Jewish concentration camp inmates. She wanted to 'turn the violence against herself so as to show that she can equal the oppressors with her self-inflicted oppression', as Alvarez noted. In her poem 'Lady Lazarus' she revels in the experience of dehumanisation as much as in opposing it. This was a dubious way of applying Holocaust traumas to our own lives. It diminishes the sufferings of concentration camp victims to use them to provide an identity for us. The ultimate indignity to the victims, which involves a terrible inversion of priorities, is that their sufferings should be used to bolster *us* up. It does not redeem them; it demeans them by reducing them to the level of our 'identity' crises. It takes away the meaning of their fate.

9

COMING OUT GRADUALLY

Modernity arose early in the 20th century, around the time of the first world war. The Russian Revolution took place at the same time. Totalitarian regimes ushered in the uncertainties of our times while at the same time claiming to have a solution to them. They postponed the plunge into modernity by offering old fashioned meaning and transcendence. The dissident's desire to be spiritually free had not taken hold. People in the East were now being lowered into the dissonances caused by modernity after many decades in a state of suspended animation. The normal problems of modernity – weak beliefs, no coherence, isolated individualism, self-obsession, no means of transcendence – were now upon them. A pattern had set in: at each stage the Communist rulers, after a short period of liberalization, withdrew reforms which looked like toppling over into freedom. In the Soviet Union and its East European satellites crises occurred about every dozen or so years: 1956 (Hungary, 1968 (Czechoslovakia), 1980 (Poland) and 1990 (all). Khrushchev's 1956 de-Stalinization speech was a limited loosening of the reins, but this liberalization in turn led to the Hungarian uprising and its brutal suppression by the Soviet army. The curtain had been lowered again, but certain new developments had occurred. A whole people had risen against imposed repression, with the Soviet invasion revealing the overlords could not subdue a people by propaganda means alone. The Soviet regime had exposed its illegitimacy.

The next, more radical break-out, occurred in Czechoslovakia in the later 1960s. Writers, thinkers, artists and worker activists led the revolution in the Czechoslovak lands. A reform government under Dubcek came to power in 1968. Quite free in attitude, its atmosphere broke the old mould; humour, satire and ridicule were now effectively employed by the literary contingent and others to discredit those in power. For the first time authors were acting not just as writers but as leaders of a burgeoning counter-government. Dubcek and his confreres' moderate ideas were too radical for the Soviet leaders, so after some months of hesitant negotiation the Soviets invaded again. The rebel's leader, the playwright Václav Havel, and others of his ilk were eventually imprisoned. The split between rulers and ruled was getting wider with every change. Each time a swing occurred the new status quo looked less convincing. Credibility was being eroded.

From the 1960s onwards a new spirit of freedom was abroad in east and west, symbolized by the youthful, cool President Kennedy in contrast with the badly dressed, old fashioned Soviet leader Khrushchev with his past track record of brutal behaviour. This efflorescence in the west was admired in the east, with many there yearning for a less uptight, more liberated style of life. In this vacuum, groups of writers and thinkers, no longer trapped like the wary dissidents of the past, threw off the shackles by ignoring their overlords. They decided to chance their arm in public. By ceasing to act as a recognized opposition they changed the rules of the game. Let the regime flounder in its own slough, keep away from it, do your own thing. They gradually developed, as much by trial and error as by a preconceived plan, a new strategy: by acting independently they would surreptitiously bring into being a new type of society in the bosom of the old. Literature had come into its own, playing a leading role not just in describing the regime's failures but in eroding it from within.

Václav Havel's literary works were satires on bureaucratic inertia, a prelude to his political activities. In his play *The Garden Party* (1963) a group of public servants incongruously arrange a garden party to help the bureaucratic Liquidation Office carry out its unappetizing work. The dutiful Hugo Pludek succeeds in this work whereas his brother Peter is sidelined as a 'bourgeois intellectual', but the action of the play reveals it is Hugo who displays true bourgeois tendencies. (Jean and Berenger have similar roles in *Rhinoceros*.) The Liquidation Office wages paper warfare with another outfit, the Inauguration Service. Finally, to end this pointless squabble the authorities establish a new higher layer of organization, a Central Commission for Inauguration and Liquidation, containing within itself two mutually exclusive goals. During the play nothing happens but office talk; there is no action to progress the aims of the organizations. There is inertia, the appearance of change while running on the spot.

Havel's play *The Memorandum* (1966) also satirizes rampant bureaucratic power games. The action centers on a public service unit given the task of introducing a new language (like Orwell's Newspeak), supposed to be rational, scientific and precise, a language without nuances. But in practice it is hopelessly complex and difficult, in other words an artificial project which ends up as the opposite of its original intention. One staff member makes a double-think claim: 'It is a paradox, but it is precisely the surface inhumanity of an artificial language which guarantees its truly humanist function!' (p. 45) This is Catch-22 type obfuscation. The new language, meaninglessly detached from reality, functions mainly as a control device. Gross, the well-meaning Managing Director of the unit, is treated with disdain by his apparatchik staff, who are on the make; this amounts to an inverted power structure. At the same time other staff are more interested in food, smoking and flirting than work. Gross, like Ionesco's Berenger, is worried and unsure of himself; he confesses his inadequacy and guilt in a 'show trial' confession, and is demoted to a minor position. Then in a further role reversal the new introduced language is itself purged in a similar 'show trial' demolition. As with the regime's propaganda in *Nineteen Eighty-Four*, yesterday's messaging is the opposite of today's. What really matters is who is controlling the shots, not the validity of the enterprize nor the content of its utterances. As everything is fluid, there exists no firm basis on which to make judgments. It's a vicious circle, with apparent change but no real change, with another artificial language introduced overnight.

Those who had won out by vilifying the first new language are now themselves vilified. In this crazy merry-go-round everyone alternates between dominant and loser roles. All are eventually destabilized by powerful unseen bureaucrats who use these language games to consolidate their power. The inherent unreality Communism makes these games worse. Havel's later *Three Vanek Plays* are dialogues between a mild, dispassionate Havel-like figure, Vanek, and an interlocutor who is self-satisfied with his supposedly independent stance, but who unwittingly reveals through his garrulous dialogue how compromised he really is. In order to survive and thrive he has developed an ability to keep in his mind contrary attitudes at the same time. He illustrates Havel's insight that such people are 'both the victims of the system and its instruments'.

In his ground-breaking essay 'The Power of the Powerless' (1978) Havel explained how a vice-like lock had been imposed on society, and how it could be broken. In the past regimes imposed themselves by force; now *petit mal* or post-totalitarian societies internalized complicity by using ideology as a bridge between rulers and ruled: 'this line of conflict [between normal life and the system] runs *de facto* through each person, for everyone in his or her own way is both a victim and a supporter of the system'. Havel showed how ideology creates 'a world of appearances, a mere ritual, a formalized language deprived of semantic content with reality', and transforms it into 'a system of ritual signs that replace reality with pseudo-reality'. To counter this citizens should set up, Havel recommended, small scale communities on their own initiative, which become parallel structures: "pre-political' events and processes provide the living humus from which genuine political change usually springs'.[41] In others words, Burke's 'small platoons'. Ordinary people should decide not to play the party's game. Instead they should set up social organizations outside its orbit, but inside society's orbit, by utilizing the 'power of the powerless'. Such activity was not just opposition or dissent, but a positive initiative. It builds an alternative culture in the bowels of society. The growth of these networks enabled Havel to eventually become President of his

---

41 Václav Havel *Living in Truth*, Faber and Faber, London, 1987, pp. 53, 47 & 68.

country.

The emerging civil society became an alternative form firstly of community, then of society and later of government. Private life was re-established – liveliness, spontaneity and multi-faceted activities flourished; over time real authority accrued to these activities. When this became evident to all, the regime atrophied. This activity was a true rebuttal of the cry for *politique d'abord*, politics first, which plays into the hands of those who wish to wield total power. In Poland Solidarity, aka the Polish people, gradually recreated a true public sphere on an even larger scale. The Gdansk trade union leader Lech Walesa, with Solidarity backing him, eventually became, like Havel in Czechoslovakia, President of his country. Writers and thinkers, sensitive to the currents bubbling away beneath the surface, were natural leaders in guiding these new moves.[42]

In line with these currents the Czech novelist Milan Kundera introduced in his writing a more relaxed modernist mood, with a potent mix of Eastern and Western attitudes, and of politics and sex. Kundera was alive to new ways in which public and private activities were linked. In his novel *The Book of Laughter and Forgetting* (1979) he noted:

> In times when history moved slowly, events were few and far between and easily committed to memory. They formed a commonly accepted *backdrop* for thrilling scenes of adventure in private life. Nowadays, history moves at a brisk clip…No longer a backdrop, it is now the *adventure* itself, an adventure enacted before the backdrop of the commonly accepted banality of private life. (pp. 7-8)

The relationship between public and private life, and between politics and love, had been upended. Public life now took centre stage; people now saw their own personal dramas enlarged and given meaning by being enacted in the public arena. The constantly changing views of politicians reflected their own fluid personalities. People were

---

42 One the best accounts of this process is Jeffrey Goldfarb's *Beyond Glasnost: The Post-Totalitarian Mind*, University of Chicago Press, Chicago, 1989.

unfaithful to each other in the same way as regimes easily shrugged off past allegiances. Kundera recalled how in 1948 the Czech Communist leader Clementis was airbrushed out of a photo of him appearing with the Czech leader Gottwald, after Clementis was unfairly charged with treason and hanged, just as we suppress uncomfortable incidents from our own past. Life is a 'struggle of memory against forgetting' (p. 3).

We oscillate, in Kundera's view, between over-immersion in utopian hopes and over-immersion in despair: 'If there is too much uncontested meaning on earth (the reign of the angels), man collapses under the burden; if the world loses all its meaning (the reign of the demons), life is every bit as impossible.' (p. 61). Communism was an example of 'too much uncontested meaning', a 'world losing all its meaning.' Both produced unsatisfactory outcomes. In combination these extremes led to a feeling of *litost*, an undefined and unbearable longing, 'a state of torment caused by a sudden insight into one's own miserable self' (p. 122). This is a basic emotional condition of contemporary life, Kundera believed, even more starkly revealed when an artificial imposition, like Communism, is removed. The modern existentialist dilemma is that there are no overarching answers, one has to survive, not just a regime, but the lonely, often brutal world of personal relationships, where hedonism is all, and where sex can kill love as much as it can promote it.

Kundera was forced to move from the east (Prague) to the west (Paris) in 1975; as a result his later novels compare life under both aspects. As an author he was now in the territory of Bellow, Roth and Updike as much as that of his previous colleagues. In Kundera's novels no stable world nor stable personality structure exists; both are fleeting and incomplete. We are given only slices of characters and incidents; plot and narrative are disconnected, life does not have continuity: 'Prague in his [Kafka's] novels is a city without memory. It has even forgotten its name.' (p. 157) In both west and east authors write stream of consciousness works, Kundera explains, because today we live primarily inside our own heads: 'Ever since Joyce we have been aware of the fact that the greatest adventure in our lives is the absence of adventure. Homer's *Odyssey* now take place within man'. (p. 90) Authorship, the act of revealing this, can come to take the place of life.

The Unbearable Lightness of Being (1984) is a novel of East-West comparison, published after Kundera moved to France. The book mixes detached philosophical musing with lightly sketched characters, each approach throwing light on the other. It employs detachment and objectivity: the author describes his characters in the third person, as though they are marionettes under his control or at least under his playful observation, a little like Mailer describing himself in the third person in *The Armies of the Night*. This makes it a novel of full blown modernism, an aspect represented by the character Tomas who, somewhat like Kundera himself, is emerging out of the earlier, more restricted, type of society in the east, which is represented by the character Tereza. Public and private life are contrasted. The personal and the modern are now dominant; political aspects and the past are less evident than in *The Book of Laughter and Forgetting*. It is still a world of paradoxical opposites: political betrayal is still linked to betrayal in private power games. (p. 87). These opposites can't be put together and reconciled, which renders modern life absurd and uncomfortable.

In Kundera's world lightness is the momentary feeling of sexual release and transcendence common in bohemian life in the West, immediately pleasurable but not deeply satisfying. Heaviness, such as the anxiety caused by public events in the east like the Russian invasion of Czechoslovakia, is deeper, but is also soul destroying since it drags you down. It is a life lived too densely, with no space or privacy. We need lightness, release and individuality, qualities the west provides, but which are also unsatisfying in the long run, the modernist weakness. Heaviness and lightness are each required to balance the other, the libertine Don Juan to balance the forlorn lover Tristan, the remoteness of *vanitas vanitatum* to balance the immediacy of *carpe diem*. In older, stable anachronistic societies everything repeated itself as an eternal return, whereas today events and personalities tend to be transitory one-offs: 'The individual 'I' is what differs from the common stock'. (p. 199)

In the decades of the 1970s and 1980s Czech writers and thinkers had been breaking new ground and gaining confidence. The Poles took things a stage further by linking the reforming movement of writers more closely with workers' organizations. This new combination led to the formation of the Solidarity movement, a trade union morphing over time into a civil society. The whole Polish nation was now involved, not just the elites. The previous split between ordinary people (the *pays réal*) and the political class (the *pays légal*) was being overcome. Civil society grew from below, led by leaders such as Adam Michnic (a thinker) and Lech Walesa (a unionist) in coalition. The proles were an essential ingredient. Polish society was in the process of being socially reconstituted by Solidarity as a prelude to its political re-birth.

In the absence of any overall belief system, where could a new consciousness and selftranscendence come from, and how could these overcome social isolation? Tadeusz Konwicki asked these questions in his novels *A Minor Apocalypse* (1979) and *The Polish Complex* (1982). The protagonist seeks a moment of instant transcendence, an epiphany, to illuminate his drab life. At the start he considers immolating himself (like Jan Palach in Czechoslovakia) as an act of incendiary defiance of the regime; he then reflects on the precise significance of his intended act. Will this be just an individual's act, or how can it be made a symbol to galvanise an indifferent nation? Will it be an artificial apocalypse like the false brouhaha of official celebrations (Russian-Polish unity ceremonies occur throughout the novel) which lift nobody? Is it just an escape from boredom and routine? How can it be a circuitbreaker and not just another contribution to self-immolation on the same level as alcohol-induced hallucinations, and the oscillation between reality and fantasy that induces subservience? Will it be just another form of death, adding to the ever present inhumanity of Communist and modern day society?

The opposition party in Poland, the protagonist believes, has become stale, careworn, like the ruling party: 'You are just a shadow cabinet of the crew in power.' (p. 139) The dissidents are compromised, enslaving themselves by in-fighting. People want to breakout from their isolation: 'Someone had to break this lethargy. To wake the sleepers with a wild cry' (p. 220), like Zamyatin's 'wild simian echo'. People desire to become genuine citizens again. Everyone is looking for a minor personal apocalypse. In his novels Konwicki lays down conditions for a successful change of the political system: the movement must be spontaneous (not politically organized), communal (not just individual dissidents) and national. Konwicki believes any such action must be linked to the nation's subconscious understanding of its history, and that it must be voluntary and instinctive, in contrast to a society where everything was blunted by endless premeditation. These conditions were potentially fulfilled in the realm of fiction with Orwell's proles in *Nineteen Eighty-Four*, and in actuality with Solidarity in Poland.

Konwicki's pre-conditions were created in Poland by the coming together of two groups who were outside the regime's power vertical. It was a bottom-up coalition of uncompromising thinkers and industrial workers, a mirror opposite of Lenin's top-down revolution of 1917. Each group needed the other. The thinkers mapped out a route to cultural change, and the workers carried it out. The first, pre-political task was to build up communal networks, which could then expand to fill the vacant public space. In Poland civic structures themselves had for some time taken on a new fearless, open position. The word 'dissident' is not a good description of these activities, implying as it does a negative disposition, like the West's adversary culture. Those who were re-building the middle realms of society were creating new oases of cultural freedom. The next move was for the whole society to act in the way these groups had; this happened first in Poland when the Solidarity movement became the basis of the new non-Communist Polish government. Konwicki's prophecy was being fulfilled.

Acting through Solidarity, the Polish people expressed themselves in the 1980s in an act of national transcendence. The Polish novelist and journalist Kazimierz Brandys captured this development in his *A Warsaw Diary 1978-1981* (1984). Brandys traced the origins of this resurgence by showing how it arose as a pre-political force, replacing pessimism with optimism. Brandy was lifted out of depressingly reflecting on his own and his nation's somnolence by a sudden change of mood in the late 1970s. After three decades the captive mind disappeared. Limbs long since atrophied felt the pulse of life in their veins; the dross and trivia of the past fell away. These were great days, as Brandys and his wife Maria noticed around Warsaw:

> Three days later, at the end of Krolewska Street, as I recall, M. and I both suddenly cried out in wonder. The streets surging with life, loose, swarming crowds, a certain nonchalant undulation to their movements, free in all directions. A great city, splendid, alive... My spirits are better here. Absolutely and totally contiguous with reality. After seven months, I'm back in my own boots again. But it didn't happen in a day...These are the same crowds about which six years ago I wrote that they lacked faith, for they were under the sway of material desire and indifferent to the ideas of freedom and justice. Everything is so unexpected and arresting. 'A worker with a crucifix,' said M. 'It's not what I had dreamed about, I who am an intellectual and practice no religion. (pp. 204-5)

Through an unorganised, almost subconscious upsurge of the people, the nation was able to express itself as a more than physical entity. This was the dream of Russian nationalists like Dostoievsky last century. Brandys' passage on the role of the miracle in the often defeated Polish nation ends:

> The Baroque and Romantic predilection for the miraculous has been encoded into Polish thinking about life and literature. It grows darker, then dawns again; it is oppressive, then radiant again. We feel its tickle on our heels, that breathtaking possibility of leaping beyond ourselves. (pp. 26-7)

The closest equivalent to the Polish events which comes to mind is George Orwell's time in Barcelona during the Spanish Civil War, recounted in *Homage to Catalonia*. Orwell was enormously lifted in spirits to find in Catalonia a gregarious populace, and a genuine workers' revolution uncontaminated by ideological elements. It was an 'emotionally widening experience' for him. Similarly for Brandys, but even more so as it was happening in his own country. The glorious memory of these moments could never be dimmed, even when both were indirectly crushed by Moscow. Orwell ended his Spanish account with the reflection: 'Curiously enough the whole experience has left me with not less but more belief in the decency of human beings'.[43]

A Warsaw Diary speaks with a voice recognisable in the best recent literature. The author is not intent on criticising others to justify himself. He scrutinises his own enlightened position and finds it inadequate. We come across something of this tone in Camus *The Myth of Sisyphus*. Calm, unideological and unillusioned, the author tries to put together from basic materials a world which exhibits no ready coherence. He crawls painfully towards meaning, yet is enormously steadfast in his provisional beliefs. There is no attempt to artificially heighten tension by imposing meaning on things. The sages of Victorian times offered to interpret the whole world. Brandys acknowledges no overarching truths and is reduced to the smallest details:

> I am no longer actually writing, only taking notes. In this siege-like situation it is beyond me to tackle any large theme. It's cold in the apartment. M. has more and more difficulty obtaining food. Six-hour lines. Some start forming at five o'clock in the morning'. (p. 233)

And so on. Prose is invested with the clarity one finds in the literature of extreme situations. Personal (and national) survival is at stake, and in this elemental state one hangs on to very basic things:

> Those days when you wake up without a glimmer of hope are painful days. You have to tough your way through them, control them somehow with words or actions. What gives people hope in Poland today? Or, to put it more modestly, what arouses their interest? Timeless human affairs, of course, like love for a woman, raising

---

43 George Orwell *Homage To Catalonia*, Penguin, Harmondsworth, 1962, p. 220.

children, and, let's say, the results of work, study, and so forth. What else? After that, the view flattens out. (p. 50)

During his time in a Russian labour camp Andrei Sinyavsky collected, in *A Voice From the Chorus*, the sayings and anecdotes of other prisoners, and put them together with his own reflections, and with passages from books which he had memorised, an anthology of the teeming life around and within him. Daily life for Brandys consists of meals and shopping with his wife, reading and talking, meeting at clubs, absorbing the day's news, and noting the mood of the streets in his diary. Brandys realises in relation to his own novel writing:

> I was constructing stories that seemed increasingly further from my experience, and finally the time came to wonder whether the story that was happening all around me was not more interesting than my own fictions. (p. 150)

Brandys finds that living and assimilating each day becomes his true occupation, and the subject matter of his writing: 'The events of the day become one's inner life.' (p. 216) Kundera and Lowell also realized that assimilating public events into the pattern of everyday life presents itself as subject matter for authors, and their greatest task and adventure.

Brandys had the inestimable good fortune of being part of a vibrant folk society, something which many thinkers have yearned for. He is released from the isolation caused by 'man's closing in egotistically on himself, death limited to the solitary, self-regarding ego', he overcomes his lassitude by being caught up in a wider exhilaration which breaks down the boundaries of the self. Totalitarianism destroys public and private life; both have to be reconstituted. This happened for the first time on a nationwide scale in Poland. Instinctive feelings need a structure to give them expression, which was provided by Solidarity, which soon became the new Polish government.

Poland had been a victim nation, dismembered in the later 18th century by Russian, German and Austrian territorial encroachments.

Two Polish revolts against its Russian overlords in the 19th century were unsuccessful. The country was overrun by Nazi and Communist militias in 1939; in 1940 Soviet hit squads massacred in the Katyn forest 20,000 of the Polish officer corps, the cream of the nation's governing class, deliberately rendering the nation leaderless. An elite group in one country, Russia, knocked out its counterpart in another, then Communism was imposed. In the 1980s this most victimized country became, not coincidentally, the first to throw off the totalitarian yoke from within. Poland had developed a new leadership group during the Communist decades. Two members of the Polish proletariat, Wojtyla (later known as Pope John Paul II) and Walesa, previously unknown to the wider world, mobilized church and state to restore the national community. Two Western authors who helped bring knowledge of Eastern and Russian writers to wider audiences were Philip Roth and Al Alvarez, who respectively edited the Penguin series 'Writers From The Other Europe' and 'Modern European Poets'. Roth and the English thinker Sir Roger Scruton set up below-the-radar structures to help writers and thinkers in Eastern Europe.

Countries further east had not developed to the stage of such a clean break. Drawbacks in traditional societies which have not embraced modernity are highlighted in the writings of the Nobel Prize winning Romanian novelist Herta Müller. She was a dissident who left for Germany in 1985 just before the Ceauşescu Communist regime collapsed. Her novel *The Land of Green Plums*, published in 1993, alludes to Ceauşescu in describing why she left Romania: 'If only the right person would have to leave, everyone else would be able to stay in the country.' (p. 60) Her family were double outsiders in Romania, originally Banat Germans as well as dissidents. By the 1980s the Stalinist cult of personality in Romania was worse than in the USSR, who by that stage had lacklustre leaders.

The novel's female narrator is friends with Lola and Tereza (the latter turns out to be an informer), and the young men Edgar, Kurt and Georg. These people live uncomfortably in crowded rooms in segregated communal huts in large cities. Theirs is a streetscape of bleak squares with dead rustling leaves, cold winds, and dilapidated buildings. Random sexual 'one-night-stands' occur. People huddle inside themselves, atomized by the lack of normal social interaction. Society provides no natural extended communities beyond the young people's own limited circle. Every activity is contaminated by the Party: children yearn to grow up as policemen or guards, the only cushy jobs available, but in reality work in factories or animal slaughter houses. Lola, a party loyalist depressed by her sexual encounters, suicides. After her death she is formally expelled from the party at a show trial enacted by higher party authorities, drummed out *pour décourager les autres*. Many of the older generation live in villages in the provinces, poor, repressed, with bad memories of war, including the Nazi takeover, but with a residual companionship. Life there is not as artificial as in the cities, as some residues of pre-Communist society remain.

Müller's novel reveals a nation deformed by a repressive regime. Society doesn't naturally congeal; there exists an eerie separation between personal experience and mainstream life. Disconnection and silences dominate, as characters look on life objectively as though from outside. A sequence of meaningless routines ensues. Characters emit staccato sentences, since their thoughts keep breaking off, mimicking life. The narrator is a translator who understands words have lost their moorings: 'This word [love] isn't honest even with itself.' (p. 153) Talk has become an inadequate substitute for activity, with speech itself having lost its punch, being used to obscure rather than define. In *The Land of Green Plums* there is anxiety but no relaxation. People even walk apart from each other: 'We still knew how to walk slowly or quickly, we could still sneak or pursue. But strolling was something we had forgotten how to do'. (p. 77) The characters act furtively, hiding letters, and using codes. People have private lives and work lives, but there is little in between, and no bond between citizens, except constant fear generated by widespread police investigations. The awful atmosphere acts as a solvent: 'the ticking of the clock was breaking her into small pieces.' (p. 98) The novel is itself broken up into short sections which don't coalesce. Everything, including nature, is desiccated, and running out of energy: 'No cities can grow in a dictatorship, because everything stays small when it is being watched'. (p. 44) The three men lose their jobs, become parasites and illegals in the regime's eyes, and apply to leave the country. The main characters are forced to be Beckettian figures intent on survival, with a minimal existence, and with no luxuries, demands nor satisfied longings. Confined to their own bubble, life amounts to mere existence. But in contrast the narrator's tone is lively not bleak, a coping intelligence, curious, noting everything. It goes back to basics, rebuilding a world from scratch, like the *Stunde Null* writers of East Germany. The overall effect is not depressing: in Müller's novel motifs are repeated and eventually joined up, producing a quilt-like effect. A limited form of private world grows up in the absence of normal society.

In the 1980s the Soviets were too lacking in self-belief to invade Poland. In their terminal stages Communist regimes were run by the deep state military bosses, police and the security organs, the only structures still functioning, a sign of terminal bankruptcy. When things came to a head, the regime's structure quickly disintegrated, having the rigidity not of firm control but of death. This appeared to happen quickly in 1990, but the necessary groundwork had been proceeding unseen for decades. Andrei Sinyavsky had advised in 1989: 'Just blow on the whole structure and it will fall down.'[44] The Soviet regime had lost confidence in itself. Every attempt at liberalization had failed. Liberalization had previously taken place only within strict limits – a threshold was soon reached beyond which it could not go. Further freedoms meant it would topple over into democracy, with alternative political parties and a network of communal groups. The Communist system worked continually to drag itself back from that precipice. But in Poland in 1989 for the first time, a liberalized system did topple over into freedom, and the game was up. It happened in the Soviet Union only two years later. The regimes looked strong externally, but within the dead carapace of the old order, an embryonic lively civic culture was thriving underneath.

Since George Orwell published *Nineteen Eighty-Four*, the novel

---
44 *Time* 10 April, 1989

has been widely acclaimed but one thing puzzled its readers. Why did Orwell say, 'If there is hope, it lay in the proles'? This seemed a weakness in the book; it looked a long shot that demoralised, unorganised ordinary citizens, outside the power hierarchy, would eventually triumph over it. Change would more likely come from disgruntled thinkers and apparatchiks within the *nomeklatura*. Yet Solidarity in Poland was made up of proles, ordinary Polish people united for communal ends. A totalitarian regime might try to renew itself if a coalition of regime middle managers and liberals took over as reformists, the Gorbachev model, but this proved not to be viable. In the late 1980s the Gorbachevites were swept along by events swirling out of their control. The leaders successively installed during the crisis – Kardar, Husak, Jaruselski, then Gorbachev himself – believed in working within the system to rationalize and improve it as much as possible, so that Communism would work more effectively. They failed in their own eyes.

Yeltsin swept away the old ramshackle edifice with refreshing confidence. In the sombre wasteland of Soviet officialdom he cut through with his exuberant public persona, in contrast with the line of grey Soviet bureaucrats in the Brezhnev, Andropov and Chernomyrdin mould. Other Orwell predictions, such as inefficiency leading to a revolt by the masses, and the regime losing self-confidence and the will to govern, came to pass. Solidarity proved Orwell's predictions true. The proles awoke to their historic destiny. Russian and East European writers and thinkers like Solzhenitsyn, Havel, Konwicki, Walesa, Müller and their ilk, much more than Gorbachev, brought down the Soviet regime. Solzhenitsyn worked on the principle that 'one cannot accept that the disastrous course of history is impossible to undo, that a soul with confidence in itself cannot influence the most powerful force in the world'. There was a clean break – it wasn't endless and unchangeable. 'The cunningly wrought chain' of unfreedom was broken, thus undermining the totalitarianism structure from below.

The Byelorussia author Svetlana Alexievich, like Herta Müller, won a Nobel Prize for literature. Herta Müller wrote novels based on imaginatively reconstructing her Romanian life. Alexievich's *Secondhand Time* (2013) consists of interview material carefully shaped as a novelist would. In contrast to East Europe after 1990, there existed in Russia no free civil society, few bonds except private ones, and few natural links to wider social organizations. Alexievich's book shows people reduced to a basic, atomized state, still not truly citizens. Life is experienced at a distance, at secondhand, with suffering not happiness foremost. Russia's lost great past has become a binding source of sorrow: 'We are neighbours in memory.' (p. 5). The present is always transitional, there's no real permanent life, everything is fluid and unstable, with little hope for a better future. Political transitions have not improved things: 'They were afraid of change because every time there had been a change, the people had always got screwed.' (p. 109) As a result people are trapped in misery in every period, as one of Alexievich's informants reveals: 'I don't know any happy people other than my three-month-old daughter.' (p. 381) 'Our language is the language of suffering.' (p. 31) The women stick it out better, as they are more resilient, more family oriented, and form some rudimentary social networks. The men are feckless and unstable; one women recalls: 'I am filled with horror when I consider how hard you have to work to keep someone in your life'. (p. 346)

Some of those interviewed in *Secondhand Time* romanticize the Stalin period where most succumbed to its ethos and were minimally provided for, but others wryly send up its propaganda: 'We used to live in a great country where we stood in line for toilet paper'. (p. 36). The state was so dominant it 'blocked out everything, even their own lives'. (p. 4) Sovoks (true believers) couldn't adjust when Communism disappeared: "Born in the USSR' is a diagnosis…you're branded for life'. (p. 338). Many despised Gorbachev for destroying the Soviet Union. In the 1990s kitchen talk dominated: 'our nocturnal life had nothing in common with how we lived during the day.' (p. 59) Books replaced life for many people during the Gorbachev and Yeltin periods: 'The country turned into a debating society.' (p. 60) One person comments: 'Russian life is supposed to be evil and base, that's what elevates the soul…The cruder and bloodier life is, the more space there is for the soul'. (p. 332) This is the yearning for the great Russian soul, the fallacy (indulged by unbridled modernists like Mailer) that going down into the depths brings liberation. Instead the smart move was to get real, drop the books and imagined past greatness. A young girl says to her mother: 'Mama, put your soul away'. Instead they try to understand real life economics, including market forces, and the importance of producing and selling, not just consuming, activities downplayed during the Soviet period: 'Too much about our lives has changed, and these weren't things you could read about in books. Russian novelists don't teach you how to become successful.' (p. 29) 'The market became our university.' (p. 159). But on the other hand they come to despise the Yeltsin years in the 1990s for bringing in sybaritic capitalism: gold bathtaps, salami, the new rich with Versace and Adani clothes, holidays in Cyprus and homes in Florida.

An optimistic view of history leads to Fukayama's 'End of History' idea: all nations converge to a democratic model. A pessimistic view is that the destruction virus continues, the black hole yawns wider. Douglas Murray's *The Strange Death of Europe* documents the tiredness of a Europe weary of the burden of history pressing on it from which it cannot escape. A whole continent is suffering burnout, with dwindling cultural capital, threatened by mass immigration from poorer societies, with all these factors together dragging it under. As in the scenarios described by Müller and Alexievich vital human well springs dry up – there are few inputs cushions and connections. A whole society can wither, a very unusual phenomenon.

In *The Dean's December* (1994) Saul Bellow describes the US and Eastern Europe converging from opposite directions, the former from chaos, the latter from restrictive ideological maladies. A deeper problem caused by these bouleversements emerges. Kundera wrote in *The Book of Laughter and Forgetting*: 'None of us knows what will be. One thing, however, is certain. In moments of clairvoyance the Czech nation can glimpse its own death at close range. Not as an accomplished fact, not as the inevitable future, but as a perfectly concrete possibility. Its death is at its side.' (p.159) Brandys caught a whiff of this in Poland. As 1980 passed into 1981, the Russians threatened, shortages became endemic and suppression reappeared. Things began to close in. The force that moved a whole people was, Dostoievsky wrote, 'the spirit of life, as the Scripture says, 'rivers of living water', the running dry of which is threatened in Revelation'. This running dry portends a new connection between the personal and the communal, as Brandys noted:

> Every grownup must come to terms with the prospect that he will cease to be. Now however for the first time I see a new kind of phenomenon – society fearing the end of its own life as a society. For some time now, nightmares have been troubling society's unconscious. Everyone is afraid, afraid to think about the void that threatens them. For the first time in my life I feel a fear that is more than personal, fear on a national scale. Yesterday the government announced that it was withdrawing a few dozen trains from service and that production has declined as much as fifty per cent in certain branches of the industry. After this bulletin, there was a deadly silence in the television room. You could feel the fear in the air – fear of collective death.[45]

In Brandys' view Central Europe preserves a truly European culture which is threatened with desiccation from both East and West. From the east the Russians apply 'that grinding down of small souls, that degrading burlesque of despair'. (p. 47) This is a pressure that Brandys believes the West will not resist. In a much-quoted passage he writes:

> It is not only Poland that the eastern empire seems to be ingesting into its monstrously distended belly. All Western Europe seems diminished by it, as if shrinking in fear. If you listen and read carefully, you can hear the West's faint-hearted recognition of its own biological weakness; they know their fatigue, the exhaustion of an old race that has to preserve carefully what strength it has. They don't want to perish. They see no values in the world worth dedicating their lives to…Today the West is emitting cries of horror; the intellectuals are grumbling; the consciousness of impotence is everywhere. They know already and are preparing themselves to be raped. All that matters now is that that rape not be a sexual mur-

---

45   Kazimierz Brandys *A Warsaw Diary 1978-1981*, p. 224.

der but that it happens calmly, in some comfortable French bed.⁴⁶

When the totalitarian system collapsed in Germany in 1945 and in the Soviet Union in 1990, there were significant differences. After some time Germany taught its children the truth about the past, and did not allow Holocaust deniers a guernsey. In contrast Russia remains in denial, it has had no lustration, no openness, no coming to terms frankly with its past. The Russian government has decommissioned its Memorial group, and attempted to extinguish historical memory of past outrages. As a result it teaches its children a false version of the Stalin and war periods. To let those who misbehaved off scot free, as happens in Russia, is a form of collective amnesia, and an evading of justice.

In this situation long-existing webs of complicity cannot easily be untangled. No breakout has been possible in Russia, as it has in East Europe. More likely is a continuation of the old war of all against all, a bleak, basic struggle, as the work of Alexievich reveals. When the party and state crumbled in Russia, authors showed us not a civic society underneath, as in Poland, but an implosion, with many of the old tensions, envies and anxieties given new rein under new auspices. The Russian sociologist Lev Gudkov began to use the word 'totalitarianism' again. Not just individuals but whole sections of society become unable to cope with great prolonged trauma: 'psychic numbing... emotional shutdown...endless return to loss...lifelong immersion in death' are some of the terms used by contemporary Russian psychiatrists.⁴⁷ This feeling can be passed on from generation to generation so that a whole society becomes depressed. In this way some strains of the totalitarian virus may survive the demise of Communism, Bolshevik-like behaviour without Bolshevism itself, as Adam Michnik has described it.

It's no accident that Russia is now run by a KGB operative, Vladi-

---

46   Ibid, p. 166.
47   See Gessen, Masha *The Future Is History: How Totalitarianism Reclaimed Russia*, Granta, London, 2017.

mir Putin. An intelligence service can for a time prop up a regime from behind the scenes. Secret policemen like Putin can never be open with their own people. Any government has two basic functions: to keep its country secure, and to promote economic advancement. Russia now has precisely the wrong mix: ex-spooks like Putin and his KGB entourage put too high a value on security, though their country is not under external threat, to the detriment of economic prosperity and freedom. Putin acts more as a successor regime to the Soviet Union and Stalin than as a clean break from it, as Svetlana Alexievich's book reveals. He has adapted the mindset of his original KGB/Communist background, incorporating a 'managed democracy', post-modernist rhetoric and cyber disinformation into his battery of control devices. There is the facsimile appearance of a proper society, with a veneer of elections and free press, but no independent groups are allowed, while corrupt elites and oligarchs flourish,

As concert-master, Putin, is not unique: he belongs to a recognizable group of post-war dictators (Peron, Nasser, Idi Amin, Castro, Ceauşescu, Sukarno, Lukashenko, Chavez and so on). They are authoritarians who exhibit an incongruous mixture of up-to-date tactics and atavistic drives. They can't be defined as left or right, as they have replaced discredited Fascism and Communism with confected nationalism, while retaining the trappings of those ideologies, such as the cult of personality. Destructive of their own economies, they embark on external adventures to divert attention from failures at home, and end up destroying their own side as much as their opponents. There is something faintly ridiculous about the cavortings of these rhinoceroses, a feature Charlie Chaplin caught so accurately in his classic film 'The Great Dictator'. They are tin-pot totalitarians, hard to take seriously as personalities, self-inflating egos in whom insolence replaces substance, cardboard cut-outs of the real thing. But Putin differs from the others because he commands a world power, which gives him immensely more leverage.

10

THE AMERICAN PUSHBACK

Two contrasting critiques of society dominated the second half of the twentieth century in the US. The old US establishment, symbolized by President Eisenhower, had ruled in the United States in the 1950s, but beginning with the swinging sixties a new radical movement with a contrary agenda had arisen. United States society seemed about to explode: the assassinations of the Kennedys and Martin Luther King, the Newark and Watts race riots, student invasions, anti-Vietnam protests, teach-ins, the great march on Washington, the Kent State killings, Black panthers, Cold War tensions, Watergate and so on. The United States seemed to be in a proto-revolutionary situation. One form of civil chaos reached its apogee at the 1968 Democratic convention in Chicago. After its long march through the universities, media, politics and the public service, a new, politically acceptable amalgam of the new class and the radicals began to reach the commanding heights of society, wielding great institutional power.

Radical commentators were happy to predict our societies were developing signs of repressive tendencies, or were even going fascist or totalitarian. Mass society, propaganda saturation, censorship, the military-industrial complex, curtailment of civil liberties, racism, the air-conditioned nightmare of modern living spaces, lack of freedom, repressive tolerance, and so on, were, it was claimed, endemic. The 'system' in our societies was considered unbreakable. Adventures abroad like the Vietnam War were the international face of this curtailment of freedoms. Reagan, Nixon and their like were leaching our liberties away. Repeated predictions of the collapse of our way of life did not eventuate.

Some US authors so embraced every new frenzy that we now understand them not as acute analysts of American society, as they saw themselves, but as dupes of its constant twists. Who was really running the show? Most societies naturally lag in self-understanding. During our lifetime virtually all satire has been directed against the old establishment, even after it has lost its monopoly position, whereas the new trendy establishment has for many decades escaped equivalent scrutiny. It was the source of many of our self-created troubles, fomenting destructive onslaughts on society for which there was no deep-seated reason. Though the US was a disturbed society for a time from the 1960s onwards, tensions subsided, society showed resilience and did not fall apart. Our societies have had a remarkable record of routine, democratic equanimity.

The novelists and commentators Saul Bellow and Tom Wolfe, with many others, resisted this attempt to be at one with the new *zeitgeist*, becoming beacons of sanity in the prevailing disorder, like Solzhenitsyn in Russia at the same time, and George Orwell in England in the 1930s. They were among those who prevented the West going into a quasi-totalitarian phase, just as writers in the East were helping their societies coming out of theirs. They pushed back against the new liberal hegemony they were initially part of. Chicago was Saul Bellow's home town, but he never succumbed to the madness of the times. Bellow and Wolfe opposed what is now misleadingly called political correctness, the move by influential progressive groups to gain power for themselves by excluding others, the very misbehavior they had held against the previous power elite.

Bellow and Wolfe were both liberals with bohemian tastes and satiric instincts; as the later decades of the 20th century progressed they became more uncomfortable with the trendy consensus, and were eventually mugged by reality into realizing the new liberal establishment was a danger to the proper ordering of society, to be undermined with satiric scorn. Each wrote four novels on this new development, Bellow from 1964 until 1982, and Wolfe from 1988 to 2012, the eight covering a span of almost five decades. Their themes were sub-political at the start, beginning with inhabitants of normal society who were dragged, often unwittingly, into higher social echelons, celebrity culture and the public sphere in general, a displacement which disoriented them. Their characters' actions have political ramifications.

Both novelists wrote in addition sharp socio-political essays drawing attention to the defects of the social group from which they had come. Bellow read widely, confessing 'I am of course an autodidact, as modern writers always are',[48] and his two selections of essays, *It All Adds Up* (1994) and *There Is Simply Too Much to Think About* (2015), place him among the best social analysts. Wolfe wrote *The Painted Word* (1975) and a book of essays, *Radical Chic & Mau-Mauing the Flak Catchers* (1970), on extremist attitudes among cultural commentators. Bellow revelled in modernity, but was never a complacent liberal and always exercised discrimination about the new. He gradually developed a critique of his times, but always from the inside as a rueful survivor. A quick learner, he was too wily to fully accept the kaleidoscopic chaos whirling about him. The two authors did not think in outmoded left versus right terms. Wolfe popularized the term 'radical chic' to show it was the contradictory convergence of adversarial and fashionable behaviour, such as Leonard Bernstein associating with the Black Panthers, the extremes against the sensible centre, which constituted the new disaster. Both believed the ideas underlying liberal modernism – the acceptance of chaos, liberality and lack of inner judgment – were ruining US society. With constant change modern society was becoming chaotic, and as a result people were losing their bearings. Both authors' novels describe concerted attempts to disorient populations; by these means disruptive elites were taking from them the capacity to act as citizens. Both novelists opposed the idea that reality is socially constructed, so that in the long run nobody is guilty of anything. They were ground-breaking in directing their satire

---

48   Saul Bellow *There is Simply Too Much To Think About*, p. 353.

at a new group, which was largely their own.

Like Mailer, Kundera and many other modern authors, Bellow wrote novels loosely based on his own experiences. In the works of his middle and best period, *Herzog* (1964), *Mr Sammler's Planet* (1969), *Humboldt's Gift* (1975) and *The Dean's December* (1982), the Bellow hero can't help ideas and impressions racing relentlessly through his mind. These notions come from his reading, from his own disturbed state, from media bombardment, and from observing a fragmented world where nothing adds up. The information superhighway has become polluted with overload. The hero takes in scrambled data of dubious veracity, trying to make some sense of it. Bellow wrote in an essay on 'The Distracted Public: '[TV] is the principal source of the noise peculiar to our time – an illuminated noise that claims our attention not in order to concentrate it but to disperse it...It is the agitation level that matters, not this or that enormity. And because we can't beat distraction, we are inclined to join it.'[49]

Bellow's *Herzog* is in the line of novels like *The Outsider*, *The Ginger Man* and *The Clown*. In a stream of consciousness mode, the principal character initially conducts a lone struggle against society, but here the anti-hero is more self-scrutinizing and self-satirizing than in previous novels in this mode. Bellow was preternaturally sensitive to the new mood. The messy early 1960s were, he sensed, a premonition of great changes to come, destabilizing to individuals (including himself), to society and to the whole American nation. The full force of these changes would be felt from later in the decade onwards. As with Kundera, sex and ideas are intertwined in Bellow's novels. Herzog's own notions, which are in some instances aligned with Bellow's own, are satirized. For example Herzog debunks Spenglerian and similar worldview-type thinking, which he (and Bellow) indulged in: 'The canned sauerkraut of Spengler's 'Prussian Socialism', the commonplaces of the Wasteland outlook, the cheap mental stimulus of Alienation, the cant and rant of pipsqueaks about Inauthenticity and Forlornness.' (p. 81) We know from Bellow's essays these were

---

49   Saul Bellow *It All Adds Up*, pp. 159 & 161.

notions he himself wrestled with. Herzog is a complex, many-sided creation.

The contemporary intellectual speculator (such as Herzog) feels obliged to examine his every move, which can become a pathology. Herzog oscillates between polarities: private and public, thinker and husband, initiator and victim. He is given to sudden outbursts of indignation and rage. Ideas plucked from anywhere are drafted for use in power struggles: 'Emancipation resulting in madness. Unlimited freedom to choose and play a tremendous variety of roles with a lot of coarse energy.' (p. 223) He notices that strange opposites, such as sentimentality and brutality, co-exist in society. Herzog (like Bellow) understands devious modern manoeuvring: 'modern consciousness has a great need to explode its own postures...and while moved by these beliefs he [an adversary] steals you blind.' (p. 201). Such mobile, manipulative personalities are difficult to counter in personal power struggles. Herzog has to contend with wide-ranging changes in his own life and in society, and he has great trouble reconciling these, as each destabilizes rather than heals the other.

In *Herzog* Bellow exploits to great comic effect the disconnect between Herzog's wide ranging intellectual interests and his messy daily life. Bellow himself often wryly observed that when a crisis hits you, all your reading and learning may be of little use:

> When that higher education was put to the test, it didn't work. I began to understand the irrelevancy of it, to recoil in disappointment from it. Then one day I saw the comedy of it. Herzog says, 'What do you propose to do now that your wife has taken a lover? Pull Spinoza from the shelf and look into what he says about adultery? About human bondage? You discover, in other words, the inapplicability of your higher learning, the absurdity of the culture it cost you so much to acquire.[50]

In *Secondhand Time* Svetlana Alexievich reveals many Russians had similar realizations about the uselessness of the books they had

---
50 Saul Bellow *It All Adds Up*, p. 322.

been reading during the Gorbachev and Yeltsin years, which diverted them from reality around them. Czeslaw Milosz noticed in Polish literature a similar gap between a higher layer of cultural pursuits and a lower level of down-to-earth necessities:

> People go to a store, they use a dish, a spoon, and a fork, sit down on a chair, open and close the door, in spite of what happens up there, 'above'. They communicate in a language indifferent to correct grammar and syntax, in an idiom of half words.[51]

Herzog tries to make sense of his shattering experiences, to put the pieces together, and to painfully build up again a serviceable personality. We now know from the biography of Bellow that the novel's genesis was in part his wife's leaving him and his own difficulty in coping with this. So writing the novel was probably therapeutic for him as well as Herzog.

Mr Sammler's Planet (1969) has a different type of narrator, an elderly Polish Jew born in Europe and living in New York, the epicentre of American life and of its new insurgency. Sammler is a generation older than Herzog, a detached survivor/observer, past active life, looking on the younger generation with sadness mixed with disdain. (In this he is like the aged Steppenwolf who, having been through the wringer, reflects at some distance on his troubled youth.) The focus of *Mr Sammler's Planet* is more on the new radical public atmosphere than on private human entanglements. The novel scrutinizes contemporary developments in the 1960s, such race riots, drugs, violence and student demonstrations, all of which Sammler (with Bellow) finds unappetizing. Early in the novel Sammler is let down by a young leftist activist Feffer, who, being middle class, go-getting and frivolous, abandons Sammler to a baying university audience which closes down Sammler's lecture with insulting behavior. Sammler is then accosted in a lift by an African-American pickpocket who sexually exposes himself as an act of intimidation and power. Near the end of the novel Feffer and the pickpocket are involved in a violent altercation with

---

51 Czeslaw Milosz 'Ruins and Poetry', *The New York Review of Books*, March 17, 1983, p. 22.

each other. We initially identify them as opposites by their divergent class and ethnic backgrounds, but in fact they two sides of same coin, both being radical, power crazy, and disruptive. Bellow was writing about student insurrections at the same time as Mailer, but was horrified not admiring.

The novel begins with one of its main themes, the opposition between inner being and intellectual accounts of the world: 'The soul had its own natural knowledge. It sat unhappily on superstructures of explanation, poor bird, not knowing which way to fly.' (p. 5) The narrator notices that commentators are obsessed with words and analyses, being distracted by ideas and the consequent 'strain of unrelenting analytical effort' which paradoxically takes them away from reality. (p. 18) Among the students there is much talk of rights, and many complaints and demands. Their public conversation becomes endlessly self-regarding, both the subject and object of its own deliberations: 'Mankind watched and described itself in the very terms of its own destiny.' (p. 60) Strange contradictions become apparent. In the 'opulent sections of the city…you opened a jewelled door into degradation'. The trick 'consisted of obtaining the privileges, and the freeways of barbarism, under the protection of civilized order.' (p. 8) Reactions against former internalized modes of proper conduct produce startling inversions: 'People justifying idleness, silliness, shallowness, distemper, lust – turning former respectability inside out'. (p. 9) Things invert themselves at the slightest pressure: 'All postures are mocked by their opposites.' (p. 96). In place of a stable personality structure, people 'wish to visit all other states of being in a diffused state of consciousness, not wishing to be any given thing but instead to become comprehensive, entering and leaving at will.' (p. 189) (We have seen this type of behavior with Mailer.) The contemporary personality becomes fluid, adapting to all, rather than forming an identity with grounded beliefs.

A yearning for originality, change, meretricious excitement, and extremism takes hold. At many stages a new version of things sweeps through society, a form of mythomania. Journalistic worldviews, likened to 'ideological hashish', are invented by 'bourgeois aristocrats', gurus and worldview thinkers like H.G. Wells, 'who set the terms...and then history follows their words.' (p. 170) They 'substitute words for acts' and become destructive, 'inheriting everything in a debased state...liberal views did not seem capable of self-defense.' (p. 29) Gnosticism takes over from rationality. Revolutions end up in the hands of madmen. (p.175.) Bellow provides here a description of what Lionel Trilling called the adversary culture, later known as political correctness: 'The high principled intellectual who must always be applying the purest standards and thumping the rest of his species on the head.' (p. 62). The theme of intellectual superiority also surfaces at the end of *Herzog*: 'the chief ambiguity which afflicts intellectuals (is)...that civilized individuals hate and resent the civilization that makes their lives possible. What they love is an imaginary human situation invented by their own genius.' (p. 311) Sammler in contrast is a tough realist, who, having been through of the Holocaust, retains his own calm, steadfast spirit. He is not carried away from his true soul by frenzied, distracting longings.

Universities were subjected to a form of show trial during teach-ins. In these endless exhaustion sessions, interrogation and denunciation of opponents ruled the day; in a characteristic inversion, the incessant hectoring went under the name of a 'free speech' movement. The teach-ins were little capsules of self-induced totalitarian frenzy – trial runs for the future. A take-over operation was in progress, the existing authority system was being destabilized and another put in its place. Though not victims, student protesters had to appear so, since it is a mark of the adversary culture that it must always put itself in a dissenting stance, no matter how powerful it is; it must never appear as an authority system in its own right. It follows from this that the struggle must be endless. So a cannibalizing tendency set in – students attacked their own free institutions.

In *Humboldt's Gift* (1975) the hero Charlie Citrine is a Herzog-like figure a decade later. The same confusions over sex, love and ideas appear. But Citrine has overcome Herzog's extreme self-deprecation.

He is more confident in his understanding of the weaknesses of the currently accepted liberal worldview, which he is still exploring, but also moving away from: 'Under pressure of public crisis, the private sphere is being surrendered.' (p. 245). Kundera had the same insight. Citrine gives context to his dilemmas by realizing that generations past and future are present to us, part of a larger dimension, and at the same tine connected to our essential selves, not torn away from it by diversions. (p. 140) There exist ways of knowing beyond our earthly limits. (p. 223)

As the 1980s and 1990s wore on, society, like a Bellow hero, somehow survived, and he in turn chronicled this calming down, nowhere better than in *The Dean's December* (1982). In this novel he compares the United States with Eastern Europe, specifically Romania (which he had visited with his current Romanian wife). Both are broken societies, but in contrasting ways: the United States fragmenting at the lowest level, with underclass deprivation, Romania at the highest level, with the Communist Ceauşescu dictatorship and its tight politico-bureaucratic power elite preventing the growth of a genuine society. Two parallel story lines continue through the novel: the death of the young, lower class Lester, murdered by a gang in Chicago, and the dignified death by natural causes of the aged Valeria, the protagonist's mother-in-law, a former Romanian government minister, long expelled from the *nomenklatura* for dissidence. In Romania the government 'sets the pain level for you', whereas in the US 'a tender liberal society has to find soft ways to institutionalize harshness'. (p. 275)

The central character and hero is a university humanities dean, Albert Corde, a decent humanist, radical in his youth, who, like Bellow himself, is undergoing a sea change in his views on American society. Events profoundly shatter his self-assurance, spawning doubts which echo through his mind. Lester is killed, and two blacks, Ebey and Hines, are implicated. But Corde's nephew the activist Mason, playing a role like Feffer in *Mr Sammler's Planet*, reverses the scenario, claiming the blacks are victims of the social structure, and that Corde, and Lester and his wife, are the problem. Here victim status is much more complicated than in earlier novels like Camus' *The Plague,* as people have learnt how to manipulate the notion. Corde writes a series of articles raising these problems for *Harper's* magazine.

The focus of American society's attention came to be on the underclass, who were genuine victims. Drugs, violence, robbery, racial animosity and death were the reality of their lives. But they were supported for the wrong reasons by would-be revolutionaries like Mason, who came from privileged backgrounds. University campuses were the prime sites of some of these misunderstood tensions. Corde becomes involved by writing on these problems, and in supporting the dead man's widow. He does not look at these events through the lens of the social construction of reality, which results in blaming society not individual actors. For political activists, taboos on facing reality 'set aside the immediate data of experience'. (p.204) While sympathetic to the plight of the underclass, Corde is horrified by the violence of urban life and the seeming hopelessness of the situation. He now opposes both the old liberal nostrums and the new aggressive 'victim status' ideology advanced by underclass supporters. In his articles Corde praises two black social workers who recommend blacks taking tough, common-sense measures themselves. Corde notices strange conjunctions: 'the vices of Sodom coexisted with the adoration of the Holy Spirit', and 'cynicism joined with purity in the heart' (pp. 130 & 161) This leads Corde/Bellow to endorse Dostoievsky's insight that the combination of 'apathy and intensity', or 'the rage for goodness (being) so near to vileness and murderousness', is a really scary development in modern societies.

Romanian society is admired by Corde, in contrast to the US, because it has retained an earlier layer of Balkan/Byzantine decency unbroken by the imposition of the Communist blanket. The Romanians 'came out with a sort of underfed dignity in what was left of the presocialist wardrobe…the old European life which at it most disgraceful was infinitely better than this present one.' (p. 214) Unlike male-driven Chicago, here in the East women keep the wheels of life turning: 'In the deeper life (Valeria) was traditional, even archaic... She had made up for Marxism...by a private system of atonement, setting up her mutual-aid female network'. (p. 105) Bellow admires the stoic women of Eastern Europe who remain a culture-bearing and culture-enhancing group, compared with brutal go-getting America, where psychopaths are on the loose.[52]

A number of characters in the novel are burning with moral, visionary zeal which Corde/Bellow distrusts. The student Mason backs the radical insurgents, with 'moral excitement' undermining his 'practical judgment.' (p. 59). The scientist Beech goes on a monomaniac, apocalyptic campaign claiming that lead poisoning is responsible for many ills in society. It is the crusading scare-mongering pessimism of environmentalist doomsayers that Corde/Bellow objects to: 'The doubtful part of his proposition is that human wickedness is absolutely a public health problem, and nothing but. No tragic destiny, no thickening of the substance of the soul, only chemistry or physiology.' (p. 227) Bellow includes a satiric portrait of a world-travelling journalist, Dewy Spangler, a John Pilger/Geoffrey Robertson/Michael Moore type, always trying to rev things up and to make himself the centrepiece of his own copy. An international celebrity, Spangler sells a willing public the fashionable worldviews of the day, 'a kind of event-glamour' which forms modern public discourse. As a result the audience 'has been deprived of the capacity to experience' events. Public intellectuals, Bellow believes, are 'now totally political, have gone over to junk culture...The sounds of junk culture are heard over a ground bass of extremism. Our entertainments swarm with spectres of world crisis. Nothing moderate can have any claim to our attention.'[53] Bellow dislikes the slick manipulations of this media breed, who serve to stir up trouble, not to understand or ameliorate it:

> They're extremely influential people and they are opinion-makers and even celebrities, and at the same time frivolous, irresponsible and silly, many of them...They are the creators of public excite-

---

52 Saul Bellow 'The Women of Eastern Europe', *The London Review of Books*, Vol. 4, No. 8, May 1982.
53 Saul Bellow *It All Adds Up*, p. 326.

ment and distraction. They are the people who make all the nations feel they're in the act – while what there really is is a chaotic mass of distractions which makes information impossible.[54]

The media is used to create 'reality' rather than to report it. A heightened, hot-house atmosphere is artificially created, in which people soon become disoriented, and open to instant change, in a way they normally wouldn't be. Reality is endlessly bombarded to alter its shape. Analysis, instead of being an account, becomes a vehicle of instant transformation. This kind of 'analysis' can become efficacious, so that what begins as desire ends as reality. The proponents are so changeable and their targets so shifting it becomes a moveable feast, like the propaganda shifts in *Nineteen Eighty-Four*. This is makework, the appearance of activity, change without the dynamic of change: '*Strenua nos exercet inertia.*' (We work hard at doing nothing). Bellow wrote: 'It is the agitation level that matters, not this or that enormity. And because we can't beat distraction, we are inclined to join it.'[55] We are today so bombarded by foreground chatter, crises, information overload and media blitzes that we're constantly distracted: 'Each of us stands in the middle of things, exposed to the great public noise.'[56] So taken up are we by public events that our very personalities have been, as Bellow shows, appropriated by our own history: 'waves of disintegrative details wash over us and threaten to wear away all sense of order and proportion'.

Excitement and distractions have cut people off from their basic identities. We become so 'totally plastic…that the material of which we are made will take any (improving) shape we choose to give it.'[57] Under the pressure of modern life our personalities can become flaky. Bellow was himself a bohemian liberal and a non-observant Jew. But, destabilized by a world crumbling around him, and liable to crumble himself, he would, he tells us 'fall back instinctively on my first consciousness [Jewishness], which has always seemed to me to be

---

54 Saul Bellow 'The Women of Eastern Europe', op. cit,
55 Saul Bellow *It All Adds Up,* p. 161.
56 Saul Bellow *There is Simply Too Much To Think About*, p. 271.
57 Saul Bellow Ibid., p. 388.

the most real and most easily accessible...To turn away from those origins, however, has always seemed to me an utter impossibility. It would be a treason to my first consciousness to un-Jew myself'.[58]

The task of the soul is, Corde reflects, to 'recover the world that is buried under the debris of false description or nonexperience.' (p. 243) Bellow has spelt out in simple terms the fact that literature's role is to rediscover:

> certain essences permanently associated with human life. These essences are restored to our consciousness by persons who are described as artists. You hear a voice, or, more significantly, an individual tone under the words. It seems to issue from the bosom, from a place beneath the breastbone. It is more musical than verbal, and it is the characteristic signature of a person, a soul. Such a writer has power over distraction and fragmentation, and out of distressing unrest, even from the edge of chaos, he can bring unity and carry us into a state of intransitive attention. People hunger for this.[59]

In this disturbed, ideology-driven world the writer, Bellow believes, must discard preconceived superstructures, immerse himself in mainstream life, absorb a lot and draw his own conclusions. He has to recreate his world from the ground up, putting it together as a coherent whole by acts of informed imagination as well as by cognition.

Violent dissent of the 1968 kind was exposed by the passing of time as mere *petit bourgeois putschism*. The commentariat kept wanting more change for its own sake, but citizens de-escalated the tensions, Reagan offered them assurance, the Cold War faded, race ceased to become a headline issue, and Reagan democrats, who wanted practical improvement, not symbolic dissent, appeared. Benign neglect proved a solvent for many problems. The Rodney King riots of 1992 did not spread to the whole society, as they might have two decades earlier. Tom Wolfe's four novels, *The Bonfire of the Vanities*, (1987) *A Man in Full* (1998), *I Am Charlotte Simmons* (2004), and

---

58 Saul Bellow Ibid., pp.356-7.
59 Saul Bellow *It All Adds Up*, p. 168.

Back to Blood (2013) which followed on in time and theme from Bellow's *The Dean's December* in the mid 1980s, capture this change of atmosphere.

Tom Wolfe invented a new way of composing novels, a new take on cultural commentary, and a new style of dress and living, all of which dovetailed with each other. His novels broke new ground, as the focus in these works is a distinctive metropolitan milieu which he foregrounds, a city such as New York, Chicago, Atlanta or Miami, in all its complex articulations, ethnicities, snobberies and social strivings. Wolfe captures in his novels life as public entertainment. He believed that in the arts modernity had been pushed too far. In painting artists elevated annotations and explanations of their paintings to the same status, or even higher, than the works themselves, as he demonstrated in *The Painted Word*. Self-obsessed novelists paraded a facsimile of themselves as the hero of their 'fictions', inviting the reader to join the mutual admiration society.

A noticeable thing about a Wolfe novel is that he is absent; he stands aside, using his detachment to accurately pinpoint changing social mores without himself moralizing about them. His characters do the character assassination for themselves. Wolfe's own taste in clothing signalled that a key determinant in contemporary life was not class nor wealth nor status nor ethnic background, but style, an ability to carry things off with a certain creative panache in contrast to the philistinism of the faux modern. Wolfe would not have been out of place as a *flaneur* in fin de siècle Paris, the culture from which his demeanour ultimately derived. He was literally a *boulevardier*, an observer who strolled around the streets of big cities, accurately taking in the sounds and sights and current idiosyncrasies.

In Wolfe's first novel *The Bonfire of the Vanities* (1987) the central figure is Sherman McCoy, a New York bond dealer and 'Master of the Universe' involved in a traffic accident in which an Afro-American is killed, an event whose ramifications soon spiral out of control. The case against McCoy is taken up by Rev. Bacon, a Harlem activist who, like Mason in The *Dean's December*, claims to be defending the underprivileged poor. He knows the money the old establishment gives him is protection money. An Afro-American who has been run over is turned into a model citizen, with a dubious media campaign mounted to get a Great White Defendant put on trial. The agitators alleging a racially-motivated cover-up are using this claim to pillory a man innocent of the crime. Wolfe understands that groups who claim to be disadvantaged can wield great power as part of a new establishment. There now exist pseudo-victims as well as real ones.

Wolfe's recurrent image for New York is that of a jungle, chaotic, dangerous and out of control. All civilizing restraints and instinctual renunciations have gone, the cushioning effect of manners, unspoken rules, authority and the daily deference needed to keep human beings safe and sane has departed, with the vacuum filled by naked force and brutal self-seeking. From all this we instinctively recoil. No trust exists between people. Sherman McCoy falls out not only with his wife but with his lover Maria Ruskin when he secretly tapes her for evidence in his case. Maria, with her southern upbringing, understands the rules of the jungle: 'Right there on the line everybody's an animal – the police, the judges, the criminals, everybody.'[60]

Wolfe shows what it is like to be on the receiving end when the media hounds a public figure. To get McCoy arrested, crowds are whipped up into a frenzy, then voracious TV cameras and journalists arrive to record, but in fact to victimize, their targets. They are the witch-hunters of the modern world, the true inquisitors, the purveyors of show trials. We are led by Wolfe to feel some solidarity with McCoy, since he, like the police, has to face the crowd, and face it down:

> When one's self ...has suddenly become an amusement park to which everybody, *todo el mundo, tout le monde*, comes scampering, skipping and screaming, nerves a-tingle, loins aflame, ready for anything, all you've got, laughs, tears, moans, giddy thrills, gasps, horrors, whatever, the gorier the merrier. (pp. 491-2)

---

60 Tom Wolfe *The Bonfire of the Vanities*, p. 264.

Sherman McCoy, the person at the centre of the scandal, is the victim of a personal case, like those in the Soviet Union, as for example in Voinoich's novel *The Ivankiad*. At the start the reader feels unsympathetic to McCoy. He begins as a standard WASP bond dealer making meaningless megabucks on the stock exchange. He lives in an opulent but lifeless Park Avenue apartment with a high mortgage, and goes to fashionable parties at the Bavardages where *tout le monde* (that is, the narrow New York social set) attends, like the parties at the Makarygins in *The First Circle*. It is an unnatural milieu and McCoy feels vaguely dissatisfied with his life.

McCoy is subjected to extraordinary pressure as he descends from Wall St to a Bronx courthouse and finally to gaol, losing all. It is at the point when he spends a day in remand prison, a modern chamber of horrors, that the reader first becomes sympathetic to him. McCoy is not charged with what he is guilty of (being part of the shonky bond market scene) but what he is not guilty of (manslaughter of a black student). As he undergoes his *purgatorio* he becomes freer in his own mind, like Innokenty Volodin in *The First Circle,* even though he is on his way to imprisonment. Both figures start out as part of a powerful establishment and lose their place completely, ending up in gaol. They are plunged into the underworld world of all against all. They endure suffering at the same time as losing materially. But both undergo a significant personal rebirth, from vacillation to strength. Both end spiritually free. Sherman is now becoming the real McCoy. Another phenomenon which distorts public understanding is that of the transnational, syndicated reporter. In *The Bonfire of the Vanities,* Wolfe creates a smart-arsed British journalist on the make in the novel, Peter Fellow. Saul Bellow created an equally obnoxious journalist, Dewey Spangler, in his novel *The Dean's December.* Both authors show how world-ranging activists posing as celebrity journalists sensationalize and propagandize events they are supposed to be merely reporting.

In the novel *I Am Charlotte Simmons,* the heroine comes from a lower middle class family in a small mountain community, which naturally sees a university education as a means of advancement in the world. She goes to wealthy Dupont University whose massive nineteenth century imitation Gothic architecture is a symbol of education system which is a facsimile of true learning. French literature like *Madame Bovary* is taught in English. The tone of the campus is set by the sports/gymnasium group and the drinking/sex group, both male dominated. The restraints of civilization have collapsed; early on Charlotte comes across a naked couple making love in public in a common room. Sex trumps all other activities. Life has been hollowed out at the core. Charlotte, repulsed by the unnatural milieu she has been unwittingly thrust into, finds temporary solace in a course on the new field of evolutionary biology, which sets off sparks in her brain and promises the intellectual stimulus she has been seeking. But other stimuli blot this out. Her seduction after a formal dinner exactly replicates the dramatic scene in Wolfe's novel *A Man in Full* where a prized stallion impregnates a mare trapped in a frame. In both the encounter is artificial, with the male totally dominant and the female cowered and passive. Good old time America is being date-raped by new priapic elites. Wolfe piles his satiric scorn on to the bankruptcy of the higher education scene.

Bellow and Wolfe's novels are not directly about politics. They begin with characters who inhabit the middle levels of society but are drawn into the public realm by influential ideologues who distort social movements in their own favour. As these novels demonstrate, we are caught in a pincer movement: modern ways of thinking erase older beliefs and ideological rigidity enforces a new position on us. The adversary culture and its brainchild, political correctness, are part of a new, wider syndrome for which there is as yet no generic description, though the term 'totalist', which is sometime used, implies that this development is a *petit mal* variant of full-blown totalitarian behavior, in that it aims in a smaller compass for a knockout blow. It is more than a matter of certain ideas, as it involves a distinctive personality type, and a distinctive mode of behavior. Herzog realizes 'modern consciousness has this great need to explode its own postures'.[61] When an issue arises, the totalist escalates things by means

---
61   Saul Bellow *Herzog*, p. 201.

of aggressive defense, itself a contradictory, double-think response, which heightens the tension, which can then be utilized as a destabilizing device. Escalation makes resolution less likely. A reasonable compromise usually ends tension, but totalist urgers like the Rev. Bacon and Mason can never be satisfied, they want the *bouleversement* to go on forever. As a result an apology or compromise is seen as weakness and only incites more demands. There's always a new log of claims around the corner.

Indignation mounting to hatred is the main motive of the adversary culture, but your target also has the same qualities as yourself. Big Brother must have a mirror opposite, a Goldstein/Trotsky, as a focus to attack. There must be a malign element to be eliminated, in oneself as well as in society. Trust is replaced by suspicion of others. It is the role reversing victim-aggressor combination, which is characteristic of contemporary soft 'totalitarian' activity, not the separation of victim and oppressor as in the past. Media blitzes and language games enforce this unsettlement. It's an atmosphere of synthetic, undifferentiated anger, it's just a need to get worked up. The switching means you have no permanent beliefs, just permanent anger and rage. In the past if you wanted control you tried to attain a dominant position. But a more subtle way is to manoeuvre yourself into the posture of a victim. This gives you immunity from attack, and at the same time enables you to disarm your quarry, who is blindsided and incapacitated by this strategy. Process is all, the journey not the end result is the aim, the show trial not the prison sentence is the real punishment, as we see in the McCoy and Lester cases. Once the previous equilibrium in society has been degraded, a fashionable ideology can rush in to replace it, with complicity achieved by ideological brainwashing rather than by force.

In this atmosphere bizarre notions, such that objective reality is a mere facsimile, are dressed to become the new currency; literature is superseded by literary theory. The final aim is power and control, the takeover of previous belief systems, and ultimately society itself. Even specific ideological content isn't crucial in the long: *politique d'abord* trumps status, fame or wealth. The Bellow and Wolfe novels reveal how quasi-governmental tribunals act as cultural policemen with coercive powers. They replace the independent, intermediate bodies which a normal society needs as a cushioning device between citizens and state. Power elites radiating down from above suborn middle level, mediating structures. The views of ordinary people are often quite different from those of the opinion formers of the media-academic-celebrity nexus. The public voice of this class creates a misleading impression of what public opinion is by constructing a one-sided narrative. The true role of public voices should be to listen as well as transmit, but they have ceased listening. As a result the state ceases to hear its own citizens.

Philip Roth's *The Human Stain* (2000), the third novel in his trilogy, satirizes political correctness in the later decades of the century. A Dean of the Humanities, Coleman Silk, at a college in the Berkshires in New England, refers to students who never appear at class 'spooks', an understandable designation. However the word has a secondary slang meaning of 'black' or 'Negro'. This trivial incident is escalated into an accusation of racism against Silk, whom we later find has black ancestry. Since his appointment Silk has cleared out time-serving plodders and recruited young trendy staff, many newly minted literary theorists, led by a feminist French lecturer Delphine Roux, who is ambitious, attractive, conniving and successful, but hollow at the core. Silk admonishes her: 'To have nothing to say about them [two plays by Euripides] other than they are 'degrading to women' isn't a 'perspective', for Christ's sake – it's mouthwash.' (p. 882) But Roth also deftly depicts her as desperate and conflicted, a victim of her own wiles (like Stalin in *The First Circle*). Instead of displaying gratitude for their positions, the new staff play the racism card against Silk, until, under pressure of an unstoppable political correctness campaign and with his wife dying from the strain, he has no option but to resign. Male academics are satirized as weakly going along with this blackballing, themselves emasculated by the feminist onslaught.

Silk first reacts with rage and a desire for revenge. Like Bellow

Roth shows how in a personal crisis education can't teach you how to live: 'All the education and nothing helps. Nothing can insulate from the lowest level of thought.' (p. 866). On the contrary, it can get in the way. He has to get over being expelled from his previous life and to settle into 'dignified contemplation...To live in a way that does not bring Philocetes to mind. He does not have to live like a tragic character in his course. He has to get away from 'the ridiculous quest for significance. From the never ending campaign for legitimacy' (pp. 862-3) But he does learn from ancient Greek writers lessons which parallel his present state: 'the many horrors can that can ensue when the highest degree of indignation is achieved and, in the name of justice, retribution is exacted and a cycle of retribution begins, (p. 763) (Writers in East Europe had at the same time understood that a revenge cycle extends, not ends, the original disturbance.)

Silk gets over has rage principally through his love affair with Faunia Farley, a cleaner at the college. She is uneducated, basic, open, close to the natural world and with an innate decency (qualities opposite in every way to Delphine's.) Faunia is stalked by her former husband, Lester, a disturbed Vietnam veteran. Faunia and Lester are both from the underclass, rural hill-country poor. Both are victims, living invisible lives: 'These are people whose fundamental feeling about life is that they have fucked over unfairly right down the line.' (p. 779) Silk now sees his own unfair treatment in perspective. The Vietnam vet syndrome at first blush seems awful. Lester's Post Traumatic Stress Disorder is not alleviated by fashionable psychiatric treatments but by fishing alone in the woods and mountains which are his home. The novel ends like a Greek tragedy – the human world, unlike the world of nature, leaves an indelible stain.

In his trilogy Roth links the decades of the 1940s, 1960s and 1990s, all times when political fanaticisms causing mental mutations swept through public life. Roth convincingly aligns right wing McCarthyism with later left wing political correctness, each dominated by 'the malevolent puritanism with which you will be tarred and feathered. (p. 775), by 'America's oldest communal passion...the ecstasy of sanctimony.' (p. 706). Silk is ostracized on false grounds, as McCoy is in Wolfe's *The Bonfire of the Vanities,* and Mr Sammler in Bellow's novel. Roth, once a radical liberal, has now also been mugged by reality. Bellow, Wolfe and Roth led the resistance to the madness of the age. They and others of their ilk saved a society poised on the brink. They were like Ionesco's Berenger, it was the bohemians, not the old bourgeois nor the new trendies, who took a stand against the derangement of the times.

In recent literature the idea that society itself is dying, and that the planet is tired, has been documented by Douglas Murray in *The Strange Death of Europe* (2017) We have noticed this in recent East European and Russian literature. In Bellow's *Herzog* the main character remembers his friend Nachman saying: 'Perhaps people wish life to end. They have polluted it...So that we loathe the daily bread that prolongs useless existence...Death himself must be tired of us.' (pp. 139-40) In *Mr Sammler's Planet* Sammler asks the scientist Lal: 'Do you think the species doesn't want to live?', and Lal replies: 'Many wish to end it...There is no sovereign obligation to one's breed. When biological destiny is fulfilled in reproduction the desire is often to die.' (p. 176) Later Mr Sammler reflects: 'New York makes one think about the collapse of civilization, about Sodom and Gomorrah, the end of the world. The end wouldn't come as surprise here. Many people already bank on it.' (p. 244) In *The Dean's December,* the possibility is raised that a whole society can move into anarchy and die, dissolving its connections, with no cushioning devices: 'there is no culture, it's only a wilderness ...we are talking about a people consigned to destruction.' (pp. 206-7). The idea that the earth itself is running out of energy features in Robert Lowell's poetry:

> No weekends for the gods now. Wars
> Flicker. Earth licks its open sores,
> Fresh breakage, fresh promotions, chance
> Assassinations, no advance...
> Only man thinning out his kind
> Sounds through the Sabbath noon, the blind

> Swipe of the pruner and his knife
> Busy about the tree of life...

Lowell, like Bellow, avoids self-indulgence and adopts an appropriately elegiac tone:

> Pity the planet, all joy gone
> from this sweet volcanic cone;
> peace to our children when they fall
> in small war on the heels of small
> war until the end of time
> to police the earth, a ghost
> orbiting forever lost
> in our monotonous sublime.

In Wolfe's novel *The Bonfire of the Vanities* a similar foreboding is evident. A bonfire originally meant a bone-fire, the great late autumn feast when all the animals which couldn't be carried through winter were roasted and consumed. This was *mardi gras*, a last gorging before a long period of hunger and other deprivations. In the dinner party scene in the novel, the elderly English poet Lord Aubrey Buffing shocks the gathering by stating, via the medium of Poe's story 'The Masque of the Red Death', that American society is dying from satiation:

> The Red Death has entered the house of Prospero. Now the exquisite part of the story is that somehow the guests have known all along what awaits them in this room, and yet they are irresistibly drawn toward it, because the excitement is so intense and the pleasure is so unbridled and the gowns and the food and the drink and the flesh so sumptuous – and that is all they have. Families, homes, children, the great chain of being, the eternal tide of chromosomes mean nothing to them any longer. They are bound together, and they whirl about one another, endlessly, particles in a doomed atom – and what else could the Red Death be but some sort of final stimulation, the *ne plus ultra*. (pp. 355-6)

In Bellow's *Humboldt's Gift* the central character realizes there exists a wider realm which gives comfort against these grim forebodings, the idea that generations past and future are present to us, part of a larger dimension, yet connected to our essential self, not torn away from it by distractions:

> I do not believe my birth began my first existence.... I am obliged to deny that so extraordinary a thing as the human soul can be wiped out forever. No, the dead are about us, shut out by our metaphysical denial of them....Our ideas should be their nourishment. We are their grainfields. But we are barren and starve them. Don't kid yourself, we are watched by the dead, watched on this earth. (p. 140)

This is Bellow speaking too through Humboldt. There exist ways of knowing beyond our earthly limits: 'there's something in human beings beyond the body and brain and we have ways of knowing that go beyond the organism and its senses. I've always believed that. My misery comes, maybe, from ignoring my own metaphysical hunches.' (p. 223)

Similarly Wolfe developed in one of his essays the notion of serial immortality, how 'the great chain of being, the eternal tide of chromosomes' operates fruitfully:

> The husband and wife who sacrifice their own ambitions and their material assets in order to provide a 'better future' for their children...the soldier who risks his life, or perhaps consciously sacrifices it, in battle... the man who devotes his life to some struggle for 'his people' that cannot be possibly won in his lifetime...people (or most of them) who buy insurance or leave wills...are people who conceive of themselves, however unconsciously, a part of a great biological stream. Just as something of their ancestors lives on in them, so will something of them live on in their children...or in their people, their race, their community – for childless people, too, conduct their lives and try to arrange their post mortem affairs with concern for how the great stream is going to flow on. Most people, historically, have not lived their lives as if thinking 'I have only one life to live'. Instead they have lived as if they are living their ancestors' lives and their offsprings' lives and perhaps their neighbours' lives as well. They have seen themselves as inseparable from the great tide of chromosomes of which they are created

and which they pass on.

As Edmund Burke understood, past, present and future generations are linked together in time by the longitudinal glue which constitutes 'the great stream'. Serial immortality elevates civil society to a higher order of reality, available to those of a secular as well as religious frame of mind. This can overcome the threat of the imminent death of society, as even in dark times the deep underlying structure is likely to prevail.

11

THE AFTERLIFE OF LITERATURE

In the battle over ideas authors were crucial. Many endured oppressive regimes, which gave them little space to breathe. A few supported the oppressors, but most opposed them. The two sides battled it out throughout the twentieth century. The struggles of our times were fought over words with words. Words are properly used for analysis, and to create deeper insights. But the world was awash with compilations of words which had lost their meanings and their associations. Words were designed to obscure rather than to elucidate. They were turned into sentences but not into sense, into ideologies but not into ideas. Words were weaponized, becoming agents of mental coercion. Propagandists came to believe words were inherently efficacious, relieving them of the necessity of explaining. Words were used to block action, and as a replacement for it. In repressive regimes, batteries of words eventually took over from torture as the authorities' preferred instrument of persuasion. Facile wordsmiths working in teams were employed by regimes to suborn civilian populations by producing false literature, 'rivers of blather' in Brandys' phrase, 'this string of eveready words' which Dostoievsky detested. On the analogy of diarrhoea Milan Kundera believed modern writers were suffering from verbal logorrhoea, word overload, a surfeit squirted out endlessly by paid literary stooges in high octane, low density solutions. Devious formulations were used to bamboozle audiences of ordinary people. Propagandists stampeded them into changing their mental universe. Their endless strings of words lacked resonance and an ability to rise above themselves. Since they had no lift, no poetics, they remained on the same base level, stifling the imagination. In Old English the root word *makar* meant a maker, a creator, and by extension a poet. Many writers became fabricators, not poets.

A later retrograde step was 'sophisticated' literary theory. Like a snake consuming its own tail theory became comfortably self-referential, spinning out endless variations on its chosen themes in virtual reality, without being tied to its moorings. Academic and political theorists often failed in their vocation; the Slovenian wordsmith Slavoj Žižek became inseperably a high literary obscurantist and a totalitarian apologist, indefensible in both roles. Literary theory became a *petit mal* version of the original control virus, perverting judgement by means of devious formulations. We experience life, then read accounts of it, then imaginative renderings of it called literature, then literary theory, then meta theory, each step a further remove from reality, and eventually from sanity. Many authors from Byron to Mailer saw themselves as a bohemian dissenters – it went with the territory. In the mid 20th century meltdown, mature writers discarded this outmoded posture, as we notice with Orwell, Camus, Ionesco, Brandys, Havel and like-minded souls. Like Berenger in *Rhinoceros* they opposed the old conservative conformism and the new radical conformism; they scrutinized all attitudes equally.

A majority of authors, sensitive to the ugly subliminal currents which the virus was generating in society, came to the fore in opposing it. They anatomized its subversive workings, and in doing so brought it to the surface. When it saw the light of day, little further comment was necessary as it exposed itself. Existentialism arose from the 1940s onwards as a reaction to actors and regimes trying to aggrandize themselves through complex prose. *Catch-22* anatomized bureaucratic inanities. The absurdist playwrights showed how words could lose their discreet meanings, operating instead as a blanket of sound to waylay the listener. In response authors combined with others as an intelligentsia to reconstitute civil society, where free speech resumed its proper place. Moreover authors moved into the public realm as a key countervailing force. From Bulgakov and Zamyatin to Bellow and Wolfe they provided the genuine literature the public thirsted for, and the *polis* required. For this reason literature came to occupy a more central public role than in the past, and eventually triumphed. Brave authors with sharp political antennae became for the first time regular Nobel Prize recipients: Camus, Pasternak, Solzhenitsyn, Böll, Grass, Hesse, Milosz, Pinter, Golding, Brodsky, Műller, Bellow and Alexievich; Sartre turned his down. Many resisted verbal webs of complicity, survived and rose above their condition. They refused easy ways out.

Domination, both personal and institutional, worked through the beguiling ambiguities of artificially heightened thinking. Brecht's smart paradoxes defending Stalin's show trials eventually got us nowhere, or worse. In an era drowning in false prose, author/victims like Borowski, Shalamov and Herbert refused to be indulgently expansive; they employed clear formulations with sparse resonances to defend their own, hard won, limited territory. The Underground Man understood that notions previously deemed virtuous could be a trap: 'consciousness is the greatest plague' and that 'too great a lucidity is a disease'. (pp. 118 & 93) The Logician in *Rhinoceros* entangles himself in a self-deluded 'logic' which leads him away from, not towards, understandings. Orwell wrote: 'We have now sunk to a depth at which the restatement of the obvious is the first duty of civilized men'. We notice in such authors a recognizable tone of equanimity, the voice of those who have been through the cauldron, and have come out the other end clarified, even if damaged, by the experience. Instead of fretting, their psyches schooled themselves to move to a realm beyond the destabilizing currents swirling around them. Though admitting to a general uncertainty, they remained curious beings trying to make sense out of things. It's as though they had emerged into a new existence, a kind of afterlife, on a different plane from what had gone before. Authors trained themselves to see things 'with a calm and very clear eye'. During the period of heightened ideology the best writers felt the need to put the world together again from its elements, from its words. Writers separated out discrete words and objects in order to reposition them with greater objectivity. Orwell, though not having undergone experiences as horrific as his continental counterparts, did something similar by ignoring the conventional thinking of the 1930s and instead patiently building up his own world from scratch.

These virtues were especially needed in Central and Eastern Europe and Russia because whole populations there had to manage the destabilizing intrusions of modernity and political madness simultaneously. Brandys's *Warsaw Diary* documented the rise of the Solidarity movement in Poland, which created a new natural society-wide culture displacing the stale official one. There is no attempt in his diary entries to artificially heighten tension – the vast material at his fingertips is sufficient subject matter. He is part of his world and does not seek to escape from it, only not to be in its thrall. He retrieves some minimal consolation from limited possibilities.

We inhabit cultures which operate horizontally, having lost their capacity for transcendence; they spawn endless webs of functions on the same level, but are incapable of a clean break, of lifting themselves above the circling make-work. This causes uncertainty and anguish. Humour is one way of achieving lightness in the dark, and of overcoming rancour, as it can be a detachment device, by which one breaks clear and see things anew without the distortion caused by one's (often legitimate) disgust. The Russian critic Mikhail Bakhtin understood this: 'Laughter destroys fear and piety in the face of the object and of the world, makes them available for familiar contact and thus prepares the way for an absolutely free investigation of their nature.' Voinovich realized something similar at the start of *The Ivankiad*:

> I tried to maintain my composure, but I wasn't always able to. What saved me was that at a certain point I decided that one must look at everything with a sense of humour, since all knowledge is a blessing. I calmed down; my hatred gave way to curiosity, which was satisfied by my adversary, who always revealed himself as in a striptease. (pp. 7-8)

In tyrannical societies, everything is designed to prevent breakout, since the regime can't bear anything to be outside itself; it can bear no *other*. Humour transcends the usual blaming of others or playing their game. Characters in literature act intuitively, outside the prevailing mentality, to momentarily at least lift themselves above its entanglements, even if not in control. This is a quality of spirit, of magnanimity, of 'unacknowledged soul'. When higher values cease to exist, the ego can expand into megalomania and turn into a destructive force. In Herbert's poem 'The Pebble', stone is acknowledged as having achieved self-restraint, and is therefore invulnerable to rapid personality changes. Purified by the ordeal it has moved beyond to the 'dungeon's supreme freedom'.

Modern events, especially in the media, tend to hype us up. In this unrelaxed state we are prone to messy judgements, caught up in the slipstream of others' and our own turmoil. Excessive political involvement engulfs whole swathes of the population. There is a realm of legitimate activity outside politics, as political literature insists. Not to be politically obsessed is the basis of a sane life. As Orwell insisted: 'The fact to which we have got to cling, as to a life-belt, is that it is possible to be a normal decent person and yet to be fully alive'.[62] On the other hand we may need to engage in politics to make sure it doesn't eliminate activities which cause us to flourish. Societies from the Anglosphere did not fall for the totalitarian temptation, since they had built up over centuries the countervailing bonds which protect civil society.

The best modern literature may often have an apparent clinical coldness about it, in order to cope with overheated situations. We see this in the detached, eerie clarity of Borowski's death camp stories in which all else is removed so events are allowed to speak for themselves. For an author to capture this there must be a certain distance in time and place, like camp inhabitants who saw themselves as object and subject at the same time. That was the only way Borowski could both survive and capture the true horror of Auschwitz; he didn't need

---

62 George Orwell *Collected Essays*, Vol. I, p. 226.

to impose his own lesser meanings on it. The true heroes of political literature follow a dual-track strategy, finding it necessary to be uncompromising and detached, outside and beyond events, yet at the same time being inevitably immersed in them. Those who adapt too readily can become collaborators; those who resist utterly can become outright rebels or *musselmänn*, marked out for extinction. This dilemma persists in a diminished form even in normal society. Internal emigration is sometimes essential if one wishes to avoid being a casualty.

Solzhenitsyn pointed out how disappointing it is that we remain slack for long periods, then make an heroic attempt when it is almost too late. How much better to be vigilant in small matters from the start, to avoid a great final effort which is less likely to succeed. Solidarity showed how an alternative non-political society can to be painstakingly created over time. Zinoviev listed the types of necessary self-restraint which serve as a basis for public morality:

> Do not coerce anyone and let nobody coerce you. Resist. Do not humble yourself. Do not be a lackey. Pay tribute to those who deserve it. Having nothing to do with bad people. Avoid their company. If there is no need to speak, be silent. Don't draw attention to yourself. Don't thrust your help on anyone. Refuse undeserved honours. Keep your word. Do not preach at people. Do not gloat over the misfortunes of others. Take no part in power and do not cooperate with it.

George Orwell was an enlightened modernist, but he retained in his being the old virtue of decency. Philip Larkin understood this: 'But superstition, like belief, must die,/And what remains when disbelief has gone?' Cynical transgressive stances are not helpful; some residual beliefs are necessary. Nerzhin, whose voice is close to that of Solzhenitsyn, realizes in *The First Circle:*

> No matter how clever and absolute the systems of scepticism or agnosticism or pessimism, you must understand that by their very nature they doom us to a loss of will. They can't really influence human behaviour because people cannot stand still. And that means they cannot renounce systems which affirm something which summon them to advance in some direction...One can cer-

tainly doubt, one is obliged to doubt. But isn't it also necessary to love something?

In his *Notes Towards The Definition Of Culture* T.S. Eliot wrote that scepticism is the 'habit of examining evidence and the capacity for delayed decision...we need not only the strength to defer a decision, but the strength to make one.' Gertrude Himmelfarb has shown in *The De-Moralization of Society: From Victorian Virtues to Modern Values* how many Victorian values, widely caricatured since the 1960s, contain that substratum of common sense all societies have found necessary to survive. For the last two centuries thinkers in Europe, feeling themselves superior to the traditional values which had held society together, ridiculed them almost out of existence. But what, if anything, replaced those downgraded values? Brandys reflected:

> My generation grew up in an era when lies were overturned. The lies were stripped away from relations between women and men, from religion, love, history, and literature. A little while later, when the blows from the totalitarian beast beat down upon that generation, it turned out that a humanity freed from lies, in order to survive, had to fall back upon ideas and values that we had considered the noble platitudes of generations past, generations that had not been free of lies. A mind liberated from prejudice was not enough; one also had to recall the old mottoes about honor, sacrifice, and hope. (p. 88)

American liberals were similarly mugged by reality, as Irving Kristol (Himmelfarb's husband) neatly put it. Once past beliefs were destroyed there was little to take their place. Under pressure many of the new beliefs were exposed as inadequate, or worse as dangerous. The sceptical stance adopted by liberals of Brandys' generation proved insufficient. Brandys' and Solidarity's stance of unillusioned steadfastness showed the way ahead in Poland and beyond.

In a fickle world one finds security in nature, in memory and the past, and in everyday human decency. The past is an important touchstone of stability; it can't be changed in spite of attempts to do so, as with the Memory Hole of *Nineteen Eighty-Four*. Tyrannies acknowledge the importance of the past through their attempts to supress it. A memory of different times and circumstances can tell us that claims made in the present may be dubious, and that arrangements different from the present have flourished in other times and places. Double-think relies on vacillating perceptions, which a sense of the solidity of the past can refute. In the absence of religious belief, serial immortality, the survival of the species beyond individuals, becomes paramount. Animals don't panic as they have a steady, cyclical existence of their own, as exemplified in Yeats' poem 'The Wild Swans at Coole'. The swans allayed his disturbed state during the troubles of the Irish Civil War:

> Unwearied still, lover by lover,
> They paddle in the cold
> Companionable stream or climb the air;
> Their hearts have no grown old;
> Passion or conquest, wander where they will,
> Attend upon them still.

Then:

> All suddenly mount
> And scatter in great broken rings
> Upon their clamorous wings.

Nature can bring relief and uplift, not spiritual deadness. For Shalamov surviving in the Artic wastes, the emergence in early winter of the dwarf cedar, which endures extreme deprivation, was his emblem of resistance, new life and hope:

> Only one tree was always green, always alive – the dwarf cedar. The tree was a weatherman. Two or three days before the first snow…the dwarf cedar would suddenly stretch out its enormous five-yard paws on the ground, lightly bend its straight, black, two-fist trunk, and lie prone on the earth. (p. 22)

In her poem 'Mushrooms' Sylvia Plath lays bare the *modus operandi* of the takeover merchant, using an analogy from the world of nature. We find an opposite reaction in the poem 'Thistles' by her husband Ted Hughes:

> Against the rubber tongues of cows and the hoeing hands of man
> Thistles spike the summer air
> Or crackle open under a blue-black pressure

The thistles have decided to resist, and so to survive, even to rebel and to rise above their condition:

> Every one a revengeful burst
> Of resurrection, a grasped fistful
> Of splintered weapons

The past is something worth preserving; it is able to resurrect itself like an old, long suffering race or language. The thistles believe in themselves and won't be deflected from their course. On the most basic level, this is a determination to resist at any cost. The thistles are not subtle; they are quite open about their basic strategy, with their survival genes operating with military precision. Their resistance is intuitive and instinctive. In contrast to the 'soft fists' of the mushrooms, their 'grasped fistful' is spiky and defensively aggressive, like cats which defend themselves when attacked. The thistles are not a threat to anyone, they just want to hold their own ground and reproduce themselves: 'Their sons appear,/Stiff with weapons, fighting back over the same ground'.

In the best writers we recognize the clear-sighted calmness of an consciousness which has been through it all. I first noticed this distinctive tone in the writings of early Camus. He began (like St Augustine) exulting in the erotic sensuality of north Africa, as in *Summer in Algiers*. But when he moved north to continental Europe he faced new problems, which led in *The Myth of Sisyphus* to his notion of a provisional attitude to events. What are our consolations, Camus calmly asks, in this puzzling and apparently meaningless world? What relieves existential angst? His tone betrays an inner serenity, against the embrace of the *vita periculoso*. Among the many examples of breakout in political literature are Julia's sovereign gesture of contempt in

Nineteen Eighty-Four, Bobynin in *The First Circle*, and the blond camp victim in Borowski, all of whom exhibit an 'unaccountable spiritual superiority'. Anton Schmid was a German guard at Vilnius who spontaneously tried to protect Jews, for which he was executed. These are individual actions, exemplary and worthwhile, but ineffective in the short term. Communally we have the optimistic atmosphere of *The First Circle,* and in real life Solidarity in Poland, which constituted a successful society-wide breakout. The consolation is that bad times are not endless.

Breakout is the quality badly needed to overcome a prevailing malaise. It is crucial in lifting a situation out of the doldrums, as Saul Bellow understood:

> The principal characteristic of the survivor is that he has made himself lighter by putting off, by setting aside, the ideas and doctrines that have dominated this century, its leading psychologies and philosophies, its wilder political beliefs, the endless horrible comedy of public lying. What is observable in our best contemporaries is a lightening, a divestiture. They lighten themselves not because they care less but because they care more...Perhaps they have come to see that the theories they accepted for decades had nothing to do with their most significant intentions and actions. We 'square' ourselves with our ideas, but in time we recognize that the unacknowledged soul has somehow saved us from the worst effects of those ideas.[63]

It is an episodic transcendence which may not last but gives us a glimmer of better things to come. Breakout can be an epiphany, like Lowell's 'O to break loose...' During the same period Solzhenitsyn was producing *The First Circle*, a novel which for all its subject matter of people unfairly imprisoned is surprisingly light and hopeful, because the prisoners, divested of everything, are able to break the linked chains of repression tying them down. As Emily Dickinson expressed it: 'After great pain, a formal feeling comes'; we experience a calm, 'A Quartz contentment, like a stone'.

---

63   Saul Bellow *It All Adds Up*, Secker & Warburg, London, 1994, p. 135.

Oppressed Russians and East Europeans admired Hamlet's ability to overcome his and his county's fate.[64] Hamlet weighed up all possibilities in devising the right mix of thought and action to relieve the disturbed political situation in his country without prolonging it. In Russia under Stalin, audiences at poetry readings cried out to Pasternak: 'Give us the 66th', Shakespeare's Sonnet No. 66, as they recognized in it the present atmosphere in the Soviet Union where every value had been inverted:

> And art made tongue-tied by authority,
> And folly (doctorlike) controlling skill,
> And simple truth miscalled simplicity,
> And captive good attending captain ill.

A sense of more than breakout, of final relief, pervades Boris Pasternak's poem 'After The Storm':

> The air is heavy with the passing storm
> The world revives and breathes in paradise...
>
> Transcendent power lies in the artist's hand
> That cleanses all things from impurity...
>
> This century outgrows its tutelage
> To clear the way for all the years to come.

Similarly in his prose poem 'Swans in Flight' the Czech Miroslav Holub spells out larger meanings of the saying 'the readiness is all' which ends the play *Hamlet*:

> It's like violence done to the atmosphere; as if Michelangelo reached out from the stone. And all the swans on the entire continent always take off together, for they are linked by a single signalling circuit. They are circling, and that means that Fortinbras's army is always approaching. That Hamlet will be saved and that an extra act will be played. In all translations, in all theatres, behind all curtains and without mercy.

---

64 The Polish theatre critic Jan Kott wrote *Shakepeare Our Contemporary* (1984) on this theme.

> The actors are already growing wings against fate.
>
> Hold out - that's all.[65]

Here relief is on a communal scale: stone is transfigured by the 'transcendent power in the artist's hand'. A 'single signalling circuit' joins the whole society together, an image which echoes that of Yeats' swans. Holub's poem, looking to the future in hope, creates a sense of lift-off, where old tensions drop away, replaced by a lightness of being.

---

65 *The Faber Book of Political Verse*, ed. Tom Paulin, Faber & Faber, London, p.466.

BIBLIOGRAPHY

Political Literature

Alan Bold ed. *The Penguin Book of Socialist Verse,* Penguin Books, Harmondsworth, 1970

Boll, Heinrich *The Clown*, Calder & Boyars, London, 1965

Borowski, Tadeusz *This Way for the Gas, Ladies and Gentlemen*, Penguin Books, Harmondsworth, 1982

Brecht, Bertolt *The Resisible Rise of Arturo Ui*, Methuen, London, 1981

Bulgakov The Master and Margarita, Collins and Harvill Press, 1968

Camus, Albert *The Myth of Sisyphus*, Penguin Books, Harmondsworth, 1980

----------------- *The Plague* , Penguin Books, Harmondsworth, 1960

Conrad, Joseph *Heart of Darkness*, Penguin Books, London, 1973

----------------- *The Secret Agent,* Penguin Books, New York, 1996

-----------------*The Secret Sharer in Twixt Land and Sea,* Penquin, *1912*

Dostoievsky, Fyodor *Notes From Underground*, Signet Classic, New York, 1961

Dostoievsky, Fyodor *The Devils*, Penguin Books, Harmondsworth, 1965

Etkind, Efim *Notes of a Non Conspirator,* Oxford University Press, Oxford, 1978

Erofeev, Venedikt *Moscow To The End Of The Line*, Taplinger, New York, 1980

Frisch, Max *The Fire Raisers*, Methuen, London, 1962

Golding, William *Lord of the Flies*, Faber & Faber, London, 1962

Grass, Gunter *The Tin Drum*, Secker & Warburg, London, 1962

Havel, Václav *The Garden Party and Other Plays, Grove Press, New York, 1993*

----------------- *The Memorandum*, Jonathan Cape London, 1967

----------------- *Three Vaněk Plays*, Faber & Faber, London, 1990

Hesse, Herman *Steppenwolf,* Penguin Books, Harmondsworth, 1965

Huxley Brave *New World*, Penguin Books, Harmondsworth, 1970

Ibsen, Henrik *Three Plays,* Penguin Books, Harmondsworth, 1952

Ionesco, Eugene *Rhinoceros,* Penguin Books, Harmondsworth, 1965

Koestler, Arthur *Darkness a Noon,* Penguin Books, Harmondsworth, 1946

Konwicki, Tadeusz *A Minor Apocalypse,* Faber & Faber, London, 1983

----------------------- *The Polish Complex,* Farrar Straus Giroux, New York, 1982

Kundera, Milan *The Book of Laughter and Forgetting*, Penguin Books, Harmondsworth, 1986

Levy, Primo *If This Is A Man*, Vintage, London, 1979

Mailer, Norman *The Armies of the Night*, Weidenfeld and Nicolson, London, 1968

--------------------*Miami and the Siege of Chicago*, Weidenfeld and Nicolson, London, 1969

Mandel'shtam, Osip *Selected Poems*, Rivers Press, Cambridge, 1973

Melville, Herman *Billy Budd*, Signet Classic, New York, 1961

Müller, Herta *The Land of Green Plums*, Granta Books, London, 1998

Orwell, George *Homage to Catalonia*, Penguin Books, Harmondsworth, 1962

--------------------*Nineteen Eighty-Four*, Penguin Books, Harmondsworth, 1960

Paulin, Tom, ed. *The Faber Book of Political Verse*, Faber & Faber, London, 1980

Pinter, Harold *The Caretaker*, Metheun, London, 1960

Roth, Phillip *The American Trilogy: American Pastoral, I Married A Communist, The Human Stain*, The Library of America, New York, 2011

Silone, Ignazio *Fontamara*, Methuen, London, 1965

(1) Shalamov, *Graphite W. W. Norton & Company, New York, 1981*

(2) _____*Kolyma Tales, W. W. Norton & Company, New York, 1980*

(3)_____*Kolyma Stories*, trans. Donald Rayfield, New York Review of Books, New York, 2018

(4)_____*Sketches From the Criminal World*, trans. Donald Rayfield, New York Review of Books, New York, 2020

Sinyavsky, Andrei (Abram Tertz) *A Voice From the Chorus*, Collins & Harvill,

London, 1976

Solzhenitsyn, Alexander *Lenin in Zurich*, Penguin Books, Harmondsworth, 1978

_____*One Day in the Life of Ivan Denisovich*, Penguin, London, 2009

_____*The First Circle*, Collins/Fontana Books, London, 1971

_____*The Gulag Archipelago,* 3 Vols, Collins/Fontana, Glasgow, 1974-8

_____*The Red Wheel* Penguin Books, Harmondsworth, 1990

Trifonov, Yuri *Another Life* and *The House On The Embankment*, Northwestern University Press, Evanston, 1999

Vaculic, Ludvik *The Axe*, Northwestern University Press, Chicago, 1994

Voinovich, Vladimir *The Life and Extraordinary Adventured of Private Chonkin,* Jonathan Cape, London, 1977

------------------------ *Pretender To The Throne,* Jonathan Cape, London, 1981

------------------------ *The Ivankiad*, Penguin Books, Harmondsworth, 1979

Zamyatin, Yevgeny *We*, Penguin Books, Harmondsworth, 1972

Zinoviev, Alexander *The Yawning Heights*, The Bodley Head, London, 1979

------------------------ *The Radiant Future*, The Bodley Head, London, 1981

Commentary on Political Literature

Alvarez, Al *Under Pressure*, Penguin Books, Harmondsworth, 1963

Conrad, Joseph *The Secret Sharer* in *Twixt Land and Sea,* Penquin, 1912

Des Pres, Terence *The Survivor,* Oxford University Press, New York, 1976

Haraszti, Milkós *The Velvet Prison,* I.B Tauris, London, 1988

Hingley, Ronald *Nightingale Fever: Russian Poets in Revolution*, Weidenfeld and Nicolson, London, 1982

Hosking, Geoffrey *Beyond Socialist Realism,* Granada, London, 1980

Howe, Irving *Politics and the Novel*, Fawcett Premier, Greenwich, Conn., 1967

Ionesco, Eugene *Notes & Counter-notes*, Grove Press, New York, 1964

Lynskey, Dorian *The Ministry of Truth*, Picador, London, 2019

Milosz, Czeslaw *The Captive Mind*, Mercury Books, London, 1962

O'Brien, Conor Cruise *Writers and Politics*, Penguin Books, Harmondsworth, 1976

Orwell, George *The Collected Essays, Journals, and Letters,* 4 Vols., Secker & Warburg, 1968

Podhoretz, Norman *The Bloody Crossroads*, Simon and Schuster, New York, 1986

Rühle Jürgen *Literature and Revolution*, Pall Mall Press, London, 1969

Steinhoff, William *The Road to 1984,* Weidenfeld and Nicolson, London, 1975

General Commentary

Andrzej, Franaszek *Milosz: A Biography*, Belknap/ Harvard University Press, Cambridge, 2017

Appelbaum, Anne *Gulag*, Allen & Unwin, London, 2003

Arendt, Hannah *The Origins of Totalitarianism*, Harcourt, Brace & World, New York, 1966

Baumont, Zygmunt *Modernity and the Holocaust*, Polity, Oxford, 1990

Bellow, Saul *It All Adds Up*, Secker & Warburg, London, 1999

--------------- *There Is Simply Too Much To Think About,* Viking, New York, 2015

Camus, Albert *The Rebel*, Penguin Books, London, 1971

---------------- *The Myth of Sisyphus*, Penguin Books, Harmondsworth, 1980

Cohn, Norman *The Pursuit of the Millennium*, OUP, Oxford, 1957

Gessen, Masha *The Future Is History: How Totalitarianism Reclaimed Russia*, Granta, London, 2017

Gleeson, Abbott *Totalitarianism: The Inner History of the Cold War*, Oxford University Press, New York, 1995

Goldfarb, Jeffrey *Beyond Glasnost: The Post-Totalitarian Mind*, The University of Chicago Press, Chicago, 1989

Haraszti, Miklós *The Velvet Prison*, I.B. Tauris, London, 1988

Legutko, Ryszard *The Demon in Democracy: Totalitarian Temptations in Free Societies*, Encounter Books, New York, 2016

Mosse, George *The Crisis of German Ideology*, The Universal Library, 1964

Murray, Douglas *The Strange Death of Europe*, Bloomsbury, London, 2017

Murray, Douglas *The Madness of Crowds*, Bloomsbury, London, 2019

Rupnik, Jacques *The Other Europe*, Weidenfeld and Nicolson,,London, 1988

Steiner, George *Language and Silence,* Penguin, Harmondsworth, 1969

Talmon *The Origins of Totalitarian Democracy*, Secker & Warburg, London, 1966

Trilling, Lionel *Beyond Culture*, Penguin Books, Harmondsworth, 1967

Voegelin, Eric *The New Science of Politics*, The University of Chicago Press, Chicago, 1952

Zinoviev, Alexander *Homo Sovieticus*, Gollancz, London, 1985

Biographies, Autobiographies and Memoirs

Bulgakov, Mikhail *Manuscripts Don't Burn*, ed. J.A.E. Curtis, Harvill, New York, 1992

Crick, Bernard *George Orwell; A Life*, Secker & Warburg, London, 1980

Fuegi, John *The Life and Lies of Bertolt Brecht*, Harper Collins, London, 1994

Esslin, Martin *Brecht: A Choice of Evils*, Heinemann, London, 1973

Franaszek, Andrzej *Miłosz: A Biography,* Harvard University Press, Cambridge, 2017.

Lottman, Herbert *Camus: A Biography*, Doubleday & Company, New York, 1979

Proffer, Ellendea *Bulgakov: Life and Work*, Ardis, Ann Arbor, 1984

Scammell, Michael *Solzhenitsyn: A Biography*, Hutchinson, London,1985

Wat, Alexander *My Century,* W.W.Norton & Company, New York, 1990

Acknowledgements

Earlier versions of about half the material in this book have been published in *Quadrant* and other journals. I am indebted to the *Quadrant* editors James McAuley, Peter Coleman, Padraig McGuinness and Keith Windschuttle for generously publishing my articles over the decades. *Quadrant* was originally published by the Congress for Cultural Freedom, whose history, *The Liberal Conspiracy*, was written by Peter Coleman. Jewish thinkers from Central Europe Franta Knöpfelmacher, Henry Mayer, Hugo Wolfsohn, Peter Farago and Richard Krygier, the founder of *Quadrant,* introduced me to the characteristics of that region. I learnt a lot from studying in London and Prague, and visiting Poland, Ukraine and Lithuania in 2014. Gerard and Anne Henderson of the Sydney Institute have provided helpful information over the years. My wife Ann has been an invaluable support, as have many others too numerous to enumerate. Once again I am indebted to Anthony Cappello and his team at Connor Court for allowing my text to see the light of day in book form

Index

Absurd literature 64, 72 sqq
Adorno, Theodor 21, 136, 187
Adversary culture 29, 34, 169 sqq, 186, 239
Akhmatova, Anna 104, 105, 135
Alexievich, Svetlana 63, 206-8, 210, 211, 217
Altaev, O 157-8
Alvarez, Al 101 188, 189, 203
American Pastoral 177
Amalrik, Andrei 168
A Minor Apocalypse 154, 162, 198
Anthill society 30, 109
Anti-Communism 182
Appollian spirit 29, 31
Arendt, Hannah 7, 15, 118, 119, 168
August 1914 61
Auden, W H 96, 140
A Voice From The Chorus 202
A Warsaw Diary 200-2

Bakhtin, Mikhail 240
Bauman, Zygmunt 56
BBC 114
Becket, Samuel 143
Bettelheim, Bruno 100
Bellow, Saul 208, 214-25, 233, 246
Beyond Socialist Realism 168
Big Brother 19, 21, 47, 72, 115, 230
Billy Budd 41, 81
Bloom, Claire 175n
Böll, Heinrich 130, 145-8
Borowski, Tadeusz 84sqq, 133-4, 239, 247
Bradbury, Malcolm 167
Brandys, Kazimierz 200-2, 209, 239, 243
'Bratsk Station' 139
Brave New World 111-4, 153, 188
Brotherhood, The 116-7
Brainwashing 28
Brecht, Bertold 13, 68-70, 136, 139-42, 144, 239

Bulgakov, Mikhail 61-6
Burke, Edmund 11, 20, 36, 41, 169, 236

Camus, Albert 7, 13, 15, 76-7, 80, 82, 137, 143, 144, 245
Carpe diem 143, 197
Catch-22 170-3, 238
Chicago and the Siege... 179
Civil society 11, 13, 14, 35, 195, 198
Committee for Public Safety 12
Communism 13, 182, 187, 189, 196, 205
Complicity 17-9
Concentration camps16, 83 sqq
Conrad, Joseph 8, 46-9
Control freak 15, 22, 27
Crick, Prof. Bernard 8
Cromwell, Oliver 1, 59, 60
Czechoslovakia 7, 191 sqq

Daniel,Yuri 139, 152, 165
Dante 103, 122
Darkness at Noon 20, 114
Darwin, Charles 40, 176
Des Pres, Terrence 81, 87, 93
Dickinson, Emily 246
Dionysian spirit 29, 31, 33, 49, 179
Domination & submission 16, 19, 21, 25, 89. 239
Donleavy, J R 170-1
Dostoievsky, Fyodor 11, 15, 17, 23-37, 186, 209
Dovlatov, Sergei 151, 154, 160
Down and Out in London and Paris 120
Double-think 18, 19, 20, 21, 26, 43, 186, 188
Dubček, Alexander 192

East Germany 130, 142
Eastern Europe 130, 188, 221, 223

Eich, Gunter 133
Eichmann in Jerusalem 118
Eliot, T S 243
Enright, D J 136
Enzenberger, Hans Magnus 133
Existentialism 82, 238
Extermination camps 83 sqq
Etkind, Efim 158, 160

Fascism 187
First World War 51
Fontemara 61
Frankfurt School 21, 114, 187-8
Frazer, Sir James 40
Freud, Sigmund 40, 50, 176

Gleeson, Abbott 14
Goldhagen, Daniel 14
Golding, William 77
Gorbachev, Mikhail 206-7
Gorky, Maxim 51
Grass, Günter 144-5
Great Depression 16, 19, 37, 174
Gross, Jan 162-3
Grusa, Jiri 166
Gudkov, Lev 210

Havel, Václav 192-5
Heller, Joseph 192 sqq
Hamlet 247
Haraszti, Miklós 17
Heart of Darkness 26, 32, 34, 47, 5, 18
Hedda Gabler 44, 60
Herbert, Zbigniew 107, 130, 239
Herzog 178, 216-8, 233
Hesse, Herman 49-51, 173
Himmelfarb, Gertrude 243
Hitler, Adolf 16, 37, 67
Hitler's Willing Executioners 14
Holocaust, The 189, 210
Holub, Miroslav 247-8
Homage to Catalonia 144, 200
Hope Abandoned 106
Hope Against Hope 106
Horace 138

Hosking, Geoffrey 166, 168
Howe, Irving 122, 166
Hughes, Ted *244*
Humboldt's Gift 220-1, 234-5
Huxley, Aldous 111-4

I Am Charlotte Simmons 228-9
Ibsen, Henrik 244
If This Is a Man 84
I Married A Communist 174
'Innocent Song' 67
'In the Onion Cellar' 144-5
Ionesco, Eugene 13, 73-6, 186
ISIS 8, 37
It All Adds Up 194

Jacobsen, Dan 3
Jaruselski, General 8
József, Attila 67, 70, 134

Kamen (see 'stone')
Kapo 87-8
Kennedy, Pres. John 185
Khrushchev, Nikita 152
Koestler, Arthur 20, 80, 134
Kolyma Tales 84
Konrad, George 151-2
KOR 121
Kogon, Eugen 93
Konwicki, Tadeusz 154, 161, 162, 165, 198-9
Kraus, Karl 138
Kundera, Milan 102, 119, 155, 158, 175, 179, 195-8, 237

'Lady Lazarus' 189
Lakshin, V I 93
Language and Silence 188
Larkin, Philip 242
Lenin, Vladimir 16, 37, 51-3, 60
Lenin in Zurich 29, 52, 60
Levi, Primo 84 sqq, 134
Liberation movements 176
Life Studies 184
Literary theory 8, 238
London Review of Books 3

INDEX

London School of Economics 8
Lord of the Flies 56, 6, 77
Lowell, Robert 184, 233-4, 246
Lubomirova, Natalia 17

McLean, Sorley 71
Magic realism 65
Mailer, Norman 179-83, 185
Mao Zedong 16, 37 138
Mandelstam, Nadezhda 105-6
Mandelstam, Osip 104-6, 133
Mann, Thomas 71, 139, 186
Marcuse, Herbert 21, 114, 187, 188
Marvell, Andrew 12, 59, 60
Marx, Karl 40, 14, 176l
Maurras, Charles 111
Melville, Herman 41
Memory 92, 243-4
Miami and The Siege....182
Michnic, Adam 198, 210
Milosz, Czeslaw 132-5, 218
Mirror image 44
Modernity 14, 15, 31, 39, 191
Modernism 29, 31, 39-40, 54, 170, 183
Moral inversion 186-7
Moscow Speaking 152
Mosse, George 15
Mr Sammler's Planet 218-220
Müller, Herta 203-5
Murray, Douglas 208, 233
'Mushrooms' 61, 78-80, 244
Musselmänn 88, 421
Mussolini, Benito 16, 37, 59
My Century 136

Nature 120, 243 sqq
Nazism 13, 187
Nechayev, Sergei 33
Nietszche, Friedrich 15, 30, 31, 40, 50
Nineteen Eighty-Four 7, 17, 108, 114-122, 129, 139, 153, 155. 167, 187, 241, 246
Nisbet, Prof. Robert 13
Nomenklatura 206

Notes of a Non-Conspirator 158, 160
Notes From Underground 15, 23-31, 138, 239

O'Brien, Conor Cruise 188
Oceanic feeling 133
One Day in the Life of Ivan Denisovich 7,21, 84, 87, 122
Orwell, George 7, 15, 17, 55, 72, 75, 108, 112, 114-22, 129, 139, 168, 172, 186, 187, 200, 205, 206, 239-40, 241, 242

Parvus 53
Pasternak, Boris 105, 247
Pays légal 111, 198
Pays réel 111, 198*?*
Pentagon, The 179-181
Permissive society 176, 183
Pinter, Harold 77-8
Plath, Sylvia 77-8, 134, 189
Pol Pot 18, 8, 138
Poland 198-203, 240
Polanyi, Michael 186
Political correctness 9, 21, 22
politique d'abord 56, 71, 139, 230
Pontius Pilate 63, 104
Prague 152
Pretender To the Throne 157, 158, 165
Proles, the 120-1, 205 sqq
Putin, Vladimir 211

Quadrant 7

Radical chic 215
Rates of Exchange 167
Reddaway, Peter 8
Reflections on the Revolution in France 11
Revolution 16
   Cultural revolution 60
   English Revolution 12
   French Revolution 12, 41, 111
   Hungarian Revolution 68, 191
   Industrial revolution 111

Permanent revolution 54, 59-60
Russian Revolution 191
Rhinoceros 6, 73-6, 239
Ridersin the Chariot 7
Romania 73, 203-5, 221 sqq
Romanticism 28, 39, 45
Roth, Philip 174, 177-9, 203, 231-3

Sartre, J P 144
Scruton, Sir Roger 203
Second World War 174
Secondhand Time 207-8
Shalamov, Varlan 84 sqq, 239, 244
Shapiro, Prof. Leonard 8
Show trial 44
Simecka, Milan 163
Sinyaysky, Andrei 139, 152, 165, 202, 205
Small platoons 27, 32, 94
Solidarity 198 sqq, 206
Solzhenitsyn, Alexander 21, 52-3, 84 sqq, 122-7, 242, 246,
Sonderkommando 88, 100, 152
Soviet Union 17, 108, 16, 205
Spanish Civil War 71, 144
SS 87, 89
Stalin, Joseph 16, 105, 122, 125, 126, 127, 207
Steiner, George 188
Steppenwolf 49-51, 170, 173-4
Stone/*kamen* 133, 135
Stunde Null (year zero) 129, 137, 204
Superfluous man 23, 48, 67

Talmon, J T 15
The Armies of the Night 179 sqq, 184
The Axe 155
The Birth of Tragedy 31
The Bonfire of the Vanities... 226-8, 234
The Book of Laughter... 119, 158, 195, 208
The Captive Mind 85, 134
The Caretaker 60, 77-8, 130
The Clown 145-8, 170
The Compromise 160

The Dean's December 208, 221-5, 233
The Devils 12, 32-7, 46, 54, 80, 95, 187
The Fire Raisers 60-1, 72-3
The First Circle 52, 122-7, 152, 173, 228, 242, 246
The Garden Party 192
The Ginger Man 156, 170-1
The Guinea Pigs 166
The Gulag Archipelago 86, 102
'The Heirs of Stalin' 139
The House on the Embankment 151, 164,
The Intellectuals on the Road... 151
The Inferno 103
The Ivankiad 156, 173, 240
The Joke 155, 157, 160, 161, 166, 167
The Land of Green Plums 203-5
'The Mask of Evil' *126*
The Master and Margarita 36, 61-6, 106, 108
The Measures Taken 142
The Memorandum 193
The Myth of Sisyphus 143, 245
The Origins of Totalitarianism 7
The Outsider 143, 170, 215
The Painted Word 215
'The Pebble' 130, 241
The Plague 60-1, 76-80, 130, 133, 137, 189
The Polish Complex 154, 161, 198
The Questionnaire 166
'The Power of the Powerless' 194-5
The Radiant Future 155-6
The Reality of Communism 151, 163
The Rebel 144
The Resistible Rise of Arturo Ui 61, 68, *139, 141*
The Secret Agent 48
The Secret Sharer 46
The Strange Death of Europe 208, 233
The Tin Drum 56, 60-1, 130, 144-5,
The Trial Begins 152
This Way to the Gas... 84

INDEX

'The World of Stone' 134
The Unbearable Lightness... 197
The Yawning Heights 162
There Is Simply Too Much. 215
Thought control 9
Three Vanek Plays 194
'To Posterity' 140-2
Tolstoy, Lev 92
Totalitarianism 7, 12-15, 17, 19, 22, 55, 183, 187, 210
    from above & below 14, 17, 19
    grand mal 36, 115?
    petit mal 115, 2229
    pre- & post- 14, 15, 20, 29
Trifonov, Yuri 15, 18, 164
Trilling, Lionel 4, 50, 170, 180, 220
Trotsky, Leon 54, 59

ubermenschen 31
Under Pressure 188
United States 176 sqq

Vaculic, Ludwig 155, 162, 166
Vanitas vanitatum 134, 197
'Verdict' 135
Vietnam War 122, 174, 213
Vita periculoso 50, 54, 59-60, 245
Voinovich, Vladimir 157, 160, 165, 167
Voronezh 105

Walesa, Lech 198, 203
Waiting For Godot 134
Warsaw Diary 200
Wat, Alexander 135-6
We 108 sqq
West Germany 147-9
Westling. John 17
White, Patrick 7
Will The Soviet Union... 168
Wolfe, Tom 214-5, 225-31
Wright, Peter 116
Writers and Politics 188

Yeats, W B 72, 184, 244, 268

Yeltsin, Boris 206
Yevtushenko, Yevgeny 139

Zamyatin, Yevgeny 56, 108-111, 199,
Zinoviev, Alexander 17, 151, 156, 163, 168, 187, 242

Printed in Australia
AUHW010847020822
367050AU00009B/9

9 781922 815132